Characters
Make
Your Story

Characters
Make Your Story

by

MAREN ELWOOD

Boston

THE WRITER, INC.

Publishers

REPRINTED 1979

ISBN: 0-87116-019-6

TO

BOYD B. RAKESTRAW

Man of Vision

THIS BOOK IS FAITHFULLY
INSCRIBED BY THE AUTHOR

Preface

PEOPLE are lonely souls. They herd and mingle and fraternize — desperately searching. They hurl themselves into the surging gabbling mob of humanity, hoping to find their own counterparts. And failing, once again fall back into their familiar armchairs, giving up the search. Here at last, in the story-people they meet in the pages of their books and magazines, they find themselves as they were and are and hope to be. They never fail them — these story-people. They live, and we, the readers, live in completeness with them!

In this book we shall meet these people. Peeping into their closet, we shall find the quickening wand that touches them to life. The secret *why* the beginning writer makes his characters hop about like puppets without souls, and why that beginner has not brought his characters out of their shadows when he has *told* his everything there is to tell, not realizing the full import of *Don't tell your reader, show him.*

All I can do for you is what I have done for years and years for student-writers all over the world, *show you how* — and ask you to do it. The rest is up to you, the artist, and you, the craftsman. But when you have read, and studied, and thought, and practiced — and finally achieved; then you will have built, not scenes, but experiences; not words, but living people. Shall we sit down together now and talk it over?

M. E.

Contents

CHAPTER I

The Importance of Characterization

The only subject that is inexhaustible is man.
SOMERSET MAUGHAM

You've never written a book, a story, a play, or a radio drama. But you'd like to. What do you do first? Ninety-nine times out of one hundred, you start looking for a plot.

Perhaps you have written two or three books, a dozen short stories, and a bureau drawer full of plays and radio dramas, but none of them has sold. Now once more, unaccountably, the creative spark has sputtered into flame. *This time* you are going to write something that will put your name in bright lights over the Filmarte Moving Picture Theatre at First and Main, or on the cover of *The Saturday Evening Post*, or in the Contributors' Column of the *Atlantic Monthly*, depending on your literary tastes and financial ambitions.

What do you do first? Ninety-nine times out of one hundred, you start looking for a plot.

Now plot is important, whether by plot you mean the skeleton of a 'pattern story,' or the structural basis of any one of a dozen other types of stories. But there is something more important than plot, something that gives meaning and significance and life to plot.

That something is character.

This matter of learning how to create characters so that they seem actual flesh-and-blood people to your readers is of supreme importance to you as a writer. For until you have *characters responding characteristically to stimuli* — that is, to whatever happens to them — you have no story. Actually, the *characters* are more important than their problems; more important than plot; though both of these are *essential* to any worth-while piece of fiction. Think of the stories and books you read ten or even five years ago. Which lives with the greater clarity in your mind, the characters or the plot? Dickens' Oliver Twist, Thackeray's Becky Sharp, Conan Doyle's Sherlock Holmes, James Hilton's Mr. Chips, and Margaret Mitchell's Scarlett O'Hara, they live in the minds of readers with all the sharpness and vitality of real people, even though the plots of the stories in which they figured have faded into the shadows of the past.

You may have the perfect plot, but if you do not give the illusion of life, of reality, to the characters *who act out* that perfect plot, the resultant piece will eventually take its place in the limbo of the bureau drawer; or, better yet, for your peace of mind and the peace of mind of harried editors, in the eternal oblivion of the wastepaper basket.

Plot is secondary to characterization. Events and action, *in themselves*, have no significance and consequently no interest. It is only as events and action *affect* people that they become really interesting. Even then, interest is slight until we know something about the people — that is, until they are characterized and, therefore, become for us *alive*.

For example, suppose we read in the paper, 'There was a heavy storm at sea last Thursday.' Well, who cares? No one. But suppose the item reads, 'Last Thursday there was a heavy storm at sea, in which five people were drowned.' This rouses a flicker of interest. Now amplify it to read:

> There was a heavy storm at sea last Thursday. Five bodies were washed up on the beach at Santa Barbara. Four were identified as Mr. and Mrs. J. A. Redfield, and their twin daughters, Anne and Shirley, aged about four years. Mr. Redfield was the head of the Fruit Growers' Association in San Bernardino, while his wife will be remembered as Anita Shelly, who, before her marriage, was a famous actress on the New York stage. The fifth body was that of a young man, about twenty years old, well-dressed, six feet one inch tall, with wavy blond hair and gray eyes. Calluses on the tips of the fingers of his left hand indicate that he was a violinist. His body is being held today and tomorrow in the morgue at Santa Barbara. If he remains unidentified, his body will be interred in the potter's field.

While the characterization of each of the above persons is brief and 'static' — that is, without action — yet interest is held because, by means of specific devices, the people have been made to take on the semblance of reality. You know the sex and approximate age of each, their social status and occupation. You know the relationship to each other of the first four, and the fact that the fifth is unknown adds pathos and curiosity. They might be people you know. And you are emotionally involved because of the sudden deaths of these specific people, all in the full tide of life. The storm that caused their deaths falls into the background of consciousness, while the spotlight of interest is focused on its *effect* on these *people*.

Events, pure and simple, should not be overemphasized in your story. They are important only as they effect changes in the lives of people who have become real to the reader through convincing characterization. Unless your characters are real and, therefore, interesting, no sequence of dramatic events, no amount of original and astounding plot will help in the least. Your reader will remain totally unconcerned as to what happens to the puppets in your story. Frankly, he will be bored. When this happens the writer will have accomplished nothing. Making the reader *care* what happens to the characters should be the writer's first purpose. It is the emotion toward which all other emotions are built.

On the other hand, the events of your story may concern themselves simply with familiar experiences of everyday life. These events, however, may be made vitally interesting, if you take care of two things: first, create real, convincing characters and, second, have *something of great significance to your main character depend upon the outcome of the story*.

The following is an example of the way a very simple, almost commonplace person — commonplace because familiar — can be made so real by characterization that the reader willingly follows him through a series of events that are not in themselves dramatic:

> He has his pension and a small farm. I used to go there when I was a kid. He's rather a grand old boy; but all you'll get out of him will be some eggs and butter. He'll probably bring them with him. These were precisely what Grandfather Rogers did bring when Tony met him at the station.

Careful analysis will show you how much characterization has been done here in about fifty-five words. The character is a man. He is old. He served in the Civil War. He lives on a small farm. He is thoughtful, kind, and generous. He has old-fashioned ideas about how to express these characteristics. He is independent, not self-conscious, and doesn't care what others think of him. And the characterization is written *interestingly*, so the reader is unconscious of the fact that he is being given information he must have to understand the story-action.

Why do people read? 'Oh,' you say, 'that is simple. They read to be entertained.' And you are right. But until we have taken the trouble to discover *what it is* that makes any piece of creative writing entertaining, we have not arrived at the root of the problem. Make no mistake about it. A simple, practical answer to the question, 'Why do people read?' can put you, the writer, on the right track, save you months and years of wasted effort, and be worth thousands of dollars to you.

All art is concerned with the creation of an emotional reaction on the part of the beholder. As one of the arts, a piece of creative writing is entertaining only as it moves the reader emotionally. The reader wants to *feel*, he does not want to think. *The foundation of all emotional response in the reader is characterization.* It is only when a story-actor is characterized as good or bad, likable or unlikable, admirable or despicable, that the reader cares what happens to him or what he does. You can have an actor hanging over a thousand-foot cliff by a rope that is being rubbed in two by sharp rocks, and the reader will feel nothing unless you have characterized that actor so the reader either likes him or hates him. He can fall to his death; the reader will remain unmoved. He may be drawn to safety at the last moment; the reader will be utterly indifferent.

On the contrary, suppose you have previously characterized this same young man as a likable chap, industrious, honest, and brave. The villain, a dastardly knave, has lowered him over the cliff to rescue an old prospector who had broken his leg and is lying in a cave halfway down the cliff. The villain wants both the helpless trusting old man and the brave young man out of the way so he can win the gold and the girl. Is the reader interested? He certainly is, if the material has been presented at all skillfully and the characterization done in a convincing manner. Why is the reader interested? Because he feels liking for the young man, hatred for the villain, fear that the villain will succeed, pity for the old prospector. Not one of these emotions could have been built without the foundation of characterization.

Before we proceed further with the subject of characterization, it should be explained that, if other aspects of writing are mentioned, it is because of the utter impossibility of segregating each in its own watertight compartment. The art of writing is really all of a piece, and every aspect bears a close relationship to and a mutual dependence upon the other. Apparent subdivision is made for the sole purpose of enabling the student of writing technique to obtain a clearer picture of one particular phase by having his attention focused upon it exclusively for the time being.

It is as if the student of oceanography turned his attention to the Indian Ocean. He is concerned for the moment with that particular body of water, but he cannot entirely disregard the other oceans that encircle the globe, intermingling their waters and influencing their tides and currents. So it is with the study of characterization. While turning the spotlight of our attention to this, we must, at the same time, not forget plot, action, setting, motivation, dialogue, mood, and many other aspects of writing that are indissolubly bound up with characterization in the production of a worth-while piece of fiction.

Actually, there are only two sources of drama: first, man's relation to his environment, and second, man's relation to man. But the first exhausts itself because the author must keep searching for some other environment; the second is inexhaustible in that man's relation to man is infinite in its variations. Man in clash is always dramatic material for the writer. Somebody has well said: To set the maximum desires of a character, at maximum intensity, against maximum opposition results in maximum drama.

The successful story, novel, stage play, movie, or radio drama, whether designed to entertain an adult or juvenile audience, is one in which people react characteristically to situations and to opposition, to love and to hate, to pleasure and to pain. This is as true of the story published in the pulp-paper magazines as it is of the literary story. The only difference is in the subtlety and richness of the characterization. The degree of that difference is gauged by the perception and understanding of the group toward which the story is *slanted*. No story can possibly be of interest to the reader, whatever his intellectual level or capacity, neither can it be a successful one from the point of view of the author, unless the characters give the *illusion of reality*.

For this reason, both the mechanics and the art of making fictional characters live are of paramount importance to the writer who hopes to succeed in his chosen field of authorship, whatever that particular field may be. I say 'mechanics' and 'art' advisedly. Writing is a profession, and every profession has its mechanics as well as its art. A surgeon must know the mechanics of making incisions and tying ligatures. But the profession of surgery comprises a far wider field of accomplishment. The mechanics of incision-making and ligature-tying is merely the handmaiden to an art, the art of mending bodies and saving lives, the art known as the practice of medicine.

The sculptor must learn the mechanics of building his armatures, of handling wet clay, and of using hammer and chisel. But to master those mechanics is not to become a sculptor. The sculptor uses these mechanical skills as *channels* of his art; his genius, if you will, flows through them, creating undying forms of beauty.

There is a strange fallacy abroad among laymen, as well as among writers who have not yet become commercially successful, to the effect that writing is an art, pure and simple, that is in no way dependent upon or subservient to mechanics. By mechanics I mean specific procedures, methods, and acquired skills. Nothing could be further from the truth. Worth-while writing is produced by an almost equal blend of mechanics and art. Moreover, since characterization plays such an important part in worth-while writing, it too has a mechanical, as well as an artistic, aspect. This essentially dual nature of characterization can never, of course, be actually so divided in creative work. No one can say, 'This is mechanics' and 'This is art.' The writer should remember that the mechanics and the art of characterization blend inextricably in the production of any piece of fiction: that the more highly perfected each is, and the more nearly perfectly balanced they are, the more closely will that particular characterization approach the illusion of reality.

Artistic expression in any field is possible only to the degree in which the creative artist masters his medium. The artist may have magnificent conceptions of what he would like to create, he may be inspired by lofty ideals and aspirations, but until he learns *the mechanics of how to communicate* these ideas to others, he is and must remain a 'wisher' and not a 'doer.' Ability is not enough; *ability must be developed*, and *trained*. Devices for sound characterization can be learned, just as devices for creating desired effects in any other art can be learned. A very few artists learn them quickly, almost in a flash of comprehension. The great majority absorb slowly, learning step by step. With increased knowledge comes a sharpening of perception and a more sympathetic understanding of character.

Throughout this book, the term 'character' is *not* used to designate a spiritual or moral quality. It is used exclusively to identify a story-actor in his essential peculiarity or as a distinct individual. It is used according to Webster's definition: 'The artistic representation of a personality as in fiction; description by a statement of characteristics; a trait or sum

of traits that serve as an index to the intrinsic nature of person or thing.'
The fine line between character and personality must be distinguished by the writer. He may so characterize his story-actor to make him 'come alive' on the printed page, and yet he may have failed to individualize him as a distinct personality. It is just as important for the writer to be able to accomplish the latter as to achieve the former. Let us examine the following:

> At the breakfast table, Coralie waited for Albert. Her clenched hands lay in her lap. 'If he moves his silver three inches away from his plate and then moves it back again before he picks up his napkin, I shall scream,' in a frenzy she told herself, 'I know I shall scream!' Albert, fresh-shaven and glowing from his cold shower, came in and sat down opposite. Rigidly Coralie sat watching him. He moved his silver three inches away from his plate, then back to its original position, and picked up his napkin. Coralie did not scream. She thought dully, 'I shall never scream, and he will never stop moving his silver.... We will go on and on....'

Albert's moving his silver only faintly characterizes him. But it very definitely individualizes him, and so helps to make him 'come alive' in the mind of the reader. Anything that does this is extremely valuable to the writer.

Although the purpose of this book is to examine in detail the various means that the writer uses and can use to characterize, there is nothing basically new. It has all been recognized and practiced by writers down the ages. Yet the beginning writer does not observe these devices when they appear, nor does he know how to use them. Moreover, many a professional would benefit, both remuneratively and artistically, by putting into practice this knowledge. In my years of work as teacher of student-writers and critic-adviser of professionals, I have found it of great value to repeat and to emphasize, to analyze and to correlate, so that the writer may be strongly *aware of the steps* that *build up* the effective result. That he may never wave away a hard-won success with the airy, 'Something the author just happened to do.'

An important truth that seems not generally to be grasped is that great art is *conscious* art. That Anton Chekhov, Henry James, Sinclair Lewis *planned* in careful detail the build-up of their story-characters seems to many a startling revelation.

Henry James tells us in 'Partial Portraits' that the germ of a story with Turgenev was never the plot but 'the representation of certain persons.' James goes on to explain that Turgenev started with an individual or a group of individuals whom he wished to see in action. He then followed the method that has always been the approach of the careful writer, he grew to *know his characters* thoroughly by writing a brief biography of them. This was not a mere outline of physical traits, but a record of everything of consequence that they had said and done and that had happened to them up to the opening of the story. This, he maintained, was important since it *determined* what those characters would do *after* the opening crisis of the story and *how* they would deal with their problem.

In one of his letters Chekhov gave this advice to a writer: 'Avoid depicting the hero's state of mind; you ought to try to make it clear from the hero's actions. It is not necessary to portray many characters. The center of gravity should be: him and her....' And again: 'You are either too lazy or you do not wish to slough off at one stroke all that is useless. To make a face from marble means to remove from the slab everything that is not the face.'

So wrought the great builders, the masters.

So must you work and you will master. Whether it is a story, a novel, a play, a radio or movie script, a personality sketch or a biographical article in the non-fiction field, the fundamentals of all characterization are the same. They differ only in the form of their presentation.

In China there lived long ago a very wise man who said, 'Sorrow not that men do not know you, but sorrow that you do not know man.'

Method of Study

1. What comes first in fiction writing: plot or character?
2. What is the chief aim of the fiction writer: to make people *think*, or to make people *feel*?
3. Take the following simple incident and develop it into a complex incident in which people are characterized in a way to arouse emotional response in the reader: 'Two cars collided at the intersection of Main and Sherman Streets today.'
4. Take an incident from a newspaper headline, such as, 'Millionaire sailed for Honolulu today,' or 'Truckload of ripe tomatoes spills on highway.' Develop it:
   (1) By narration, that is, *telling* the reader about it;
   (2) In a scene; that is by *showing* it to the reader. Do this so that two or more actors are characterized and a definite emotion roused in the reader toward each of them.

CHAPTER II

The Creative Process of Characterization

THE IMPORTANCE OF UNDERSTANDING THE CHARACTER

THE creative process of characterization is one of the most complicated and, at the same time, one of the simplest activities of the human mind. It is complicated in that the whole man is involved in its exercise. The sum of every experience of his life, his mode of thought, the degree of his awareness or unawareness of what goes on about him and of its significance, goes into the creation of his character. It is simple, because in the artist all this is synthesized, for practical purposes, into one faculty, and that faculty is understanding. Only as the artist or writer understands his fellow man and, to that end, sympathizes with him, can he create characters that are lifelike.

It is a curious, and perhaps to some a shocking fact, that we understand only that which is within ourselves. 'But,' you cry furiously, 'I am no murderer, no thief, no child-beater! Yet I create such characters!' No one is accusing you of being a murderer, a thief, a child-beater. But question yourself honestly on this point: Suppose your character is a most convincing murderer. If you were placed in his circumstances, and had the mentality, the background of experience and circumstance that you have assigned to him, would you not do exactly as he did? Of course you would. Under no other conditions could you make this man come alive. This may not be palatable but it is the truth. *It is only through your own understanding that you are able to create characters that interest the reader and move him emotionally.*

One misapprehension that is commonly found among writers, who have not yet got into their stride, is that they must imagine, or invent their characters. Nothing is further from the truth. Imagination and invention are almost certain to result in unreal, mechanical characters. Do as the painter or sculptor does; take your models from life.

This does not mean that you are to take someone you know and 'put him in' a story. When you do this you are being a photographer, not an artist. By that I do not mean that photographers cannot be artists, for they can be and often are. But, as in other arts and professions, it is in the skillful manipulations of the mechanics of their profession that they are able to sublimate it into an art. By selection and arrangement of *models*, by highlighting of certain details and the suppression of others, by planning and by composition, they achieve that single unified effect that is art.

This is exactly what a writer does when he creates a major character. He uses one model, or many models, selecting and combining characteristics, highlighting one or two, using others but leaving them in the shadow, testing and trying until the result gives the illusion of a real human being.

I say *illusion*, because that is what every artist creates, in order to make his work give the impression of reality. Suppose an artist painted a tree as it is, with every leaf, every twig, exactly as it exists in nature. The result, however true it might be in fact, would not be true in *spirit*, because it would not look like a tree to the observer. No artist has ever painted trees more exquisitely and more truthfully than Corot. But Corot's trees, when examined closely, are no more a factual reproduction of trees of the French landscape than the picture of a storm is a factual reproduction of water and lightning. In art we don't have reality, but the *illusion of reality*.

The same is true of people in real life and the people whom the writer brings to life in his writing. If you took someone you know and put him in a story as he is, he would not seem real and no one would be particularly interested in him. Living people are too complex and have too many contradictory traits and too many apparently unrelated characteristics to allow them to be convincing on the printed page or on the stage or screen. In writing we are 'not aiming at a transcription of life,' to quote Somerset Maugham, 'but at a dramatization of it.'

Thus certain characteristics have to be selected, characteristics that logically go together. Even these cannot be given equal importance. Almost always one is emphasized above all others. This is because the human mind is forever demanding unity, cohesion, pattern, in everything it sees. One of the major activities of the human mind, so the psychologists tell us, is that of selecting, grouping, relating one thing to another, hunting for sequences of cause and effect. In other words, trying to put all perception and experience into a logical pattern. This mental activity is apparently instinctive and never-ceasing, so that for the most part we are unconscious of it. But it goes on every waking moment, nevertheless.

The pattern of life is too vast for human comprehension. We see causes without visible effects and effects without visible causes. Life stretches into infinity on either side of us. Our past is bounded by approximately five thousand years of recorded history. Our vision of the future is no farther away than our next breath, and not always that far. Life does not satisfy the craving for pattern, for logical arrangement that is inherent in our every fiber. Only in the art of the writer can we find satisfaction for this fundamental craving of the human heart for orderly events, for a comprehensible sequence of cause and effect, for unity in character, and for a series of related happenings increasing in dramatic intensity to a climax and a conclusion.

If the writer could but realize the universality and strength of this need of the human heart for unity and coherent relationship of human characteristics and events, tending from an observable cause to an observable effect, he would make a greater effort to meet it. For this is one of the services of the writer to humanity; he gives to his readers a satisfaction that real life does not offer; he solves the problem of everyday existence; he makes dreams come true; he lifts the reader, for the time that he is reading at least, out of the monotony and the uncertainty of his own existence into a world of adventure and romance.

This difference between transcription and dramatization is the fundamental reason back of the editor's rejection of the 'true' story and of the 'true' character. 'Why, it actually happened, exactly as I have written it down!' cries the infuriated and astonished writer. And the reader's lack of interest in the 'true' story and the 'true' character is due to that very statement. *Both may be true in fact, but they are far from being true in spirit.* They almost invariably fail to give the reader what he wants most: logical relation of cause and effect, unity of impressions, and a satisfying conclusion.

Do I hear someone say, 'But look at the popularity of biographies, stories of real men and real events!' Well, suppose we look at these biographies. No one questions their popularity. But do not fall into the error of supposing that the real men and the real events of their lives are recorded here in factual truthfulness. If every thought, every act of a person's life were set down as it happens, day after day, the reader would be bored to the point of tears, and the writer's 'truthfulness' would be a tremendous lie.

Taken from the long view, the major tendencies and traits of a character and his actions fall into a certain pattern, so the clever and, therefore, successful writer of biography selects certain *dominant characteristics* in his subject. The others he subordinates, or leaves out entirely, in his tracing back from effect to cause. Of the selected characteristics the author turns the spotlight on one, two, at the most three. The others he keeps in the background where they belong, using them to enhance the spotlighted characteristics, either by similarity, or by contrast.

The successful writer of fiction uses the same technique. The nature of even the simplest man is too complex to be presented effectively and convincingly in its entirety, even in a book. Then consider how much more this is true of the short story, the play, or the radio script. The wise writer does not attempt it. He uses all the mechanics and all the art at his command to create the illusion of reality with a few character-traits, while at the same time satisfying the reader's instinctive demand for the orderly procedure of cause and effect to a logical, dramatic, and satisfying conclusion.

As I said before, invention is not necessary to the creation of characters. In fact, invention, unless carefully modified after checking it against actualities, is likely to result in the creation of unreal characters. A far better procedure is to work from the living model. But do it as the artist does, taking the hands of one person, the torso of another, the face of another and combining them to create a figure that *embodies his intention and purpose*, but that does not closely resemble any specific person. The result then is not the literal transcription of life but the *dramatization* of it.

In order to be able to do this, you, the writer, must acquire the habit of observing people, watching always the infinite ways in which the character-actor is an individual.

Take advantage of every means at your command for meeting people whose lives are as different as possible from your own. And, if possible, meet them on their own ground and as one of them. Only then will they feel at ease with you and react naturally to the impacts of opposition and situation and, by the nature of these reactions, reveal deep-seated character-traits.

But all of us cannot leave our homes and our affairs, live in strange places, either near or distant, or alter our mode of living so that we may meet people leading widely different lives from our own. What then, can we do? We can do what practically every successful writer does — we can enlarge our experience by reading of the experiences of others. Meeting characters in the fiction world will deepen your understanding of human nature every bit as effectively as knowing characters in real life.

Usually, reading is recommended to the writer as a means of acquiring style. The value of reading in acquiring knowledge of character-traits and character-reactions is little known. I do not mean to say that reading will take the place of mingling with living people. But reading can be used to great advantage in complementing such contact. No one person can ever know enough people intimately. That is why so many famous writers started out in some profession or occupation that brought them into intimate relationship with large numbers of people. The profession of doctor and the occupation of newspaper reporter are perhaps unequaled in the opportunities they offer for observing human nature in great emotional crises, with all bars of reserve let down.

But everyone cannot be a doctor or a reporter for five or six years while he is gathering experience and material for his writing.

Then next best enlarge your own experience, whatever it may be, by reading the work of writers who have wide knowledge of phases of life that you have never touched. No one human being could possibly have lived through the variety of experiences that have fallen to the lot of Victor Hugo, Leo Tolstoy, Charles Dickens, Mark Twain, Jack London, and Somerset Maugham. Yet everyone can read their books and make the essence of these varied experiences his own. He may observe and analyze the actions, the problems, the desires, the emotions, the conflicts, of those characters who would never otherwise touch so much as the fringe of his own life.

The ambitious writer of today will do well to concentrate on the character-portrayals found in the pages of the books of these, and many other masters in the art of character-delineation. In this way his own experiences can be multiplied a thousandfold and the people therein can be studied closely, repeatedly, and at his leisure; an opportunity that does not often present itself when dealing with living models.

There is another method by which the writer may enter into the characters and experiences of which he has small or no direct knowledge, and that is by his own sympathetic attitude. The writer can sympathize and, therefore, understand a character so deeply that those who have no knowledge of the process involved marvel at this miraculous ability and regard it as equivalent to genius. But neither a miracle nor genius is necessarily involved, as the writers themselves testify. The *sympathetic rapport between the writer and his character-actor is so great that the writer, for all practical purposes, becomes that character, and can then observe that character from within.* This is the explanation of how some men are able to write with such complete understanding of women, and of experiences through which, because they are men, they could never have lived, or even have observed. It explains why women writers can give true character-portraits of men, and why both men and women can characterize very young children, where memory cannot help them, and, also, people whose character traits in no way coincide with their own. Therefore, a writer should cultivate sympathy, for it is only when we sympathize that we understand; and both understanding and sympathy are dependent upon the writer's ability to identify himself with his characters.

Any task is more easily accomplished when we know exactly what it is we want to do, the end we want to achieve, the effect we are striving to create, and the limitations and possibilities of our medium. Hence, it is only when the writer thoroughly comprehends the limitations and the possibilities of his *medium* that he can use it to achieve the best effects of which he is capable.

Words are the medium used by the writer to characterize his actor. Words, and nothing else. Only one medium is more limited — that of the radio dramatist who must depend entirely on the spoken word of his actors, that is, on sound. In the moving picture and the stage play, characterization is done by spoken words, plus all the rich and varied communications that reach the mind through the sensory channels of sight and hearing: setting, clothing, facial contours and expressions, gestures, mannerisms, etc. All these are perceived simultaneously with the sound of the spoken words. These remain, with changes and variations or are repeated at frequent intervals, throughout the play. The spectator does not have to remember them. Indeed, he is reminded continually of his character through the actor's distinctive voice and manner of delivery that reach him through his own auditory nerve and sense of hearing.

These two direct channels of characterization, sight and hearing, are not available to the writer, except as he utilizes them through his one medium of communication with the reader, the printed word. By means of arbitrary symbols, the writer supplies the reader's imagination with enough, but not too much, material for the reader to *do for himself* what is *done for him* in the moving picture and stage play. This presents no limitation but a definite opportunity, since the reader derives far greater satisfaction from creating his own pictures and sounds than by accepting scenes and sounds *created for him*. In like manner, characters he creates for himself prove far more satisfying than those presented on stage or screen. Knowing this, the author, by causing the reader to remember his own experiences and people connected with them, has succeeded in *involving the reader*, both *imaginatively* and *emotionally in what he is reading*. To the degree that the author is able to do this to him, is the reader's interest intensified. Never forget this writer-reader collaboration, and you will have laid the corner stone of a successful writing career.

For characterization to approximate perfection, the writer must use words skillfully and carefully, both from a mechanical and an artistic point of view. His characterizations should always be aimed to stimulate the imaginative faculty of the reader, rather than to present in detail every facet of the story character-actor.

Characterization should show no effort, no creaking of the machinery; in other words, the fact that you are characterizing an actor should never be obvious to the reader. The characterization should be so integrated with the actions, setting, and dialogue, and the total result be so intrinsically interesting, that the reader is unaware of the mechanics and is conscious only of the art, of the 'living' quality of the characterization. To repeat, the best characterization is that of which the reader is totally unaware; that is, it is so much a part of action, so much a part of the story, that the reader accepts it as he accepts his own estimates of people in real life. This is often very difficult to do, and requires careful thought, planning, and effort, but this conscious effort should never be apparent in the story.

Yet before you can characterize a story-actor for the reader, you must have created that character. And the place to create characters is not on paper, but in your mind. The creation of a major story-actor is not, and cannot be, an instantaneous act. According to Genesis, God took seven days to create the universe. So, with our limited powers, it seems not unreasonable to allow ourselves seven days to create a major character.

Or even more. The point is, before we attempt to acquaint a reader with a character, we ourselves should know that character thoroughly. We should be familiar with the details of his physical appearance, though we may never mention them in our story. We should know what kind of clothes he wears, his mannerisms, his moods, what kinds of food he likes, the general tenor of his mind, what he desires to be, what he fears, all his outstanding characteristics and traits. This means that we should know him at least as well as we know the members of our family and our closest friends. For the writer, whose aim is to make his character-actors *live*, nothing short of this will do.

A student of mine, working by mail, was asked concerning several of her story-characters, who were little more than puppets, 'Are you sure you know these characters?' She replied, 'Yes, I know them very well. I lived next door to them in Milwaukee for three years.' I need not point out that this is not the kind of 'knowing' I mean. You can live in the same house with people for forty years and not 'know' them in the sense that a writer must know his story-characters. He must understand them so well that he will not have to stop and reason out *how* they will react to any given circumstance or situation. Think of the main masculine character in the last story you wrote. Imagine that he is sitting in the living-room of his home. From the terrace outside the open French window he hears his wife and her lover planning to go away together that night, taking with them valuable securities belonging to him. What will this husband's reactions be, mentally? Physically? If you *understand* your character you will see, or be aware of, his reactions at once, without conscious thought. Will he knock the man down? Will he shoot his wife? Will he slip away unnoticed and get possession of his securities? Will he sit quietly at his desk and plan to trap them? Will he walk into the living-room and apologize to his wife for his failure as a husband? Or will he do nothing whatsoever? If you understand this man's character, you will know instantly the answer to these questions. And this 'knowing' can come only after you have created that character fully and completely *in your mind*. Because most beginning writers, and many professional ones, neglect entirely or slight this primary activity of mental creation, their stories fail to convince and, as a result, fail to interest the reader as they should. What is of even greater importance to the writer himself, such stories often fail to interest an editor, and are, as a consequence, rejected.

While it is true that people, for the most part, like to read about people they might conceivably know; in other words, about characters who are more or less familiar to them in their everyday life, sometimes, like a dash of cinnamon in the familiar apple pie, they like to meet the exotic, the strange character whom they have never met and who would probably be repellent to them if they did meet him in the flesh. But here the writer must use care. He should never forget to endow this strange personality with one or more simple, homely traits of character, or habits, or weaknesses, or virtues, that will cause the reader to say, perhaps subconsciously, 'Why, that fellow is human, after all! And not a bad fellow, at that. Some day I'd like to meet him.'

Always establish a *common bond* of sympathy and understanding between this unusual character, who has not been met, and the everyday reader sitting in an easy chair by the radio, his feet in slippers and a pipe in his hand.

Characters must be consistent. This does not mean that a villain will always be about his villainy, or the hero continually doing noble deeds But everything a fictional character does must be the logical expression of character traits that have been clearly shown to the reader before the characteristic action takes place. Unless, of course, the action takes place in the beginning of the story and is itself designed to establish character-traits.

That is to say, once the character of an actor has been established, there must be a convincing character-trait that enters into the motivation of every act. If a normally nice husband comes home and berates his wife because the mashed potatoes are lumpy, the reader must already be aware of the fact that, along with his Sir Galahad characteristics, he has a nervous temperament that tricks him into blowing off steam in sudden bursts of irritability over trivial annoyances. Of course, being the hero of your story, he regrets these small tempests as soon as they are over. The point is, don't have the man whom you have characterized as patient, slow, phlegmatic, suddenly start throwing dishes; don't have the polite gentleman suddenly become a boor, at least, not without having planted character-traits from which such acts would logically spring. *After you have once characterized your actors, see to it that they act at all times in a manner consistent with that characterization.*

The shorter the piece of writing, the simpler the characterization should be. In a book you may develop several aspects of an actor's character, though it is better to have one characteristic predominate over the others. In a short story there should not be more than three, and two is better. In a very brief story, such as a short short, the hero will be flawless and the villain black-hearted to the core. There is no room for fine shadings of character in a short short. In life, we have to know a person some time to become aware of more than a few of his most obvious character-traits. When we meet a person briefly he is, for us, little more than a one-dimensional character. The same is true of characters in fiction. The longer the story, the more complicated and many-sided you may show your characters to be. The shorter the story, the more your characters should be simplified and the fewer the traits.

In view of the importance of characterization in the work of the writer, I believe it wise to emphasize here what I explained at some length a few pages ago, that the writer should know his characters so well that while he is writing his story he experiences no moment of doubt as to how any character will react to the circumstances of any moment. In order to achieve this degree of character-understanding *it will be necessary for the writer to know a great deal more about his actors than he ever actually tells the reader in words.* But for an instant do not think that the labor of knowing your characters is lost. In subtle ways, through overtones and nuances of which you yourself will probably be totally unaware, this knowledge will trickle through to the reader and your actors will live as three-dimensional characters, which they would never have become without this background of specific knowledge about them that you have carefully built up, bit by bit.

Method of Study

1. Is it advisable to put a real person in a story, exactly as he is? Why?
2. Should the writer confine his observations of character-expression to real life?
3. Where is the convincing story-character first created; on paper, or in the mind of the writer?
4. Observe someone you know well. Select what you consider his dominant character-trait. Write a brief scene showing this character-trait in action.
5. Write the same scene in narrative form, doing your best to make it as interesting, as dynamic, and as emotionally strong, as the scene.

CHAPTER III

First Steps in Characterization

SELECTING THAT WHICH INDIVIDUALIZES

LET US suppose that you have selected a major character who is worth the reader's time to meet, that he is sound in mind and body, and is interesting to the group for which you are writing the story. It is well to remember that you cannot hold reader-interest with an intrinsically dull person, though many inexperienced writers try to do so. Neither should you choose a character who is insane, or even a half-wit. Not until you are very skillful and have a well-known name will you use a character as hero who is seriously ill or physically handicapped. As much as you can, choose *normal* people. Don't give a gangster a major rôle in a story intended for the women's magazines, and do not feature a society matron in a story you plan to sell to a magazine for men. These are extreme examples of what not to do, yet beginning writers make these mistakes all the time.

Also, in your selection of a character-actor, the more surely you choose one with the motives, the desires, and the traits of the average mortal, the more surely your story will have a timeless quality and be universal in its appeal. Every one of us knows a Macbeth, whether in business or in national affairs, who ruthlessly sacrifices the lives of others in his will to power; a Lady Macbeth, who will do anything, even murder, for the man she loves; a Hamlet, an indecisive young man; an Othello, whose insane jealousy destroys the thing he loves. Power, love, indecision, and jealousy are strong motivating forces with which every reader is familiar. They make headlines in the newspaper every day in the week.

In your selection of material for your creation of a fictional character, there are three steps:

1. Creating a clear mental concept of the character.
2. Selecting one major and two or three minor character-traits.
3. Presenting these character-traits effectively.

The steps in creating the mental conception of a character have already been explained. So we shall consider step 2, selecting one major and two or three minor character-traits. The traits you select, out of the many possessed by your character, will depend on the kind of story you plan to write and the group of people for whom you plan to write that story.

Let us see how this works in actual practice: Your character-actor, we shall say, is a middle-aged man named Dean Crawford. He owns and successfully operates a chain of restaurants. Therefore he is practical, shrewd, far-seeing, and dominant. We know he must possess these character-traits, because he is making money in a highly practical and competitive business. He is honest and fair in all his dealings, whether concerning his business or personal relationships. He is an affectionate husband, proud of his wife's beauty and charm, and very indulgent toward her, proud of his home, his material possessions, his place in the community. He is proud of his two children, a boy and a girl of high-school age, but outwardly he is stern with them because of his sense of pride and, also, because he loves them and wants them to develop into fine adults.

You have far too many characteristics here to feature all of them in one short story. If you are planning a novel around this man, you could use them all, though even in a book one or two should be stressed over the others.

In order to make your selection intelligently, you should decide in advance what kind of story you are going to plan around this man. If it is to be a story of business, you will feature his shrewdness, his far-sightedness, and his ingenuity in succeeding where others fail. His love of family and pride of possessions would no doubt enter in, but as minor character-traits that motivate, to some extent, his business actions.

If you plan to feature him in a marriage-problem story, then his capacity for affection might well be the chief character-trait selected for expression, using his business shrewdness, pride in possessions and of his standing in the community as minor character-traits.

Perhaps you have in mind a story that deals with a parents-and-children problem. Look over the character-traits you have assigned to this man and select the ones that will best serve your purpose. There is a

wide choice here, but suppose that you decide to stress his desire to dom-
inate and rule. Minor character-traits featured in this story might be
his capacity for affection and his innate sense of fairness.

You will see that in each of the above examples, the character-traits
selected for emphasis determine, to a great extent, the course your story
will take. By choosing yet other character-traits than the ones above
selected, the resultant stories will still be very different. To the alert
student, this example should serve as more than a hint concerning a
practical method of getting story ideas and be a prolific source of plots.
One character, fully created in the writer's mind, can be the basis of
many stories. His various traits and characteristics may be used either
in a series featuring one individual, or in a number of stories in a wide
variety of unrecognizable rôles, by the mere effort of changing the name
and stressing different characteristics.

Avoid the strange, the extremely unusual, the bizarre character. The
character that most people like to read about is a known type, but he is
also an individual within the type. Our character, Dean Crawford, is an
example of this. Broadly speaking, he is the solid, dependable, substan-
tial American business-man type. But he is highly individualized within
that type. Always remember to do this, especially with your principal
characters. And the only way to do it is to create that character whole,
in your own mind, *before you fully plot your story.* Don't expect to individualize your character-actor while you are plotting and writing your
story. If you do, your story may be skillfully written, even it may sell,
but it will be 'just another story,' not one the reader will remember with
pleasure a week or even a day after he has read it. *Time spent in creating
your character-actor and in devising effective ways of communicating that
character to the reader is time well spent.*

Watch the balance, or proportion, of the characterization in your
story. Don't become interested in a minor character, give him the spotlight, and let him run away with your story. If a minor character insists
on taking the center of the stage and you find yourself building him up
into a 'round' character in spite of yourself, take him out of the story
and plot another story that revolves around him as the logical central
character. In that way you will probably have two good stories, instead
of one poor story that lacks unity of effect and proper emphasis.

Step 3, or the presentation of selected character-traits in an effective
way, will be illustrated by the examples that follow.

Just as a scientist cannot understand an atom or a molecule until he has broken them down into their component parts and discovered the relationship of these parts to each other, so the student of writing must break down major problems of his craft into their component parts and discover the relation of these component parts to each other. This sounds dull, but, on the contrary, it is extremely absorbing. Let us see what this scientific method as applied to characterization will do for us:

All characterization falls under two main headings: *Direct* characterization and *indirect* characterization. There are important subdivisions under these main headings that we shall talk about later, but an understanding of direct and indirect characterization is fundamental and necessary to the writer who seriously intends to succeed.

DIRECT CHARACTERIZATION

Direct characterization is accomplished in one way only, by the writer's *telling* the reader what sort of person the actor is. In other words, direct characterization is done by exposition. Let us see how this works with our friend whom we already know so well, the chain-restaurant owner, Dean Crawford. You, as writer, are now characterizing Dean Crawford directly for the reader:

> Dean Crawford was a hard man to deal with, if you started playing tricks; but he was honest even with his enemies. He loved his wife and children, although he did not understand them, and the fact that he owned the finest home in Maplewood gave him a rich, warm feeling deep inside, though he never put the feeling into words.

INDIRECT CHARACTERIZATION

Indirect characterization is done when you tell the reader facts and permit him to reach his own conclusions concerning the character-traits of your actor. Of course, the reader is not really 'left to reach his own conclusions.' *You select the facts to be presented, facts that will inevitably indicate the character-traits you have assigned to your actor.* And you present them in such a way that the reader *sees* what you want him to see. Indirect characterization allows the reader to feel he is free to draw his own conclusions and is, therefore, other things being equal, more interesting to the reader than direct characterization. The use of direct characterization allows the writer to tell a great deal about his character in a few words and, for this reason, is extremely valuable, especially in the case of minor characters. It should, however, always be done very briefly.

Indirect characterization is accomplished by one of the following means: description, setting or environment, action, speech, thought. First, let us see how we can describe, and at the same time characterize, Dean Crawford:

DESCRIPTION

He was a tall man with plenty of weight where weight ought to be. All his movements were swift and purposeful, yet he never seemed in a hurry. His gray eyes looked straight at you from under thick eyebrows that almost met. Today he wore a brown suit of Harris tweed, expensive and conservative. 'No pleats and no padding,' he always sternly admonished his tailor. The ring of soft yellow Chinese gold, set with carved apple-green jade and worn on the third finger of his left hand, struck an unexpected, but not unpleasant note.

Description, like exposition, while helpful, must be used with care since, while you are *describing* a character, your story is standing still. Because of this you will be brief and take care to avoid the effect of giving a list or inventory of things described.

ENVIRONMENT OR SETTING

Both environment and setting have a very wide application. Environment includes surroundings, conditions, and forces within that environment. Setting is the more immediate surroundings of a story or a character and may be anything from a town to a telephone booth. Environment and setting characterize either by likeness or by contrast. If a character likes, and fits into, his environment and setting, then characterize him by likeness. If he hates his environment and setting, then characterize him by contrast. Environment and setting are valuable means of indirectly characterizing an actor, so study them with care to the end that you may use them in your own writing.

The more obvious phases of Dean Crawford's environment are the town in which he lives, his business, his home, his family. He is so plainly characterized by these that we need not examine a specific example of how to do so. But we can profitably turn our attention to the way to characterize him by setting. Suppose we take a look at his office, though his home would do almost as well, and both would in all probability be used in a story about him.

Dean Crawford's plain desk of fumed walnut stood, foursquare and sturdy, on the thick, two-toned blue rug. It said plainly, 'Let there be no nonsense here.' It bore no frivolous vase of flowers. No photographs in Florentine frames cluttered its polished surface. But in one of the drawers, close to Dean's hand, were unframed photographs of Emily in her wedding dress, of John playing tennis, and one of Elise taken in her bath at the age of six months. The chairs were handsome, but all except Dean's possessed an incredible stiffness that did not invite loitering.

Not all of the man's character, but a great deal, is shown by the few details of his office given here; details of setting.

ACTION

Action leads the field as the chief means of characterizing a story-actor. Either alone, or in combination with other means of characterization, action is used in almost every piece of work a writer attempts. He does this largely because there exists an infinite variety of character-revealing action and also because, while in action, people reveal by facial expression, gestures, unconscious movement and physical reactions to emotional and physical impacts, the sort of characters they are.

Another reason the writer likes to use action in characterizing his actors is that action, other things being equal, interests people more than any other means of character delineation open to the writer, except speech. Of course, strictly speaking, speech is action, but speech is in itself such a wide field that we shall consider it separately from action.

How can you characterize Dean Crawford by action? If you show him in any action, that action should reveal character. Suppose you tell the reader how he drives a car. And the best way to tell the reader is to *show* him.

> Dean drove away from the house that morning, outwardly unmoved by the goggle-eyed stares of the neighbors at the long, sleek lines of his new car. He drove easily, carefully, as he always did. Halted by the red light at the intersection of Grove and Main, he waited patiently and, in spite of wild honking from a cut-down flivver behind him, he did not put his car in motion until the green light flashed on. Then he swung the big car around with one hand, gravely saluting his friend, the corner policeman, with the other.

Carefully check the above for the various character traits it discloses

SPEECH

Speech is a flexible tool with which the writer characterizes an actor. It is one of the most characteristic acts of a human being. It consists of the *words* themselves, the *way* they are said, and the *tone* of voice used. Consider how wide a difference there would necessarily be between the speech of our hero, Dean Crawford, and the man in the cut-down flivver who honked his horn. Suppose we listen to Dean Crawford give his breakfast order at a café, and then listen to our friend in the flivver give the same order:

Dean Crawford:

> 'Hot cakes and coffee, please. And would you mind telling the cook to hurry. I'm late for an appointment.'

Man in Flivver:

> 'Stack of wheats and a cup of Java. Make it snappy. I gotta date.'

THOUGHTS

Most people, though not all, are fairly honest with themselves when they are thinking. That is why thoughts are helpful to the writer in characterizing an actor. Suppose we look into Dean Crawford's mind for a moment and see what goes on there:

> 'Two more restaurants opening next week,' Dean thought. 'I checked carefully on everything and they will both be money-makers from the start. Wish I could get John interested in the business. If only Emily wouldn't encourage him to fool around all the time in that laboratory he has fixed up in the basement. Chemistry! Sort of fiddling work. Nothing a man can get his teeth into.'

Now that we have made a general survey of the ways in which the writer may characterize his story people and so make them appear real and convincing, the next step is to start a notebook, or rather two notebooks. In one you will set down your own observations of human beings *reacting characteristically.* In the other you will keep outstanding examples of characterization that you find in published stories.

You will, of course, use any kind of notebook you please, but the loose-leaf type that carries typewriter-size paper is practical. Divide each notebook under the subheadings that have been given you in this chapter: exposition, description, environment or setting, speech, action, thought. Later you will want to add other subheadings, but these will do for the present.

Train yourself to watch the clerk in the store who sells you a spool of thread or a necktie, the conductor on the streetcar that takes you downtown, the famous explorer who has just returned from the wilds of some never-never land, the shockheaded youngster your son brings home to play. Practice getting each down on paper in a few expressive words. *This notebook is the equivalent of the artist's sketchbook.* These little word sketches are the germ ideas from which you will plot and write your stories. It may not be easy at first. You may perhaps find it difficult to recognize characteristic speech and action, or to see character as it is expressed in environment. But keep looking, keep observing. *The exercise of any faculty strengthens it, and soon you will be seeing expressions of character in the most unconsidered speech, the smallest actions of those around you.* When this happens, you may be sure that you are gaining craftsmanship in the art of characterization and are on the right path to accomplish its mastery.

Almost equally important as your personal observation notebook is your notebook of examples of characterization from published stories. When you find a clever or deft bit of characterization, either clip it and paste it into your notebook, or type it in under its proper heading. This notebook will contain your models. When you are facing a problem of characterization in your own writing and don't know how to solve it, re-read your models; see the ways in which experienced writers have solved the same problem. These examples will serve another important purpose. They will serve as hints of what you should look for; the specific detail of clothing that tells so much, the manner of walking that discovers the man, the type of laughter that reveals the woman.

Of course you cannot carry this large notebook about with you. What you will have is a small work notebook not too large to go in your pocket or handbag. This should go with you everywhere, because you never know what moment you will meet a special character who, put into a story or book, may make your fortune.

These observations should be put down while they are fresh in your mind. You may think you will remember the details that made the man in the cigar stand on the corner so interesting to you, but you will not. You will forget the deep wrinkle on one side of his hard mouth that gave his face that fascinatingly sinister expression. After you get home you will be unable to recall the details of the ring he wore, whether or not there was hair on the back of his hands, and if he said 'D'ja think so?' or 'Do you think so?' In short, you will have forgotten the exact details that would have made him live as a 'round' (major) character. All you will have left will be broad generalities and he will be useless to you except in creating a 'flat' (minor) character, to be kept in the background.

Since stories spring primarily from character, every bit of characterization you set down in your personal observation notebook contains the potentialities of a plot. If the only notebook you keep is one concerning character and characterization, you will never be at a loss for plot-ideas, and, therefore, for something to write about. So, with a notebook containing models from the best writers, and a notebook containing your own characterizations made from direct observations of living people, you should have no great difficulty in planning and writing a consistent output of marketable stories.

Remember that you cannot characterize your actors once and for all. *You have to keep characterizing them as your story advances.* The major character-trait or traits of your main character must be stressed and emphasized again and again. In a recent story that appeared in a national magazine the major character-traits of the principal character, an old woman, were courage and determination. The writer told the reader, that is the writer 'planted,' nine times that the old woman was courageous and determined. He showed her doing things in a determined and courageous manner. The reader finally came to believe that she really was courageous and determined, so when the old woman *solved her problem by means of these character-traits,* the reader accepted the ending as not only logical and plausible, but as inevitable.

One of the greatest single helps to the writer in characterizing his actors, both major and minor, is an ability to classify them, for himself, as mainly extrovert or mainly introvert types. Note that I say 'mainly.' The pure type of either holds small interest for the majority of fiction readers. Generally speaking, the pure extrovert and the pure introvert are good only for background characters. Rather strangely, these pure types are given main rôles only in the so-called 'funny papers,' in the pulp magazines where the extrovert flourishes, and in the 'quality' magazines where both appear for psychological character-analysis, though the introvert is more often examined and emphasized.

Simply stated, though the definition is sufficient for our purpose, an extrovert is one whose energies are outgoing; who acts first and thinks afterward, if at all. An introvert is one whose mind turns inward on itself; who thinks, analyzes, weighs, and almost never acts.

This definition is placed here in the hope that it will keep the person who previously did not know the difference between an extrovert and an introvert from rushing to the nearest library and demanding a ponderous volume on psychology. There is, also, the hope that what is said here will deter the person who already knows what an extrovert and an introvert are, from reading more ponderous volumes on psychology than he has already read and, thereby, becoming more confused than he already is by their scientific terminology and analysis.

You may conclude from this, and your conclusion will be right, that I am decidedly opposed to the creative writer's making an exhaustive study of psychology in the abstract, as it is usually presented in most texts on the subject. By making him befuddled and self-conscious, the damage that can be done to the unbiased observation and to the creative instinct of the serious writer is often irreparable, because the dyed-in-the-wool psychologist takes living, breathing, laughing, weeping, feeling, human beings, catalogues them with neat, pedantic labels, and files them away in a psychological columbarium where they promptly become desiccated cadavers. Instead of studying emotion, motivation, stimulus and response in the abstract, what you, the writer, must do is to observe living people around you, in clash, intent on their individual activities, problems, loves and fears, hopes and petty jealousies. That done, you should acquire your own knowledge of psychology by observation of your own mental, emotional, and physical reactions to those of other people. That is the best way of finding out why you and others act like human beings. You can't let someone else tell you; you must know for yourself. There is no substitute for your own living and your own reflecting. And your own jottings in that notebook.

Method of Study

1. How many dominant character-traits of one character can you safely feature in the short story?
2. How do you decide which character-traits, out of all those possessed by your actor, to stress in your story?
3. Do readers prefer familiar, or unfamiliar, types of characters in stories?
4. Write a brief characterization of someone you know, using the indirect method of characterization.
5. Write a brief characterization of an imaginary character, or one whom you have observed but who is otherwise unknown to you, using the direct method.
6. Begin both of your notebooks.

CHAPTER IV

Appearance Only

STATIC CHARACTERIZATION

THE fullest, most truthful expression of man's character is man himself. As well try to tell someone the nature of the earth without mentioning its shape, its seas, its mountains, its rain and sunshine, its colors at dawn and sunset, as try to express the nature of man without taking into consideration his physical appearance, clothing, belongings.

These are static expressions of his character; that is to say, character expressed without action. They betray his true character to the observant onlooker. We do not always read the legend correctly, but that is because we fail to draw correct conclusions from what we see. The full and accurate record is there; but we are sometimes not wise enough to decipher its message.

In order to write static characterization well, you must train yourself to observe with meticulous care, to be aware of the significance of what you see, and to *select* out of the mass of detail observed the one, two, or three details — that is, the most significant details — that will make the character you wish to create come alive for the reader. Your task is to furnish material from which the reader can create his own imaginative picture, but this picture must be, in its broad outlines, *the one you want the reader to create*. Generalizations will not do. Nor can you give these necessary details unless you first observe them.

For example, if you say, 'She had the face of a discontented, petulant woman,' you mark yourself as a lazy, inefficient writer. The writer of such a sentence attempts to force the reader to imagine the details that make a woman's face reveal a discontented and petulant character instead of *giving* the details and allowing the reader to imagine the face.

Most readers subconsciously refuse to imagine the details when such a vague picture is given; the result is the readers are bored and they know not why. But given a few specific details, the reader enjoys exercising his imaginative faculty to build up the whole picture. Instead of being bored, he is interested, and an interested reader is the end and aim of all writing.

Suppose, instead of the vague descriptive phrase given above you say, 'Her small mouth was pulled together tightly, as if with a drawstring. Her eyes, once bright blue, were now the color of the sky at noonday and in them was a constant look of hurt surprise.' Now you have given your reader material from which to make his own picture, a characteristic picture of your actor.

Age is an important means of characterization, just as gender is important. People in different age-groups react differently to situations and emotional impacts. Men, generally speaking, will act in a different manner from women, and girls from boys. For this reason it is important that the writer let the reader know as soon as possible the approximate age of his character and whether his character is a boy or girl, a man or a woman.

When using static characterization, the tendency of the beginning writer, and often the professional writer as well, is to give a list or inventory of physical details of appearance, for example:

> Millie was plump. Her eyes were brown and her straight hair was also brown. She wore a blue silk dress with a jabot of white lace. Her shoes had low heels.

Never permit yourself to do this. If such pale gray passages as this should ever get by the blue pencil of an editor, and they do sometimes, the reader will be painfully bored. True, there is specific detail here, but the details chosen are not significant. They give neither a clear picture nor a clear characterization and, to make matters worse, they are presented in a dull manner.

Be sure that you write entertainingly at all times. Merely because it takes brains, skill, and thought to write static characterization arrestingly is no excuse for writing it in a dull manner. Put life into your static characterizations, and, if possible, write them so that they build an emotion toward the character described. This may be anything from quiet liking to intense admiration, violent hate, or any one of a dozen other emotional reader reactions.

Never forget that the reader of fiction reads to feel. He doesn't read to think and most certainly doesn't read to be bored. So, in all characterization, and especially in static characterization, watch carefully to see that some emotional value is present and that your writing has life, vitality, and freshness of presentation. The only time it is safe to list details of clothing, et cetera, is after the character has been fully characterized and you want merely to paint a swift sketch of the actor's appearance at that moment.

Now let us see how the dull, static description of Millie — it cannot be truthfully called a characterization since no clear-cut character-traits appear — can be written in an interesting way, a way that will characterize Millie and rouse at least a slight emotional reaction in the reader toward her:

> Millie wore a blue silk dress that she must have 'picked up' at a sale — one of those sales where you see a placard saying, 'No Try-Ons — No Exchanges.' The white lace jabot hung dejectedly crooked and the shoulders were too wide, even for Millie's plumpness. Her low-heeled shoes were as uncompromisingly honest as her candid brown eyes, looking at you from under soft brown hair that had never known the steaming rigors of a permanent-wave machine.

The same details are used as in the previous description, but now they have been related and given significance. The reader is enabled thereby to create his own mental picture of Millie and through that picture to reach a conclusion regarding her character. Just as he would have reached it had he actually seen Millie, except that his conclusion is probably sharper and more accurate now than it would have been without the assistance of the writer in pointing out the specific details of Millie's appearance. Reader-liking is built for Millie, because she is completely honest and without pretense.

The major divisions of static characterization are as follows:

1. Name
2. Lineaments
3. Habitual posture
4. Habitual expression
5. Clothing
6. Surroundings, such as house, belongings, etc.
7. Occupation or profession

First, we shall examine these means of static characterization sep-arately, and then learn how to combine two or more to create and in-dividualize a character-actor that 'lives.'

1. NAME

The importance of names in characterization is not nearly so well understood as it should be. Usually it is the first means of characteriza-tion that the writer uses in a story, since in almost all cases characters are named as soon as they are introduced. The serious, intelligent writer collects names as other people collect postage stamps, first edi-tions, or Egyptian scarabs. *The name chosen becomes a character-tag;* the first means by which the reader begins to become acquainted with the particular actor in the story. The name chosen should be in keeping with the dominant character-trait, dominant emotion, age, race, general background, and occupation or profession of the person.

You do not necessarily have to use strange or unusual names to characterize your actors, though such names are sometimes very ef-fective. In your notebook you will have a list of the unusual, along with names that are more or less commonplace.

For example, note the different characters indicated by the following contrasted names: Tip Reilly and Algernon Blackstone; Marie Tipton and Maggie Kennedy; Paul Howard and Chuck Spangler; Mellie Slat-tern and Brenda Winston. These names not only indicate character; they also indicate social status and, in some cases, personal appearance as well. The name, Lulie Jones, for instance, indicates a small, simple, pleasant small-town girl, while the name Brenda Winston creates a picture of a tall, sophisticated, poised girl who knows her way about.

The sound of names has to be taken into account in characterization and, in some cases, the pictorial effect or spelling of a name makes a great difference in the image built or memory evoked by the name in the mind of the reader. Look at the three feminine names that follow and you will see at once what I mean: Marie — Mari; Betty — Bette; Sarah — Sara.

Use harsh consonants when you wish to express rugged strength, and soft vowels and consonants when you wish to express softness and in-decisiveness. Under *Posture* you will see that we use a man named John Hacker to represent strength and a man named Ollie Whimbledon to represent the opposite characteristics.

So select names for your characters after thoughtful consideration, suiting the name to the character, unless your purpose is to characterize by contrast. In that case you would select a name that expresses the opposite traits of character to those you have assigned to your actor. This technique is often used in humorous stories, where sharp contrasts are especially desirable. For example, in a humorous story you might name your huge, powerful, vile-tempered villain Eddie Meech, and the mild little soul of timidity whom he tortures Jacobus P. Turkingbutch.

2. LINEAMENTS

Under this heading we shall consider both the lineaments of the face and the lineaments of the body. We are accustomed to think of the face contours as expressing character, but we do not so often think of the contours of the body as also expressing character, though of course we all know that this is true. A writer cannot afford to be ignorant, or even vague, regarding any means of character-delineation.

An extremely fat man has a basically different character-appeal from an extremely thin man. This is so obviously true and generally conceded that no proof need be offered. Other characteristic physical details are not so well-known. For example, a man with bony hands and enlarged knuckles is usually classified as thoughtful, philosophical, a worker and a thinker. A man with small plump hands and smooth fingers, as a rule, takes things as they come, is more or less indolent and inclined to let the world go by with a shrug. Countless details such as these a writer must know so well that he can use them almost automatically and at a moment's notice. And the only way to learn them is by repeated, almost constant, and careful observation.

Now let us see how we can do this. Suppose we are walking down the street. A woman is approaching us. We concentrate our attention on the lineaments of her face, disregarding for the moment everything else about her appearance. We notice her wide forehead, large eyes set far apart, straight nose, a rather large mouth, firm yet full lips, a round chin with a dimple or indentation in it. The general contour of her face tells us she is in her early thirties.

What do these lineaments of her face tell us about her character? They tell a great deal — probably more than we shall want to use when we put her in a story. But we need to know everything we can about her character so we can make her really 'come alive' for the reader, and show her acting plausibly and convincingly at all times and in all situations.

Her wide forehead and eyes set far apart tell us that she is highly intelligent. Looking at her straight nose, we know that she is firm in her beliefs and convictions. Her large mouth denotes generosity, sympathy, and versatility. Her chin corroborates the testimony given by her nose, and the dimple shows that she likes admiration and appreciation.

How can we use these details as means of individualizing her as a character and at the same time not bore the reader to extinction? There are literally thousands of ways, but let us try this one:

> Lucia's face was an autobiography of uncut pages. It challenged attention, but defied scrutiny. When a man first saw her, he beheld a blonde madonna exquisitely masked with an inscrutability that both intrigued him and compelled reverence. Later, he discovered a wide inviting mouth, a faintly dimpled chin and ventured — as who would not — to explore. Then, at last, those dark hovering eyes flashed into action like an intermittent stop signal, alternately beckoning and warning.

Remember the steps:

1. Observation of all possible details.
2. Selection of the significant details.
3. Presentation in an interesting manner.

Follow them in every phase of characterization and you can't go wrong.

3. HABITUAL POSTURE

The habitual posture of a person can be very significant of character. Think of someone you know who holds himself erect. Now think of someone who never really sits in a chair, but always lolls. How do these people differ in character? Consider this carefully. There is no doubt that they do differ and in very outstanding ways.

The woman who habitually holds her head tipped to one side is a different person from the woman who holds her head straight and her chin up. Even a tyro in observation and character-analysis knows the general type to which each of these women belongs.

Let us go back to the man who habitually holds himself erect. How can we use this posture to characterize him? There are, of course, countless ways, but this time suppose we avoid actually mentioning his posture and use a figure of speech, the simile:

> Old John Hacker sat in his chair looking like an old bald eagle perched on a crag, ready to defend his right of possession with bill and claw.

The reader 'sees' the erect posture of John Hacker, and is impressed with the man's dominant character-trait of determined courage as shown by his posture, without being actually told that he holds himself stiffly erect. Old John is already 'living' and would make a good Actor A (hero) for a story. The reader instantly is forced to admire him and expects him to do things; to bend forces to his own ends.

Let us return briefly to the man who lolls, and see how he can be presented entertainingly and characteristically, by means of his habitual posture:

> Ollie Whimbledon, through long practice, had achieved a spine so flexible that it permitted him to melt into what gave the effect of a supine position, even in an office chair. The complete muscular relaxation that he could achieve in a chair, even slightly upholstered, passed belief.

As in the previous example, the reader 'sees' Ollie Whimbledon in his characteristic posture and, therefore, knows that Ollie is lazy, and probably not alert either physically or mentally. He is likely a weakling and a sneak. Ollie is the makings of a villain for a story and already the reader dislikes him.

4. HABITUAL EXPRESSION

This is different from the changing expression of eyes, lips, and so on, which will be dealt with under dynamic characterization, or characterization by action. Here we shall consider only the expression of the face in repose.

Train yourself to notice people's faces when they are in repose, and their owners are unconscious that they are being observed. It is then that aspects of character are revealed that you might otherwise never detect. At such moments look carefully. Develop the 'seeing eye' by determination, analysis, and patient practice. That woman who was so bright, so vivacious, so charming a moment ago. Look at her, now that her escort has left for a moment. Her eyes are narrowed, her lips make a straight, inexorable line. If he could see her as she is now — but he won't. Here he comes and she is all softness and smiles again.

The expression on the face of a patient, loving mother is very different from the expression on the face of even the most humane foreman in a large plant. What makes them different? Wherein does the difference lie? In the specific details. Observe these details. Put them into clear, image-making words. Don't say, 'She looked like a motherly woman.'

Don't say, 'He had the face of a factory foreman.' There are many kinds of 'motherly' women. There really is no typical 'foreman's face.' Characterization such as this, if it can be called characterization, is the mark of the slovenly, careless, third-rate writer. It is easy to do better. All that is required is a few minutes' hard, careful thinking.

Let us see what we can do to characterize and individualize a mother by the expression of her face in repose:

> The look of quiet, competent expectancy in Millicent's face was the natural result of having raised four children, who had never in their lives done the expected, the conventional thing.

Now what about the foreman? How can we show him as an individual, by his habitual expression? The word 'foreman' designates his type; now we must individualize him within the type:

> The long straight line of his chin made you think of a granite cliff, and the rigid set of his mouth added to the effect of remote inaccessibility.

Watch the habitual expressions on the faces of people who are unaware that anyone is looking at them. Observe specific details that make up the effect of the face as a whole. The study of habitual expressions is a rich vein well worth mining by the writer who wants to know how to make his characters live as individuals by means of static characterization.

5. CLOTHING

Show any writer what a person wears and the writer should be able to deduce a great deal as to what that person is. Clothing is an extremely important means of characterization. People choose their clothes, and character-traits influence that choice. The way people wear their clothes also indicates character. We judge people by their clothing dozens of times each day. We do it so often that the process, except in special instances, has become automatic, and takes place below the threshold of conscious thought.

The writer teaches himself to do it *consciously*. How do we judge people by their clothes? These are a few of the details we notice and from which we reach our conclusions in probably less than a second of time: approximate cost, color, color combinations, style or lack of style, approximate age, cleanliness, suitability to the person, suitability to the occasion.

Suppose you see a man coming toward you on the street. He wears an oyster-white sport coat, complete with belt and gathers in the back, and heavily padded shoulders. A yellow feather flower protrudes jauntily from his lapel. His slacks are made of expensive flannel, pale lilac in color. His hat, a close-woven panama, is banded with folds of Kelly-green silk.

Is this a man with whom you would trust your wife, or your fortune? The answer is undoubtedly 'No.' How long did it take you to make a practical evaluation of this man's character as indicated by his clothes? Not more than five or six seconds, at the most. You didn't reason about it, you knew. Now on what did you base your opinion?

The man is obviously an extremist, lacking in balanced judgment and taste. You know that he is vain, full of egotism and self-love. His dominant desire is to attract attention through externals, rather than by sound accomplishments or true worth. He may be good-hearted enough, generous in an impulsive way, but you can never depend on him and he is probably a dreadful bore to those who know him. This man exhibits one set of specific details concerning clothing that express the character-traits set down above. Show these details to the reader in a vivid way, and he will see the man and judge him, as you did.

Of course, this man is an extreme case selected for emphasis. Character is just as surely indicated in the most subtle details of dress. One woman chooses a crisp organdy collar for a dark blue dress. Another woman selects a bizarre piece of costume jewelry to ornament the same type of dress. Both are stylish, both in good taste. But the character-traits that impelled each woman to make the choice she did are different.

Study people's clothing and try to discern the individual character-traits expressed by that clothing. The skilled technician overlooks no detail that will help him to build a 'living' character.

6. SURROUNDINGS

The surroundings in which a writer places his character have infinite possibilities for characterization. As was said in Chapter III, you may communicate the character-traits of your actor to the reader either through likeness or through contrast. When using the first method, the surroundings you choose to depict will be in harmony with the character-traits of your actor. When using the second method, the surroundings will be in sharp contrast with the character-traits you aim to show.

Let us see how this works out in actual practice: We shall imagine an actor for your story who is in harmony with his surroundings, and whose surroundings, therefore, indicate his dominant character traits:

> Most women are satisfied with one set of curtains at their bedroom windows, but Nellie Courruthers had three. First there was a gossamer-thin white silk marquisette that hung like gathered mist next to the glass. Over that, draped back at the sides, ruffled curtains of pink net embroidered in rosebuds cascaded frothily to the thickly carpeted floor. Framing this confection was a lambrequin and drapes of pale blue hammered satin. 'So French!' Nellie fluttered, as she gazed on the display of expensive yardage for which the windows were an excuse.

We know nothing about this woman except the way she has chosen to have the windows in her bedroom treated, yet there can be no doubt that at least some of her dominant character-traits are clearly indicated thereby. She likes fussy, expensive personal luxuries and is guided by what things cost rather than their beauty and simplicity. She is a woman who sees only the surface of life, and is mainly interested in the material things of living. Probably selfish and self-centered, she moves through life surrounded by lace-covered pillows, beribboned boxes of chocolates, and Pekinese dogs. Yet, let me remind you, all we have seen are the curtains in this woman's bedroom.

The following is an example of the way character is effectively indicated by means of contrast with surroundings:

> Margaret had never before seen a room like this one. The dark brown woodwork was old-fashioned before Margaret was born. Yellowed wallpaper, on which red and green and gold scrolls sprawled in a monotonously repeated design, was stained in places and peeling off in others. The tailored freshness of Margaret's trim linen suit and her smart pigskin suitcase struck incongruous notes in this atmosphere of age and decay.

For another example of characterization by surroundings, turn back to page 23 and re-read the description of Dean Crawford's office.

7. OCCUPATION AND BACKGROUND

Occupation is usually the next means at hand, after the name, for characterizing a fictional character. And an excellent and versatile tool it is. A doctor will not have the same characteristics — or at any rate, his expressions will not be the same — as a hard-rock miner. A professor of some science in a great university will have a different character from the man who runs the corner grocery store. He will approach his problem in a different way, and solve it by different means. That is why it is important that you fit your character to the occupation selected, or fit the occupation to the character selected.

The characterization given by naming an occupation is a general one, to be sure, but if given where it should be, in the very beginning of a story, it helps to narrow down the characterization and prepare the reader for the *specific detail* that will later characterize the actor *as an individual.* So, whenever your material will permit, give the *occupation* of your characters as an early part of their characterization. Furthermore, when the reader knows the occupation or profession of a character, his imagination automatically builds the correct setting and details of background for that character-actor.

Of course, when we are actually writing a story we seldom characterize by any one means. *We mix the ways of characterization,* and so give a rounder, more lifelike picture than would otherwise be the case. It is in this mixing or integrating that the art of writing characterization begins to develop. In this chapter we are deliberately limiting ourselves, for purposes of study, to static characterization. So let us turn our attention now to ways of *mixing* the different kinds of static characterization, leaving out of account, for the moment, other methods that we shall examine later.

Again I must emphasize the fact that in order to do static characterization, or any other kind of characterization, well, it is essential that you not only *observe details* with meticulous care, but at the same time be aware of the *significance* of what you see. There is no point at all in saying, 'He wore a shabby gray tweed suit with flecks of green and purple in it. His hat was green, with a soft brim. His eyes were gray and his nose straight.' You might go on like this for pages, giving detail, and correct detail at that, but if these details are not given significance by their presentation, if they do not denote character, or even individualize the actor, they are just so much lost effort, both for you and for your reader.

Now let us see what can be done with these same details by giving them significance, and *mixing* the means of static characterization afforded us by the use of a name, clothing, lineaments, habitual facial expression, habitual posture, and profession:

> Doctor Michael Arden wore the same gray tweed suit with green and purple flecks in it that he had worn at Anita's wedding three years before. And his green hat was sat at the same precise angle above his graying hair,

just as he had worn it that day so long ago. But the suit was now mended at the cuffs and the shoulders undeniably sagged. His gray eyes were no longer dauntless, and his nose, though still straight and firm, had a pinched look about the nostrils.

The same details have been used, but now a character emerges, a doctor who is growing old, unsuccessful and defeated, but refuses to admit any of these things, therefore, a man of courage and pride. The fact that he hasn't made money in the practice of his profession makes the reader feel that Doctor Arden was a kindly man who looked after the health of his patients more carefully than the condition of his own pocketbook. The man's character has been shown and an emotion roused in the mind of the reader toward him, by a mixture of several means of static characterization.

There is no easy way to learn how to characterize your story people deftly and skillfully. All I can do for you is to show you a way to make the path a little shorter and a little less hard to follow. But nothing I can do will spare you the labor of learning *how to observe the ways in which character is expressed by static impression; what to observe; how to comprehend and correlate what you see and, thereby reaching an approximately correct conclusion from the facts observed, how to communicate the result to the reader in an interesting way.* I can tell you how to characterize, but I cannot characterize your story-people for you. That is your job. There is no magic formula that will make you, or anyone else, a writer. Ability and hard work and directed effort have in them all the magic there is in the development of a successful writer. You furnish the ability and hard work, I can tell you only how to *direct* your effort.

Don't skip ahead, but at the end of the next chapter I shall give you a specific and practical plan for training yourself to observe the bewilderingly large number of ways in which people unconsciously individualize themselves. These are the ways you will use to communicate to your reader the character-traits of your story people. Remember that you are not going to do as the beginning writer does, stop at *telling* the reader that a character is bad, good, brave, or cowardly. You are going to let the reader *see* and *judge* for himself. Only when that is done is the reader really convinced, only then do your characters 'live.'

Method of Study

1. List at least eight ways in which a writer can characterize an actor by static characterization.
2. What is the difference between a static *description* and a static *characterization*?
3. What are the three steps a writer must take in order to characterize convincingly?
4. Choose three examples from published stories of each static way to characterize, and comment on them.
5. Write a static description of someone you know. Then change this description to a static characterization.
6. Write the characterization of
    (*a*) a man by means of his habitual posture,
    (*b*) a woman by means of the way she wears her hat.

CHAPTER V

Moving-Picture Technique Applied to Fiction Writing

DYNAMIC CHARACTERIZATION BY WALK AND GESTURE

OF COURSE you remember the quotation, 'Full many a flower is born to blush unseen, and waste its sweetness on the desert air.' Flowers aren't the only things about which this is true. Interesting characters are everywhere, blooming unseen, wasting their sweetness — and cash value to the writer — on the desert air of blindness and inability on the part of the writer to observe.

Never say you do not know any interesting people about whom to write. It is far more likely that you know too many. You meet people constantly, in varying degrees of intimacy, in your home, the homes of friends, at your place of business, the club to which you belong, on the street, at the movies, on the country roads. You know so many people that they have almost ceased to register on your consciousness, except in the most superficial manner. The innumerable ways in which people constantly reveal character-traits of a unique and unexpected nature present themselves at every turn if you could but train yourself to see them.

The first step in the process of waking up and beginning to develop your own 'awareness' is to practice *observing*. In this, as in every other human activity, first steps are difficult mainly because you don't know exactly how to go about taking them. It is all very well to say that 'The proper study of mankind is man,' but that doesn't help the bewildered writer who hasn't the faintest idea how to set about pursuing that study in a practical manner.

Suppose a professor of botany took members of his class for a field trip and gave them no more explicit instructions than merely to observe the flowers they saw, without telling them *what to observe*. Suppose he failed to impress upon them the significance of certain phenomena, to advise them how to judge, analyze, and correlate their observations, with a view to arriving at important conclusions! As far as increasing their botanical knowledge is concerned, they might just as well have stayed at home and looked at the illustrations of the *National Geographic Magazine*, without reading the captions or the text.

But suppose that the professor of botany had told them to count the petals of the flowers, examine the way the petals grew on the stem, observe the method of pollenization, the arrangement of pistils, stamen, and so on, and to classify the flowers according to these findings. At least the student would have received the benefit of intelligent direction.

There has been a great deal of circling about the core of the problem of the observation of action as a means of expressing and determining character. High-sounding generalities have been written, but few practical, concrete suggestions have been given. We intend, however, to approach the subject with a definite, clear-cut plan; a plan that is a good blueprint for a beginner in the practice of observation for the purpose of determining character from action, and, at the same time, capable of infinite expansion to meet the needs of every writer, even the professional. For the work of observing character, expressed through action, can never be finished for any writer until for the last time he puts the cover on his typewriter.

The first step in this plan of observing the significance of action in relation to character is to turn the spotlight of our attention on one kind, or type, of action, study that carefully, and then go on in the same way to other kinds and types of action. When we are able to observe these separate expressions of character, and to show their significance to the reader through the medium of words in an arresting manner, then we are ready to combine one or more ways in which character is expressed, thus getting a fuller, richer expression of our actor than would otherwise be the case.

Let us look closely at the ways in which human beings express character through action. Much as I dislike lists and headings and subheadings, the study will be easier if we divide action into two classifications. However, please remember that this is done only so that we may direct our attention to specific points under discussion. Never forget that *one means of characterization cannot be considered apart from all the other means. Characterization must be done with an understanding of the man as a whole.* The spotlight is turned on the première danseuse of the ballet. This serves to focus the attention of the audience on her, but the audience never forgets that the rest of the dancers in the ballet are also on the stage, the stage setting is there, so are a hundred things that influence and condition all that the danseuse expresses in her solo dance. Presently, when the footlights go on, the audience will see all these things again. That is what we are going to do; turn the spotlight of attention from one means of character-expression to another, in order that we may study each in detail. This done, we shall turn on the foot lights and study the character as a whole.

The two broad classifications we shall use in this analysis of dynamic characterization, or characterization through action, are bodily or muscular movements, and speech. Each of these is a very broad field and must be further subdivided in order to avoid confusion because of the infinite variety and complexity of the actions to be observed. The study of bodily or muscular action, as it expresses character, can be more easily studied if the action is grouped under the following headings: walk, gestures, mannerisms, changing facial expressions.

Now that this brief survey of the field is concluded, let us turn back and focus the spotlight of our attention on the ways in which character is shown through bodily or muscular action by means of walk and gestures, leaving mannerisms and changing facial expressions for a later chapter.

WALK AND GESTURES

Walking is one of the most characteristic acts in which a human being can engage. Walking is automatic and all automatic movements — that is, movements over which the conscious mind is no longer in complete control — allow more or less free expression of character, depending on the amount of control exercised. The lazy person walks in a different manner from the energetic person. A secretive man usually takes short steps, holds his arms close to his side and scarcely moves them at all. The frank, open-hearted person invariably strides along, in a decided rhythm, his arms swinging freely.

Let us look at a few examples of the different ways people walk:

> His progress down the avenue was a succession of falls, each one arrested just before it reached the point of disaster by the thrust of a foot against the sidewalk.

What character-traits does this individual way of walking indicate? It indicates that the man is headlong and precipitate in everything he does, rushing ahead without careful consideration and trusting to his strength of will and body to attain his ends. He is impetuous, impulsive, and a physical rather than a mental type.

Now let us observe a very different man in the act of walking:

> He lumbered vaguely about the room like a bear not yet fully awake after a cosy six-months nap.

The reader knows at once that here is a slow-witted man; a man who thinks as slowly and as vaguely as he walks. He is probably stubborn and completely inflexible in his beliefs and convictions.

Now watch this woman and see what her walk tells us about her character:

> She moved across the room toward Harold, not as a thistledown drifts uncertainly this way and that across the grass, but as a high cloud floats straight and sure on a steady wind.

This, we know, is a woman who is gentle and, at the same time certain in her purpose, firm in her determination.

Suppose we reverse the process, by first assigning specific character-traits to our actor, a woman, and then by seeing how we can have her show those character-traits by the way she walks. Just to make it harder, let us suppose that this person has opposing character-traits; superficially she is timid, but underneath that timidity there is a strong streak of courage. We all know that this is true to life. None of us is all one thing or all something else, we are bundles of characteristics that oppose each other, and it is the balance between that opposition that makes the character as a whole.

> Coralie tiptoed hesitatingly into Aunt Sophronia's room as if fearful she would rouse the old woman into her habitual waking state of harsh invective. Reluctantly her eyes went to the bed. It came to her with a shock that never again would the smooth expanse of the candlewick bedspread be disturbed by the bony frame of Aunt Sophronia. Aunt Sophronia was dead. In sudden decision, Coralie brought her heels down hard on the maplewood floor. She went clicking briskly about the room, gathering up the bottles of medicine, drinking-glasses, wisps of gauze; all the miserable evidences of Aunt Sophronia's bitter fight. Death had won in the end and so had put a dramatic period to Aunt Sophronia's domination of Coralie.

Now, just to prove to you that *showing* the reader is far more interesting and effective than *telling* him, suppose this scene were presented without allowing the reader to see how Coralie walked:

> Coralie went into Aunt Sophronia's room. At first she felt timid, but when she realized that Aunt Sophronia was really dead and would never again order her about, courage began to come back to her.

No one will deny that this is flat and dull. The difference in presentation between these two passages is definitely the difference that marks the gap between amateur and professional writing. Therefore, learn to *characterize by action.*

I want you to write down your impression of the character whose walk is described in the following paragraphs. Then check it with the paragraph marked with an asterick (*) at the end of this chapter to see how much I have communicated to you of the character I had in mind as I wrote these paragraphs. Don't fudge. Read. Then write. Then check. This is going to be a test of me as well as of you.

> Elbert lunged down the steps of Science Hall and propelled himself across the campus. His long, muscular arms swung wildly in unison with his legs.
> 'Hi, El!' boomed Hob Englewright, emerging from behind the trunk of an old elm. 'Wait!'
> Simultaneously Elbert's legs stopped swinging, his arms hung motionless at his sides.
> 'Whadja stop me for, twerp?' he scowled. 'I only got forty seconds to make Psyc B. Outa my way.' Elbert leaned forward and the purposeful rhythm of arms and legs began again.

What are the dominant character-traits of this young man? Think. Write. And then turn to the end of the chapter. I fully expect you to get a grade A on this.

Now I shall give you two examples of the wrong way, and of approximately the right way, to present character-traits by means of describing the actor's walk. By 'right way' I mean a manner that will clearly and unmistakably communicate to the reader the character-traits you have in mind, and do it in an entertaining way. In order to accomplish this you will avoid trite phrases and overworked figures of speech, striving always for fresh, timely presentation, some new way of saying the same old thing that writers have been saying for hundreds of years and will continue to say for hundreds of years more.

Just to show you what I mean by trite expressions, here are a few sentences out of the many that cause editors to turn pale and reach for the antidote to relieve the headache and dark brown taste caused by an excessive intake of trite phrases:

> She walked listlessly to and fro.
>
> He walked as if the weight of the world rested on his shoulders.
>
> She tripped merrily down the street.
>
> She tripped along like a young girl.
>
> He walked slowly, dragging his feet like an old man.

Remember that you have really nothing new to say. All you have to sell to the editors is skill in saying the old things in new ways. Yet there must never be the slightest straining for effect.

Let us look at a man, whom we shall call Everard Dashiel, as he walks down the street. This is how the beginning writer would tell about him:

> Everard Dashiel walked buoyantly, with a decided springiness in his step.

There are the bare facts, correct but dull! If the reader works hard he can deduce from them the dominant character-trait of the gentleman. But the reader is a lazy fellow who doesn't intend to work yet, on the contrary, is expecting to be entertained by you. So suppose the beginner discards his first feeble effort and decides to give this matter at least as much thought as he would give to the ordering of a dinner for a beautiful blonde, if he is a man, or to the selection of that combination of impracticable materials put together in a completely idiotic way, the result of which is called a hat, if the writer is a woman.

After mental travail of no mean order the following result might be achieved, using, you will observe, the same basic facts:

> Everard Dashiel walked with the springy, confident stride of a man who is sure not only that the universe is God's gift to him, but that he is God's gift to the universe.

Which version is the reader going to like better and, what is still more important as far as your bread and butter is concerned, which one is the editor going to like better? I'll give you one guess. If you need more you'll never make a writer.

Another example and we shall leave this pedestrian subject of walking and go on to other, though not more useful, means of dynamic characterization.

Here is what a beginning writer would tell us about the way Owen walks:

> Owen slouched listlessly along.

Now there is nothing really wrong with that except that every month approximately a thousand writers have approximately a thousand characters who 'slouch listlessly along.' The 'tired business man,' the 'busy housewife,' the 'general reader' weary of this in time, while the state the editor reaches is past telling about.

So what can the writer who wants to rise above the gray dead level of mediocrity do with 'Owen slouched listlessly along'? Well, his first effort might go something like this: 'Did you ever see a sag walking? That was Owen...'

This would have been good once, but not any more. This has been done — with variations — too many times. If you are writing a story that might possibly see publication within a few months, you could try to use a popular song hit of the moment. If this doesn't work out, better chuck the idea and see what else the brain will give up on demand. After some profitless scribbling the following is evolved:

> Owen is the only man I know who can walk with an approximately erect posture, and at the same time give the effect of a cold, overcooked piece of macaroni.

Or this:

> Owen walked toward us with all the firmness and vigor that one associates with a jellyfish out of water.

After this, any direct naming of the dominant character-trait that Owen shows by the way he *walks* is, I am certain, superfluous. Or of the dominant emotion, roused in the reader by this account of Owen's peregrinations, that is, I suspect, profound loathing.

Now we come to another means by which persons continually give away their characters to prying writers, who are the most ruthlessly curious set of Peeping Toms in the world. And that is through *gestures*. These, like walking, are almost entirely the product of subconscious impulses. This is true even in the case of the political orator and professional lecturer, for all the training in the world cannot induce a man or woman to make one fully uncharacteristic gesture. And as for people in everyday life, their every gesture, or even the fact that they refrain from gestures, is an open book that the writer who runs may read, provided he is literate in the language that characteristic action speaks. If he doesn't know that language, he had better start at once to learn it by the only possible means — observation of others and of himself, by analysis and synthesis.

The public speaker, either consciously or unconsciously, usually exaggerates his natural gestures for the purpose of emphasis. The classic example is Theodore Roosevelt, pounding the rostrum with his clenched fist, waving an imaginary 'big stick' and clenching his jaws until the muscles of his cheeks and neck stood out in knots. Some people, who never saw Theodore Roosevelt, might take exception to the idea of any man being able to gesticulate with his jaws, but anyone who ever saw Teddy speak knows that he did just that — and very effectively and characteristically. The man's power and determination and purposefulness was expressed in every gesture. The most distinguished bearer of the Roosevelt name in this generation uses a very characteristic gesture of which he is probably unconscious — a toss of the head for emphasis at the end of every significant sentence. This, while more restrained than the gestures of his predecessor, is none the less revealing of deep-seated character-traits.

But not many of us are going to use orators or presidents in our stories. More often we shall use, as character-actors, the proprietor of the drugstore where we buy our shaving cream, the banker who renews our mortgage or doesn't renew it, the man with whom we are falling in love, or the lady receptionist in the dentist's office.

In order to identify an individual gesture with an individual character-trait, we shall reverse the process. Instead of observing other people, let us *observe ourselves*. This is a very important procedure, because you can use it at a moment's notice while you are sitting at your desk. I advise you to be alone when you employ it, however, otherwise, well-meaning but mistaken friends or relatives may rush you into court for a sanity hearing:

Imagine yourself to be the proprietor of a drugstore that has just opened in a suburban shopping center or a small town. You are a kindly, genial sort of fellow and you want to make a good impression on the people of the neighborhood. Mrs. Smith comes in to buy a package of cigarettes for Mr. Smith, some tennis balls for Junior, and an alarm clock. What gesture will you make as you swing the door open for Mrs.

Smith? Probably you will bow and wave your free hand in a sweeping outward arc that is mainly accomplished by shoulder and wrist movements. The palm of your hand will be exposed, fingers slightly flexed, thumb parallel with the palm. Mrs. Smith's subconscious mind will register this and she will instantly, and also consciously, decide that you are a man to be trusted and that she will trade with you in future instead of that stiff crabbed old Hawkins across the street. And that evening when Mr. Smith asks her how she knows that you are a better man than Druggist Hawkins, who has never yet been caught cheating the Smith family, she will say, 'I just feel it, Henry. And you know my intuitions are always right.'

Now imagine yourself to be your competitor, Druggist Hawkins. You are seated at the desk in your little office at the back of the store. A salesman comes in, tries to sell you a line of drugs you have never before handled. The salesman is fluent, persuasive. He tells you these drugs are purer, better, more attractively packaged than your present line. But his talk irks you. There is just one thing you want to know. (Remember, you are a selfish, calculating man, intent only on making a profit. What gestures will you, as Hawkins, naturally make? Let yourself go at this point. Ten to one you will jab the blotter in front of you with a stiff forefinger.) 'That's all right,' you will snarl, 'but you tell me this!' Now you will emphatically jab the air in front of the salesman with the same stiff forefinger. 'Suppose I do change to your line.' Now you will clench your fingers and jab the third stripe of your tie with a stiff thumb, as you say, 'What do *I* get out of it?'

Leaving the words out of account, and considering the gestures only, we must conclude that Mrs. Smith was right in her estimate of the characters of these two men, even though we may doubt that intuition had anything to do with the way she reached that conclusion.

For the author, what is the real importance of the little object lesson in gestures given above? You cannot always be observing — you cannot always have a model before you. But you are always with yourself. So use yourself as a model, and at the same time as a guinea pig on which to practice experiments in expressing character-traits by gestures. *Your problem of interpreting your characters is exactly the same as though you were an actor. And your success, as his, will be in due proportion to your ability to identify yourself with that character.* In other words, *be* that character.

Imagine yourself to be the character in your story. You are a determined, ruthless man, engaged in a war of price-slashing with a rival firm across the street. Your competitor has come to talk over a plan of compromise. You are sure of ultimate victory so you order him from your office. *Try to feel this man's emotions. What gestures will you make?* All right, make them. Now what did you do? You probably pounded your desk with your clenched fist, then made several shoving motions with the same fist toward the door, thus indicating your implacable determination to continue the warfare and that the interview was ended.

Now reverse the process. Suppose you are by nature a quiet, self-controlled man who believes that what he thinks and feels is nobody's business but his own. But you want to portray a man who, for plot purposes, must be so overcome with enthusiasm for the leading lady in a Broadway play that he climbs on his orchestra seat, at a tense moment in that play, swings his arms wildly above his head and shouts his approbation of her performance and personal charm. Sitting quietly at your desk, you can't understand this man. But you must *understand* him if you are to make him *live* in your story. There is one way to do it. Without stopping to think how silly you are going to look, leap up on your chair, wave your arms wildly and shout that Maybelle LeMay is the loveliest creature alive, the greatest actress that the stage has ever seen and that you personally adore her. How did you *feel?* Why, you felt a great uprush of glorious enthusiasm. You forgot your inhibitions and shed your stiff protective armor of conventional behavior. You felt free and happy. That is, you became temporarily an extrovert, with energies outgoing and untrammeled. For an infinitesimal moment of time you *were* an extrovert and therefore, being an extrovert, you could understand an extrovert character. You *identified* yourself with that man; you were no longer Melville Smith.

Character and gestures, gestures and character. Like the words 'mom,' 'pop,' 'tot,' read them forward or backward, the meaning is the same. By reproducing the proper gesture you can temporarily create within yourself the appropriate character-trait, or the emotion that springs from that character-trait responding to impact from without. *By temporarily reproducing within yourself the desired character-trait and the emotion that springs from that character-trait under impact from without, you can unfailingly make the appropriate gesture.* Rembrandt is said to have painted portraits of himself seven — or was it ten? — times in one year. The writer can paint word pictures of himself seventy or a hundred times each year, and each portrait will be completely different. Because a writer is not one person. He is many persons. How many he is depends on the width of his sympathy, the depth of his understanding and the effort he makes toward comprehension.

* He is young, full of animal spirits, unthinking in the full meaning of the word, though able to memorize facts easily. He is readily influenced by habit and automatically obeys an ordinary command. Note that he stops when Hob calls to him, though he is intent on getting to Psychology B on time; not that he is interested in Psychology B, but the behavior pattern imposed on him from without demands that he be punctual at classes. He has a good deal of determination and his reactions are likely to manifest themselves first physically. In other words, he acts automatically and thinks, if at all, later. These character-traits could bring about some very dramatic story-action.

Method of Study

1. What are the two ways of dynamic characterization dealt with in this chapter?
2. Why are the automatic actions, that is, those made without conscious thought, so much more indicative of character than those made consciously, that is, planned to a greater or less extent?
3. Which is the more interesting to the reader, characterization couched in familiar words and phrases, or characterization made by fresh, original words and phrases?
4. Write a brief characterization of someone you know, by describing the way he walks.
5. Characterize a stranger, whom you have observed, by describing his gestures and other bodily movements.
6. Make a list of words or phrases descriptive of the various means used in this chapter to characterize dynamically. For example, for walk and posture: barged, clumped, edged, scuffed, shambled, scurried, wavered.

    NOTE 1. The purpose of this assignment is to *aid* the student in building a large and fluent writing vocabulary that is pictorial, active, and emotion-making. Never forget that, as a writer, words are the sole medium through which you reach your reader; *words are your tools*. It is not that you will use any of these particular words in your writing, but that by such practice you will *train yourself* to be observant and specific in your choice of detail.

NOTE 2. The following is quoted from a letter by a serious student who tells how he *studies:*

'Here is the outline of my vocabulary-building scheme:

'1. When I read a story, I underline with a blue pencil all of the words, phrases, and sometimes whole paragraphs used to characterize physically.

'2. I take single sheets of paper and in the upper right corner, in caps, I write the name of a part of the body. These sheets cover face, gesture, smile, posture, feet, etc. The sheets are then organized in alphabetical order and stacked loose in a folder, so that any desired one may be selected and put into the typewriter for additional lists, without having to remove clips or other fastenings.

'3. Upon finishing my reading of the story, I pick out my underlinings. If the first one is about smile, I select my sheet titled "smile" and on it I copy the words. I do likewise for all the other subjects I have marked. For example:

'*Eyes:*

'His gray eyes smouldered under a scowl.

'She drew back from the profanity of his eyes, shivering.

'*Face:*

'With a face eroded by decades of hardship.

'His seasoned face fringed with white.

'His face was on the homely side — the plain but honest type.

'*Hands:*

'He found a light, chill sweat in the palm of his hands.

'I have recently added more subjects to my list, taking in the various emotions, sensory appeals, types of settings, etc.'

7. Choose three examples from published stories of each of the ways to characterize dynamically.

CHAPTER VI

Look at His Face

DYNAMIC CHARACTERIZATION BY FACIAL EXPRESSION,
EYE AND GLANCE

You meet a man for the first time. It is important to you that you arrive quickly at a fairly accurate conclusion regarding this man's character. What do you do first?

You look at his face.

You do not consciously plan to look at his face. You do not reason about it. You automatically do it. Why?

Because thousands of experiences, beginning in very early childhood and continuing until the present time, have impressed upon your subconscious mind that by observing a man's face you can come most quickly and most surely to an understanding of that man's character, of the man behind that face.

We have already, in a previous chapter, considered the lineaments of the face, its shape and form, in relation to character. Here we shall consider only facial expression in relation to character portrayal.

It may seem strange at first, but the very facility you have gained through your thousands of experiences in judging character by facial expression may handicap you, at first, in your function as writer. Because the mental processes of observing, comparing, weighing, and reaching a conclusion have, by long practice, become *synthesized* into one process of almost lightning-like rapidity. You are no longer fully conscious of the specific details from which you draw your conclusions as to the man's character. In everyday, practical affairs, the conclusion is the important thing, and the details that caused you to reach that conclusion are pushed into the background, if you are conscious of them at all.

It is necessary that the writer learn to reverse this process and turn the spotlight of his attention on the details. *He should train himself to observe consciously the most minute, as well as the most obvious, changes of facial expression. By means of these details he will create in the reader's mind an accurate picture of a character, so that the reader will, in turn, form his own opinion of this character by what amounts to his own observation of these details.* Of course, this accuracy of observation of significant specific detail is important, not alone in the matter of delineation by facial expression but in every other phase of characterization.

Each of us reveals his character in every movement, conscious and unconscious, and in every word he speaks. The *expression* of character is everywhere, though the trained observer is not always present. No one can control all the muscles that come into play even in completing the simplest act. And it is in the unconscious movement of muscles that character is most often revealed. These unconscious movements are those that the writer must carefully observe, although conscious movements are also highly indicative of underlying character-traits.

The reason it is imperative for the writer to observe specific details, as they apply to character-revelation, is that the reader will believe almost nothing the writer tells him; he has to be *shown*. You may tell the reader a dozen times that a fictional character is mean and cruel, and the reader, in all probability, will pay almost no attention to you. But if once you show this character *doing* mean and cruel acts, or expressing meanness and cruelty by facial expression, the reader will not only believe you implicitly, but he will immediately hate the character and, thereby, be involved emotionally in your story.

It is a great mistake to suppose, as even some established writers sometimes appear to do, that the writer does all the work and the reader is passive. Exactly the contrary is the case. The writer and the reader must each do his part, if a worth-while effect is to be achieved. When the writer does too much of the work, leaving nothing for the reader to do, the reader is bored. This is what happens when the writer presents the reader with already-arrived-at conclusions regarding the character of a story-actor. The reader wants to be shown the facts and allowed the satisfaction of reaching his own conclusions. The reader is interested only when he is taking an active creative part in the partnership of writer-reader. That is to say, *involve the reader imaginatively as well as stir his emotions.*

If this were not so, the writer's task of characterizing his actors would be a very simple one, instead of being perhaps the most complicated and difficult phase of literary effort. All he would have to do would be to say, 'Mildred was a mean, selfish, stingy, and cruel woman,' and the whole job would be done, as far as Mildred was concerned, once and for all. But this kind of characterization leaves nothing for the reader to do. He sees no reason why the writer should be believed, he is not convinced and he finds the whole procedure excessively dull.

The fact that the reader must be *shown*, not told, is so fundamental as to require no proof, but since in the very nature of things you, as reader, are skeptical of what I say, I shall show you what I mean and so, I hope, make this important point clear.

You are sitting on a bench in the park close by the edge of a lake. I, whom you do not know at all, am sitting on the other end of the bench. A tall, elderly gentleman, thin-faced, keen-eyed, approaches slowly along a winding graveled path. I say, 'That man is very kind-hearted and loves children.'

Do you believe me? Are you interested? The answer to both questions is undeniably 'No.' But at that moment a little girl runs down the path, earnestly engaged in rolling a hoop. She collides with the tall, elderly man, falls down on the gravel, and skins both knees. Her hoop rolls on into the lake. You see the old man tenderly pick the child up, look at her sympathetically, brush her dress, smilingly pat her on the back, and give her a dollar to buy a new hoop. Now, do you believe that the old man is kind-hearted and loves children? Are you interested? The answer to both questions is undeniably 'Yes.' Why? Because you were shown the expression of character and allowed to reach your own conclusions.

Now we shall return for a moment to Mildred, because the short imagined scene, which you and I have just played, illustrates the futility of telling the reader that Mildred is mean, selfish, stingy, and cruel. What the writer must do is show the reader that Mildred is all that he says she is. Then, from the *selected specific details* that the writer offers as *proof* that Mildred is a thoroughly unlikable woman, the reader will create a picture of Mildred and feel a definite emotion toward her. Looking at this picture, or series of pictures, he will reach the conclusion concerning her that you want him to reach, by the same mental processes he would have used had he seen Mildred in person. The reader likes to do this. You are affording him a way of living, too.

EYE AND GLANCE

This is applicable to practically all characterization. But at the moment we are especially interested in finding out the best way to *communicate* character-traits as they are shown by facial expression. The chief centers of facial expression are the eyes and mouth. First, let us turn our attention to the eyes:

Suppose that you have a character in your story who is a middle-aged woman, pleasant, amiable, not especially bright, and who has lived a protected life. It will do no good to tell the reader this, unless you follow the statement with specific detail showing that what you say is true. How can you solve the difficulty, through her eyes alone? The following is an example of one way it might be done:

> Lucia Warrington looked up at me. Her round blue eyes, surrounded by tiny wrinkles in her creamy, well-cared-for-skin, were as sweet, as expressionless, as unaware of life, as those of a six-months' old baby.

Or your problem may be entirely different, because your character is different. You write, 'Jim was selfish, cold, and calculating.' Of course you know that won't do to go in your story; you merely want to get the man down on paper and his character thoroughly clarified in your own mind. After a little thought you write, keeping in mind that Jim's eyes are to be featured in this characterization of him:

> Jim looked at Elaine sharply, his dark brown eyes under bushy black eyebrows taking a swift inventory of her mink coat, the diamond that sparkled on the third finger of her left hand, and the hat that even he could see was a French model. His eyelids drooped a little, but not enough to hide the cold, acquisitive gleam that shone between the narrowed slits.

The reader sees Jim and gets a very good idea of Jim's character from what he sees.

> Miss Manners's face was as guiltless of a wrinkle as her starched white uniform, and equally expressionless.

The reader instantly senses from this that Miss Manners would be of small comfort in a sickroom.

> 'Will you take me to the elevator?' Kay asked, but her eyes plainly said, 'I must see you alone for a minute.'

You, as writer, have done your part in furnishing specific and significant detail. The reader has done his part, which is *to use the details you have given him as nuclei around which to build the completed picture that reveals your actor's character.*

A few more examples may be helpful:

Telling the reader:

> Alexis had a violent temper.

Showing the reader:

> Alexis' protruding eyes blazed into mine with an almost maniacal glare.

Telling the reader:

> Myra was gentle, patient, and kind.

Showing the reader:

> Myra's calm hazel eyes seemed not to see the mud dripping on her new beige rug from three-year-old Davie's water-soaked clothes. You could tell that she saw only a frightened child who needed sympathy and a hot bath.

Telling the reader:

> He was an honest man.

Showing the reader:

> He looked at me with clear, unwavering eyes as he told me his astounding story. It was that look, which never faltered, that convinced me he was telling the truth.

Telling the reader:

> He was a cowardly man.

Showing the reader:

> Elzy's pale blue eyes were set close together. They shifted uncertainly from side to side under Alan's accusing look. In them was confusion and a hint of fear — fear of what Alan might do next.

Before we leave the subject of eyes I wish to mention something about their treatment that has no direct bearing on characterization, but is, nevertheless, important to the writer. For some reason for which I have as yet discovered no convincing explanation, the beginning writer, and sometimes the professional writer as well, takes greater liberties with the eyes of his fictional characters than with any other portion of their anatomy. For example, I frequently find the two following sentences both in manuscripts and in published stories: 'She lowered her eyes to the floor,' and 'She dropped her eyes.' If the poor woman actually did either of these things the result would be horrifying. Fortunately, Nature has made it impossible for even the most absent-minded man or woman to be so careless. Why not say instead, 'She lowered her eyelids,' and 'She looked at the floor'? I have no idea.

As another example of the strange things writers do with the eyes of their characters: 'He plunged his eyes deep into hers.' Awful thought! If he really did it, the ferocious act no doubt blinded both of them for life. And this: 'She tore her eyes from the moon and cast them upon the beach.' A strenuous and athletic lady, if we are to believe the writer.

Watch your writing carefully for phrases that create ridiculous, impossible, or repulsive pictures for the reader. They defeat your end.

FACIAL EXPRESSION

There are two general ways in which character can be shown by facial expression. We can use the *habitual* facial expression of an actor, that is, the expression when the face is in repose. Or we may use the facial expression that denotes *mood* or *emotion* expressed in a *highly characteristic* way.

To explain in detail:

1. *Characterization by habitual facial expression*

Imagine that we are looking at three people who are sitting across from us in a doctor's waiting-room: an old man, a middle-aged woman, and a young woman of twenty-two or twenty-three. They are sitting quietly, not even reading the last year's magazines on the table. What is the character of each? Let us see what the *facial expression* of each will tell us.

We look at the old man: We see immediately that he is impatient, cruel, domineering. We write on our notebook:

> His thin lips are set in a bitter curve below a pinched, bony nose that twitches violently every time someone goes into the doctor's office ahead of him

We look at the middle-aged woman: It doesn't take long to see what kind of character she has. She is nervous, a great worrier, and emotionally unstable. We write in our notebook:

> Wrinkles crisscross her face, and she is using every one of them. Her washed-out blue eyes and the drooping corners of her mouth make her look as if she cried a great deal — and enjoyed it.

Now the young woman: We wonder what she is doing here, she looks so full of health and vitality. Her expression shows she is strong and courageous. So we write:

> Her brown eyes are bright and brave above a resolutely lifted chin. Those soft curved lips would, we feel sure, continue to smile, no matter what verdict awaits her there in the doctor's office.

2. *Characterization by facial expression showing emotion or mood*

Let us take one emotion, a simple one, that of anger, and see how three people of totally different *character* will express anger by their facial expression:

> The heavy muscles of Saylor's jaw tightened, drew into ugly knots. His heavy black eyebrows drew together, above his small black eyes, eyes that glittered now with demoniacal fury.

> A slow red mounted in Alec's face, but his cool smile did not change.

> There was one swift blaze of fury in her eyes, suddenly hidden by lowered lids. A moment later, she was twinkling and sparkling up at him, her face all gaiety and laughter.

Always remember that when you show emotion or mood in a major character, you should show it *characteristically, not in a way that it might be shown by anyone*. Often this is done for minor characters as well, but it is not so necessary as it is when dealing with characters of major importance.

The mouth is always an important means of character delineation. By the changing expressions of the mouth, the writer can show many character-traits through the outward evidences of emotion that are made evident through the muscular movements of the lips. Sincerity, insincerity, cruelty, avarice, sympathy, anger, tenderness: all these and many more are shown clearly in this manner.

Suppose you read in a story, 'Lora turned her smile on and off as if it were an electric light.' What does that show you about Lora? It shows you that Lora is an affected person; a poseur, one who tries, not very cleverly, for an effect of friendliness and warmth.

But suppose the writer had said this about Lora:

> Her smile was natural, untouched by artifice. It made me think of sunshine and warm summer afternoons and the scent of wild roses blooming in thick grass.

Here no actual details of the smile are given, only a generalization. It 'was natural, untouched by artifice,' followed by the emotional impression on the observer. But the reader has no difficulty in creating imaginatively, from the material given him, Lora's dominant character-traits, and a definite impression, not only of Lora's smile, but probably of Lora herself.

Suppose we reverse the procedure we were using before we became interested in Lora and her smile. Instead of first *telling* the reader the character of the person we have in mind, let us *show* the character first, and afterward try to see the effect, in so far as character-traits go, on the reader:

> I suppose Clint Sawyer must have had teeth, but not once during the interview did I see them. When he talked, his thin lips parted just enough to let the words slip out, then he pressed them tightly together again. His smile, a line stretching across his mouth, was distinctly alarming. It took me a moment to realize that the singular grimace was meant for a smile, no doubt self-congratulatory, since he had definitely gotten the better of me.

It would not require a very clever reader to discern from this that Clint was a decidedly unpleasant person, scheming, acquisitive, secretive, and determined. But the reader was given this information indirectly, and by implication. The reader was not bludgeoned with the information. Instead, he was left feeling free to make up his own mind about the character of Clint Sawyer, and it is this feeling of freedom, although unconscious, that the reader likes. You, as writer, must see that you do not obviously infringe on this apparent freedom of thought. Of course, the writer himself knows that it is only apparent, since he allows the reader to see that which will leave the desired impression, and nothing else.

While it is true that well-defined character-traits can be shown by the eyes alone, or by the mouth alone, sometimes the writer will get a better effect by combining details of the mouth and eyes and blending them with the expression of the face as a whole. This is by no means as complicated as it sounds. The following example begins with a generalization that tells the reader what to expect, then follows with specific detail:

> Serenity was in every line of Bella's face. It shone from her calm brown eyes, her composed smile. Only the faint color in her cheeks, and the pulse that beat in the hollow of her throat, betrayed the emotional strain through which she had just come.

We could have said to the reader, 'Bella feels deeply, is sensitive, and yet has a great deal of poise and self-control.' But the reader would have been completely indifferent, both to Bella and to the truth of what we said. Instead, in order to interest the reader and convince him that Bella possesses the character traits we have assigned to her, we put her on the stage and let her *act* them out. In other words, we *show* her to the reader.

I do not mean to say that you should never characterize an actor by direct exposition or analysis. Sometimes, especially in the case of minor characters and where brevity is necessary, either or both methods may be used. The great danger of using such methods of characterization lies in the possibility that they may produce results dull and lifeless. How to characterize interestingly by exposition and analysis will be discussed in Chapter XV.

While it is true that no facial expression can be imagined that does not express character to some degree, facial expression is sometimes used to excellent advantage for a purpose other than characterization. This purpose is that of individualizing a character, making him appear a living, breathing, human being.

The following serves to illustrate:

> Ellie shut her eyes tight and wrinkled her pretty little nose. Then she opened her eyes and stared at Paul solemnly. 'Stop making faces and answer me,' Paul said sharply.
> 'I'm not making faces!' Ellie was indignant. 'I always do that when I think.'

Of course, Ellie's shutting her eyes and wrinkling her nose does characterize her to some extent, but it accomplishes more than that; it individualizes her, the reader *sees* her thinking. Almost everyone thinks occasionally, but not many people shut their eyes and wrinkle their noses when they think. So the act tends to make Ellie an individual. Or:

> His comments were addressed to the group as a whole, but Jane felt that his smile was destined for her alone, and carried a special-delivery stamp as well.

One of the useful devices that trained writers use is this one of individualizing their characters by giving them a mannerism in keeping with their dominant character-traits. This mannerism is then repeated at intervals throughout the story, so that the reader will not forget it. Of course this mannerism may be almost any characteristic act, but, at the moment, we are considering only mannerisms of facial expression.

There are two broad divisions of mannerisms that individualize first and characterize afterward; the mannerism that rouses liking in the reader for the character, and the mannerism that rouses dislike in the reader for the character. Most readers would be inclined to like a pretty young girl who shut her eyes and wrinkled her nose when she thought seriously. On the contrary, let us see the kind of facial mannerisms we might use to individualize an unlikable character:

> Gameliel Yancy pulled the right side of his mouth down until his thin, blue lips slanted at an angle of forty-five degrees across his lined face. Then he twitched his beak of a nose and sniffed loudly. Funny thing about Yancy. He always did that just before he said a decisive 'No.' So I wasn't surprised when he barked out of the upper corner of his mouth, 'You've got your nerve, Dave, coming to me for a favor!'

It is a curious fact, and one that every careful writer should remember, that men are almost always unconscious of their mannerisms, while women are almost always conscious of theirs, and use them deliberately, in order to create an effect that they think will be advantageous to them. There is, I believe, a deep psychological significance behind this difference. Men, for uncounted thousands of years, have depended on what they said and what they did to gain their ends. On the contrary, women have been almost altogether dependent on their appearance and on their feminine appeal to men to get what they wanted. The result is that women use mannerisms consciously, while with men mannerisms are simply unconscious muscular reflexes that have become habits by repetition. This is not a criticism of either sex, but a statement of facts and conclusions of practical use to the observant writer.

CHARACTERS MAKE YOUR STORY

One word of caution before we leave the subject of characterization by means of facial expression. As always, avoid the use of trite, worn-out words and phrases to describe eyes, smiles, and all the varying facial expressions. Do not say, 'Her eyes were pensive'; 'She smiles sweetly'; 'He laughed mockingly'; He turned as red as a beet'; 'She was as white as a ghost.' These were good once, but that was a long time ago. Now they are worn out from overuse. Shabby and shopworn, they serve no purpose to the ambitious writer of today. Their use marks him as mentally lazy, careless, and inefficient. Delete and replace them with fresh, timely phrases that are pictorially accurate and, at the same time, pleasantly surprise the reader by their aptness and novelty.

Method of Study

1. Why must the manner in which the writer observes faces differ from that used by the layman (non-writer)?
2. State the function of the various details of facial expression. Is it primarily to convey to the reader the complete impression of the face, or to give him merely sufficient material with which to construct the picture the writer has in mind?
3. In characterization is it better to tell the reader the dominant character-trait of an actor, or show the actor demonstrating his dominant character-trait by action?
4. Write a characterization of someone you know by
   (a) telling the reader the dominant character-trait possessed by the person you have in mind,
   (b) showing the character-trait by means of facial expression.
5. Add to (b) above some facial expression or movement of the facial muscles or eyes that individualizes, yet is not out of character.
6. Make a list of words or phrases descriptive of the various means used in this chapter to characterize dynamically (see Chapter V, Method of Study, number 6).
7. Select three examples from published stories of dynamic characterization by means of facial expression and analyze them.

CHAPTER VII

Listen to Him Speak

TONE OF VOICE AND WAY OF SPEAKING

ONE of the first requirements of any piece of fiction is that the actors speak naturally, as people of their character, education, and station in life might be expected to speak. Natural, convincing conversation is often very difficult for writers until they have had considerable experience. Always supposing that your fictional characters are fully alive in your own mind, there is one sure, one easy way to write natural, convincing conversation.

Listen to your characters speak.

Don't write speeches and force them into the mouths of your characters. Don't tell your characters what to say and how to say it.

Let them tell you.

Until you learn to do this, everything your characters say will be wooden, stilted, uninteresting; or they will all talk alike and you will have one character, perhaps well defined but far more likely only a type, speaking through different mouthpieces. Readers feel the unreality of this at once and, as a result, are not occupied by your story. Guard carefully against letting this happen. *Let every character speak for himself.*

'All right,' you say. 'I'm game. I'll try anything once. I have a character in a story I've never sold — can't imagine why, because it has a marvelous plot — named Joe Doaks. Come here, Joe. Go ahead. I'm listening.'

Silence. Not a word out of Joe.

You feel embarrassed, not only for Joe, but for yourself. Why won't Joe talk? Something must be done to save the situation. You hastily scribble on a pad one of Joe's speeches in the story — the story that hasn't sold in spite of a plot that you believe positively is a world-beater:

> 'I am extremely depressed,' Joe says — in your story. 'Everything has been going against me lately. Life has become so painful that unless there is a rift in the lowering clouds very soon, I feel I shall be justified in bringing my unhappy existence to an end.'

You hand me this. I read it. I tear it up. I tell you: 'Joe Doaks didn't say that. You made it up. You *think* about Joe awhile. You don't *know* Joe. What does Joe *look* like? Where and how long did Joe go to school? What does he like to eat? What kind of clothes does Joe wear? What is his hobby? His favorite movie star? Answer those questions and then listen to Joe again.'

You scratch your head in your endeavor to think. In another minute Joe begins to talk. You write frantically, because Joe talks fast. He says:

> 'Everything is on the blink. I ain't had a break in years. If something don't come my way by tomorrow noon, I'm going to bump myself off.'

'Are you sure,' I demand severely, 'that Joe said this?'

'Of course I am' — you are indignant. 'I tell you, I heard Joe say it!' Fine. If you keep listening to Joe you will sell that story yet.

But you can't 'hear Joe say it' until you have him clearly characterized and individualized in your own mind. In writing fiction for today's readers there is no place for skimpy characterization, or for puppets, and even the pure 'type' character can appear only in very minor rôles.

All this means that *the writer must do very careful work in creative characterization before he starts to plot his story, and long before he starts to write it.* How can you tell how a character will speak until you yourself *know* that character through and through? Observation precedes characterization, just as characterizing your actor precedes both plotting and writing. Before you can 'listen' to your character speaking, you will necessarily have listened to many people conversing in real life.

'But I've listened to people speaking all my life!' you protest. True, but now you have to listen in a new way. *You have to listen analytically and understandingly.* It is easy to tell the writer to listen to people speak; but it is not always easy to do it, just at first, anyway. The untrained observer does not know what to listen for. Remember the old botany professor and his class that we used in Chapter IV as an illustration of this very situation as applied to the observation of action? Now we are looking for a way to observe one phase of action, that of speaking and the principle is the same.

If you will make a list of the most important points to be noted in listening to conversation and focus your attention on them, you will be able to recognize, classify, arrange, and correlate the facts you observe and so become aware of their significance. Knowing their significance in terms of character, you can then reverse the process, and by having your character speak in one certain way you can make his conversation characteristic and arresting. All of which sounds very abstract and dull, but is really intensely interesting and dramatic. Suppose we state it another way: If you know *what to listen to*, and *what to listen for*, very soon this matter of characterizing your fictional actors by their speech will become one of the easiest and most pleasurable parts of your work as a writer.

As you listen to people talk, you will watch them, too; watch their facial expressions, their gestures, their bodily movements, for *it is not altogether what a man says that characterizes him, but the way in which he says it*.

In the following examples, the words are the same, but the different ways in which they are said give them a different meaning and, hence, characterize the speaker as not the same in each instance:

1. 'Get out!' old Buck Elkins rumbled, shaking a fat, hairy forefinger menacingly at Ed. 'If you weren't so damned good-looking, I'd fire you. But' — he glowered furiously at the young man before him — 'I have to consider our women customers. A profile counts more with them than the safety of their investment. So I'll keep you on, you lazy whelp.' Buck looked at Ed as he might have looked at a dose of bitter medicine, hard to take but necessary to his well-being. 'At least,' he added, 'until a better profile comes along.'

2. 'Get out!' old Buck Elkins rumbled, shaking a fat, hairy forefinger playfully at Ed. 'If you weren't so damned good-looking I'd fire you. But' — he closed one jovial blue eye in a Gargantuan wink — 'I have to please our women customers. A profile counts more with them than the safety of their investment. So I'll keep you on, you lazy whelp.' Buck looked at Ed as an indulgent father looks at an unpredictable but brilliant son. 'At least,' he added, 'until a better profile comes along.'

In listening to people talk, the main points to watch, with the intention of learning how to characterize by means of what you hear, are as follows: tone of voice and voice modulation; choice of words; way of speaking; tempo. You will see at once how clearly and decisively these give an impression of character. It is my opinion that conversation is one of the most important ways of individualizing your individual character and making him live. Every person speaks differently, and *what* he says and *how* he says it is also a matter of age, race, emotional state, cultural background, profession and occupation, as well as his own individual interest. It is also a matter of gender. Listen to a man and a woman in conversation: They may be discussing the same topic, but the man will characteristically use a man's phrases and the woman those words characteristically feminine. Further, a man will use different words, and a different tempo, in conversation with a woman than he will use in talking about the same subject with a man. Observe, and jot down these differences in your character notebook.

TONE AND VOICE MODULATION

Train yourself to listen to the tone of voice in which a person speaks. For a moment pay no attention to the words he is saying, his facial expression, his gestures, his mannerisms. Close your eyes and so eliminate a whole group of sensory impressions that will otherwise tend to distract you from the one point on which you are trying to concentrate, and listen to the voice as it indicates the character of the speaker.

One reason you should listen carefully to the tones and qualities of voices is that these are extremely difficult to communicate by means of the printed word. There is only one other sense impression that is more difficult to communicate by writing, and that is the impression of taste. Try it and see. Yet the tonal quality of a voice is often an excellent means of determining character and, by that means, of portraying character. As with taste, voice quality is sometimes best communicated by the use of adverbs, or still better, by comparisons or figures of speech.

For example, if you hear a woman speaking in a high, grating tone of voice you may be quite sure she is nervous, excitable, irritable, and quick in all her movements. How can you communicate the sound of this voice, and with it the characterization you want it to convey, to the reader? Suppose you write, 'She spoke shrilly.' This is all right as far as it goes, but it doesn't tell the reader very much. In other words, the reader doesn't really *hear* her. Instead, you say, 'The longer she talked the more her voice sounded like a siren going to a four-alarm fire.' In spite of the exaggeration in this figure of speech, or perhaps because of it, the reader 'hears' her voice, and gets from it an impression of this woman as an individual.

Never forget the importance of *individualizing*, along with giving actual character-traits. I stress individualizing a character because it is an important part of making any fictional character come alive. Suppose you have presented the dominant character-traits of your actor, but you want further to individualize him by means of his voice. You will, of course, choose a quality of voice in keeping with your character; that is, you will not give a patient man a petulant, singsong voice, or a bully a low-pitched melodious voice.

Suppose you have a man in your story whom you want to characterize. You say, 'Albert always spoke hoarsely.' Because the word 'hoarsely' is too general, no sound is communicated to the reader, who is left unimpressed. Substitute for this ineffective way of characterizing Albert by speech, this more specific method: 'Albert's voice always made me think of a foghorn with gravel in it,' and the reader is able to imagine that he hears Albert's voice. The basic principle behind this is clear. *Relate the sound of the voice to a specific sound with which the reader is familiar*. That is the only way you will make it possible for the reader to reproduce the sound by his own imagination, and until you have done that, the reader hasn't actually *heard* the voice of your character.

The emotion of a character has a strong effect on the tonal quality of a voice. If this were not true it would be impossible to tell anything about the emotional state of a person from his voice, and even the most casual observation of people will prove the contrary.

Suppose you read the following:

Ed slammed into the house, rumbling like a summer thunderstorm.

You actually hear Ed, don't you? You haven't yet heard a word he says, only the tone and general effect of his voice. Yet the passage is packed with characterization, the very best kind of characterization, since it allows the reader to arrive at his own conclusions with no actual 'telling' by the writer. You know that Ed has a dominant personality, is strong, forceful, but without meanness or cruelty. He is an arresting personality, getting his way by force sometimes, but his black moods are soon followed by sunshine. You think you are going to like Ed and you are curious to know what he is rumbling about.

This illustrates the way character can be individualized and, at the same time, a distinct emotion be created in the reader toward that character, through the tone of voice alone. Some idea of Ed's appearance is also given. A man who rumbles like a summer thunderstorm is not likely to be slender, blond, and with classical features. He is much more likely to be big, muscular, with black, bushy hair, a prominent nose and jutting chin. This further characterizes him.

All this was accomplished, please note, in few words, the length of most telegrams. That is practicing a true economy of words.

Listen while a woman speaks and let us see how much characterization can be accomplished by letting the reader hear her tone of voice, and nothing more:

> Almost every sentence Marilee spoke was a treble arpeggio that ended in a tinkle of silver laughter.

The reader knows from Marilee's tone of voice that she is young, lighthearted, ever, buoyant, inexperienced, full of hope and happiness. In appearance she is probably small, slender, and doubtless wears a dress with many ruffles. If no ruffles, then there is certainly lace on her underthings.

What is your emotional reaction to this:

> 'How about a sandwich?' Her words were casual enough, but her voice made you feel that she was more in need of company than of food.

You feel pity, of course.

If you haven't been certain of it before, these examples should make you certain that time spent carefully choosing your words and on devising an apt figure of speech to communicate voice tone is time well spent. As editors are demanding shorter and shorter stories, with no lessening of substance or significance, writers are required more and more to make ten words do the work of twenty, and no doubt the time will arrive when the writer will be forced to make ten words do the work of fifty. To that end, any method that will enable you to characterize and individualize your actors in several ways at once, as in both these examples concerning the tone of voice, should be given your closest attention.

CHOICE OF WORDS

Your choice of the words that your character speaks is one of your best means of characterizing him. No two people use the same words and with the same frequency or in the same arrangement. A man's background, the whole sum of his experience, as well as his character, determine his choice of words. A carpenter doesn't choose the same words as does a research scientist. A law-abiding business man doesn't use the vocabulary of a gangster. These are broad divisions of which it would seem that all writers would be aware and take into account. But very few untrained writers think for a moment about the proper words to put in the mouths of their characters. Perhaps that is their difficulty. They 'put the words into the mouths of their characters,' instead of listening to the characters speak.

Suppose you're planning to write a story about a carpenter. Go listen to carpenters. Get a job as a carpenter's helper, if you can. Otherwise, make an excuse to eavesdrop. Learn something of the terminology of the carpenter trade.

When your character describes a job of carpentry, don't have him talk of it as a banker would, or as you would, but as a carpenter would and as this individual carpenter would speak. Watch very carefully, or you will have every character in your story talking as you talk. You may be a very entertaining person, but four or five duplicates of you in the same story is going to be monotonous and uninteresting. The reader wants contrast in everything, and especially in the way story-characters speak. Your first and perhaps most important way of getting this contrast is by having your actors speak in character.

TEMPO

The speed with which a character talks and the spacing or pace of his words and sentences are sound indexes to your actor as a person.

Let us see how this works out. You have a character in your story named James Buchanan. He is six feet two inches tall, weighs two hundred and twenty-five pounds, and is a successful lawyer. Listen to him speak:

'No, I haven't heard from Albers for a long time. Almost a year, I should say. Yes, it has been quite a year since my last letter from him arrived. I remember it was dated May 6th. And this is May 10th. Do you have a special reason for asking?'

You have another character in this same story named Cedric Bently. He is an 'art' photographer and gets enormous prices for prints depicting an old pipe and a slightly decayed cantaloupe resting on a broken orange crate, or a badly worn wagon-wheel leaning against a dead cactus, with something that looks like a gnawed ham bone in the foreground. He has a thin nose, long tapering fingers, and a great deal of hair like frayed rope, badly in need of cutting. Listen to him speak:

> 'Albers! Albers!' Cedric cried distractedly, and then was silent so long I thought he had forgotten my question. 'Him!' he exploded suddenly. 'Sure. I had a letter from him. Some time ago. Maybe a year — maybe nine months. How'n hell do you expect me to remember?' Cedric cleared a corner of the table by pushing a litter of brushes and paint tubes so that they fell on the floor. 'Albers,' he repeated, wiggling one foot until I thought he would dislocate the ankle. 'He was a funny guy. What you want to know about him for?'

Try giving Cedric Bently's speech to James Buchanan and James Buchanan's speech to Cedric Bently. Of course, the effect will be grotesque. The point is that a man who possesses the character, appearance, and training of James Buchanan will speak in a slow, even tempo; while a man with the character, appearance, and training of Cedric Bently will be jerky, nervous, and rapid in speech. Also, their choice of words will vary greatly as well as their way of saying them. The trained writer knows this and so he listens to each character speak and writes down not only what that character says, but the *way* he says it; thus his story-people live. But the beginning writer often allows all of his characters to speak alike, to use the same tempo, and to show no mannerisms at all. Consequently, his characters are unreal and unconvincing, as well as illogical and flatly dull.

Method of Study

1. In published stories find three examples each of characterization by the author and characterization by the speech of the character himself.

   (a) Which is more effective and why?

   (b) Rewrite the characterization by narration in scenes in which the actors speak characteristically.

2. Select six men characters from widely different backgrounds and occupations and list some of their *characteristic* words.

3. Do the same as above, using women characters.

CHAPTER VIII

When Characters Meet

CHARACTERIZATION BY DIALOGUE

THE fiction writer cannot hope to hold reader-interest for long without action, progressive action of some kind, showing conflict and clash. When I say action is necessary to hold reader-interest, I do not mean that your characters must be pushing each other around, or throwing things, or fighting, or shooting, or galloping madly to meet the enemy, every moment of the time. *Action is anything that moves your story nearer its climax or end.* Action may be thought, speech, or bodily movement. For example, the most dramatic action may take place in the mind of a man, sitting motionless and alone, miles from another human being. Of course, this is an extreme case, and one that I do not advise a writer to attempt unless he knows the devices for overcoming the difficulties of presentation inherent in such a passive situation. Yet it is often done by our best writers who are also craftsmen, and the specific ways of doing it will be presented in detail in the next chapter dealing with characterization by means of the thoughts of a character.

Dialogue, when properly handled, is one of the most entertaining divisions of action. The man who speaks even one truly *significant* word is as much in action as the man who throws the villain over the cliff from the thundering express train. Both are *moving the story forward.* The one is characterized by the word just as much as the other is characterized in disposing of the villain with one heave.

How much more, then, do characters reveal themselves to the reader and carry the story forward, when two or more talk together. Therein, if the writer knows his business, there is action and reaction; stimulus and response follow each other quickly, information is given, character is revealed, and the plot unfolds.

Thus we see that dialogue in fiction has four main purposes:

1. To show character.
2. To further the action of the plot; that is, *build* the story.
3. To convey needed information.
4. To show the emotional state of the speaker.

Other minor and occasional purposes are:

1. To build reader suspense.
2. To foreshadow difficulty and disaster; happiness or success.
3. To sum up the action of the plot for the reader.

Delineation of character is the most important of these purposes of dialogue. However, the writer must not forget that dialogue that shows character, and nothing more, is not allowable in the modern short story. For this reason you must make sure that the dialogue you write, while it characterizes, at the same time performs one or more of the functions listed above. *The more functions dialogue performs, the more skill you show as writer* and, other things being equal, the more artistic is your story.

Let us examine the following example of dialogue and see how this works out in actual practice. You are writing a story in which two young women meet. Let us listen:

'Jean,' Lucie said hesitatingly, 'I saw Andrea today ... for the first time in six months.'

'Did you?' Jean yawned, as she carefully examined her scarlet finger-nails.

'Yes,' Lucie was serious. 'She looked thin and — and sort of worried. Don't tell any of the old crowd, will you? ... but there was a crack clear across the sole of one shoe. I saw it when she knelt down to tie Junior's shoelace. She used to be so proud of her shoes before she married Jim. You don't suppose he's out of work, do you?'

'I wouldn't know about that.' Jean's words were icicles. 'But if Andrea is having to wear shoes with cracks in them it's no more than she deserves. The way she snatched Jim away from Elaine, practically at the church steps.' She paused in the minute examination of her nails. 'Say, that's funny! Elaine told me yesterday she'd just paid eighteen dollars for a pair of pumps to go dancing tonight with Ted Winston — you know, that guy who keeps a yacht at Catalina.'

'I don't see anything funny about it!' Lucie retorted. 'Andrea didn't snatch Jim at all. They belonged to each other — anybody could see

that. If you tell Elaine about the crack in Andrea's shoe, I'll — I'll ——'
Jean sneered, 'You and who else will do what? I'm having lunch with
Elaine today. She'll see the point of this joke, even if you don't.'

I need not explain in detail how this dialogue characterizes Lucie as
sympathetic, understanding, and loyal; Jean as suspicious and cruel.
Nor how it rouses decided emotions in the mind of the reader toward
both of these girls, and, to a less degree, toward Elaine and Jim, who do
not come on the stage in person at all.

If, however, that was all this dialogue accomplished it would have to
come out of your story. But it does much more than that. Though we
do not know the rest of the story, we are safe in surmising that the above
dialogue also gives the reader necessary information about what has
happened in the past; it furthers the plot, since if Lucie had not told
Jean about the crack in Andrea's shoe, Jean would not have been able
to tell Elaine; it shows immediate conflict between Lucie and Jean, foreshadows more important conflict to come, and, finally, foreshadows disaster and trouble to Jim and Andrea. Since all this is true, you are safe
in letting the dialogue remain in your story.

Let us repeat the scene with Lucia and Jean. While they possess the
same characteristics, in this instance their dialogue does nothing for the
story:

The soda-jerker slipped two chocolate ice cream sodas across the
counter. Simultaneously, Jean and Lucie reached for straws. Jean looked
suspiciously at Lucie's soda spilling over the sides of the tall glass and
making a rich brown pool on the counter.

'I'd like to know why,' Jean demanded loudly, 'you always get a bigger
ice cream soda at this place than I do. It's that fellow with the blond
hair, who always rushes to wait on us. Don't think I haven't seen you
making eyes at him. Oh well, I've always said a girl could get along — if
she didn't care how she did it.'

'Oh, Jean,' Lucie almost whispered, hurt tears in her eyes. 'How can
you say such things! Why, I never even looked at the fellow that fixed
our sodas. It just happened mine is bigger than yours. Here, you take it.
I don't want so much, really.'

As before, the reader likes Lucie and heartily dislikes Jean. But that
is all. No information is given, no trouble foreshadowed, no suspense
roused. Therefore, this dialogue is deleted from your story.

Remember that characters tend to speak alike — that is, without
showing character-traits or even individualizing traits of behavior, when

everything is going smoothly. But when characters are reacting emotionally to impacts or opposing forces, whether these stimuli rise from within themselves or from forces outside themselves, the actors will react characteristically, that is, *individually*, if you, the writer, will give them half a chance.

Suppose the two girls, Lucie and Jean, had been talking about ice cream sodas and had discovered that they both liked chocolate ice cream sodas best. They might have been individualized by their dialogue, but it is not likely that the reader would have learned much about their dominant character traits. And the emotion toward them, roused in the reader, would have been slight, if any.

But the moment Lucie and Jean clashed in the above scenes, what they said and how they said it characterized them sharply and roused well-defined emotions toward each girl in the mind of the reader. Never forget that *the real purpose of characterization is to make the reader feel strongly, in a specific way, toward the actor whom you are characterizing*.

In order to characterize fiction adequately by means of dialogue, the dialogue must, first of all, be natural and convincing. In other words, it must give the illusion of real conversation between real people. You cannot characterize actors who speak in a stilted or unnatural or illogical way. This is of such tremendous importance and is so little understood by beginning writers — and sometimes by established writers as well — that time spent in achieving a thorough understanding of the problems involved in writing natural dialogue will be well spent.

When a living person, or an actor in a story, speaks naturally, he uses only those words that a person of his age, sex, educational background, occupation, and individual temperament would be expected to use — *in talking*. Every writer who takes the profession of writing seriously and is determined to succeed in it, should take full cognizance of the fact that all of us have not one vocabulary, but several. The three most important of these vocabularies are the speaking vocabulary, the writing vocabulary, and the reading vocabulary. Your main concern as a writer is with the speaking vocabulary of your character, but, in order to keep that convincing, you have to exclude carefully from the speaking vocabulary words that he would use only in writing, or would recognize in reading, but never thinks of using in either speaking or writing. So don't write formal conversation, unless the 'talking vocabulary' of your character-actor is formal.

The following example of dialogue will show you what I mean and is a good example of what *not* to do:

Two high-school boys meet on their way to school. This is the way — with no exaggeration — that many beginners would write. Not you, of course, but the majority of the others:

> 'Good morning, Albert. Why are you shouting?'
>
> 'Good morning, William. I am shouting because I enjoyed my morning ablutions so greatly. The effect of a cold shower is distinctly exhilarating. After a brisk rubdown I donned my outer garments and sped to school shouting lustily because of the exuberance of my emotions.'

Beginners' manuscripts are full of passages like this, believe it or not. If the reader accepted the fact that these boys actually existed, he would want to kick them. But, of course, he knows they are puppets, moved by strings in the hands of the beginning writer.

The words used above are 'reading words,' words that are rarely written and almost never spoken by the everyday person. 'Ablutions,' 'donned,' 'sped,' 'lustily,' and 'exuberance.' And 'emotions,' when he is speaking of his own feelings.

Almost none of the words, except those of one syllable, are those which these boys would use either in writing or in speaking, and especially when speaking to a classmate.

Now let us listen to these two high-school boys speak and watch what words they do use and the way they use them:

> 'Hi ya, Alley, what's all the speeding and the uproar about?'
>
> 'Hi ya, Bill. Had a dash of the old frigid H_2O this morning. You oughta try it sometime. That needle spray business certainly gives you a kick. After I dried myself, I yanked on my pants and shirt and here I am, rearin' to go.'
>
> 'But what made you chase yourself down the hill and yell, Alley?'
>
> 'I dunno. Just felt like it, that's all.'

While there is no strong characterization accomplished in the above bit of dialogue, a certain feeling of liking is roused toward the boys as healthy, normal young animals and curiosity as to what form of action their excess vitality will take.

The vocabulary of the fiction character will also be influenced by many conditions:

1. Where he is when speaking.

He will select, within his own vocabulary boundaries, however limited or however wide these boundaries may be, different words to use in a church from those used in the home of a friend, where an informal party is taking place.

2. To whom he is speaking.

No person, in actual life, uses the same vocabulary when speaking to a small child as he uses in speaking to a mature person.

While there are other conditions to affect the vocabulary used at a specific time, within fixed vocabulary limitations, these will suffice to direct the ambitious young writer to further study on the subject.

It is only when you understand fully the limits and nature of the speaking vocabulary of your characters that you can write convincing dialogue, that is, dialogue that is in character.

Furthermore, dialogue in fiction is a means of characterizing, not only the character speaking, but the character spoken to, and the character spoken about.

This has its basis in a psychological fact that every writer should know so well he will never forget it. If the writer tells the reader that a character is good or bad, hateful or lovable, the reader is indifferent or frankly skeptical, unless the telling is done very deftly, as we shall learn in a later chapter. But if one character says to another, 'That old Jim Blaggep is so mean a self-respecting flea wouldn't even stay in his clothes,' the reader is convinced that Jim Blaggep is a scoundrelly rascal. You see, in the first place, the reader feels, subconsciously, that the writer *wants* him to think Jim is mean; therefore, he resents it and is on the defensive. On the other hand, if the reader knows that the character in the story doesn't care whether he likes Jim or not, he will believe what that character says. Having a character-actor say Jim Blaggep is mean is the next best way of convincing the reader of the truth. The best way, of course, is to *show* Jim Blaggep actually doing a mean act.

Let us see how this is done:

We shall select for a minor character, though this device works just as well for a major, a pretty woman, who is a devoted wife and mother, unselfish, kind, patient, and also very intelligent. You, as writer, will say to the reader: 'Amy Lawrence was a pretty woman. Always treated her husband and child well, too. More than that, Amy had brains.' That certainly isn't exciting, nor is it convincing. The reader may accept it provisionally, but that is as far as he will go. You haven't sufficient words to spare to show Amy being all these things. What is your best procedure? There are two ways you may solve your problem of characterizing Amy in an effective and convincing way, both by dialogue. First, you can give the dialogue between two characters as they discuss Amy; and, second, you can give the dialogue between Amy and another character. Which device you use will be dictated by your material. Suppose we use the first:

Mary Birch and Susan Albee are sitting in Mary's old-fashioned parlor. Susan is knitting and Mary is sewing. We listen:

'I saw Amy Lawrence at the social Friday night,' Mary said, biting off a thread with a click of her false teeth. 'She looked as pretty as the day she married Dow Lawrence, and that was eight years ago, come Thanksgiving.'

'She works hard, too,' observed Susan, moving her thin lips in time to her flashing knitting needles. 'You can tell that, the way she keeps them two little girls of hers dressed. Last time I seen Sallie Bee she was wearin' one of them little jackets made out of pink rickrack braid that her mother had made for her. And I hear Amy made Bets, the young one, a dress with ten little bitsy ruffles on the skirt to wear to June Bently's birthday party.'

'Yes,' Mary agreed. 'Amy don't mind work. And she's smart, too. Some say she really manages that feed and grain business of Dow's. Keeps the books and everything. But you never hear her say nothing about what she does. Dow Lawrence was lucky to get her.'

Now the reader has a very good idea of the character of Amy Lawrence and he has no doubts or reservations. Why? Because he *heard* two people, who know Amy well, talking about her. If Mary Birch and Susan Albee don't know all about Amy, who does?

Now let us try the other method of characterizing Amy by dialogue, this time in a conversation between Amy and her husband, Dow Lawrence:

'I wish you wouldn't work so hard.' Dow laid his big hand on Amy's shoulders that were bent over the sewing machine. 'Bets and Sallie Bee don't have to have new clothes all the time.'

Amy reached up and patted his hand absently. 'I know, Dow, but it's fun making clothes for the girls. And,' she said, suddenly smiling up at him, 'even shirts for you.'

'Just the same, you work too hard,' Dow said stubbornly. 'You're too pretty to be working all the time. If it isn't sewing for me and the girls, it's cooking, or working on the hay and grain books, or something. Amy, why don't you ever take time to do something for yourself? Why, you could write a book, or lecture or — or, why, most anything you wanted to do, I guess.'

'My goodness, Dow,' Amy said, giving him a gentle push. 'What fun would there be in writing a book, or getting up and talking before a lot of people? You go on back to the store. I guess I know what I want to do.'

Here Dow characterizes Amy for the reader by what he says about her. Of course a little is added by what Amy herself says and does, but not much. Dow could have done it all, with no help from Any, except that the necessary speech would have been long and lacking in contrast.

However, a very brief dialogue between actors may serve to characterize another actor. As is done in the following examples:

1. 'Hank Picket,' said Amby, 'is the kind of farmer who wouldn't give a pickaninny a watermelon on a hot August day, even if he was feedin' watermelon to the hogs at the time.'

'Them is true words,' Lem Patterson agreed warmly. 'If a generous feelin' ever got into Hank's heart — by mistake, a' course — it would die of this here malnutrition I been readin' about in the farm papers.'

2. 'She has three kinds of lipstick,' said Cherrie breathlessly, 'and a different kind of face powder for day and for evening, and eye shadow, and mascara. And she uses them all!'

'My soul and body!' marveled Aunt Drue. 'Wonder what her real face is like — or her real self, either, for the matter of that. Bet she don't rightly know herself.'

3. 'When do you think Lulu will consent to a divorce from Bob?'

'Just as soon as she can find a man with more money and less brains than Bob has. Lulu doesn't like brains in a man — makes him too hard to fool. And she wants more money than Bob can give her.'

Contrast is a valuable device used by trained writers in characterizing, though it does not in itself characterize; its purpose is to sharpen characterization.

Contrast is of great help to writers in many ways. It always tends to arrest the reader's attention and, if striking, to hold reader-interest. Remember this when choosing your characters for a story. Contrast them as much as possible, as to names, appearance, and dominant character-traits. This helps you to get variety into your story. Re-read your favorite author for concrete examples of this.

Let us see how we can use contrast in dialogue that characterizes. and so throw the dominant character-traits of each character into sharper relief:

> Mrs. Oswald Gunthry held back a swirling fold of her ice-blue chiffon evening gown.
>
> 'My dear man,' Mrs. Gunthry said to the grease-smeared plumber kneeling on the tiled floor of her black and rose bathroom, 'don't tell me there is a dead cat choking the drain. It's impossible — I won't have it!'
>
> 'Lady,' the plumber said, squinting up at her around the smoke of a tired cigarette, 'it ain't what you won't have that's bothering me. It's what you've got. And what you've got is a dead cat, like I told you.'

You will see at once that the above characters are much more sharply delineated because of the contrast between them than if, for example, the scene had been between Mrs. Gunthry and her husband, or between the plumber and a maid. Observe that the contrast here is one of character-actors, dialogue, emotional reaction, and situation.

Remember that in dialogue you have one of the richest means of character-delineation that your medium allows. Work hard to master dialogue in its many aspects for when you have done that editors will be fairly sitting on your doorstep asking for your stories.

Method of Study

1. Is action in a story necessarily violent physical action, or physical action of any kind?
2. Why does the reader more willingly believe characterization that is done by dialogue than characterization that is done by exposition?
3. Why is clash useful in dialogue that characterizes?
4. Write
    (a) a dialogue between two people that characterizes them both;
    (b) a dialogue between two people that characterizes someone not present.
5. Select one of the characters you have created in assignment 4 and write a brief dialogue between him and another person under each of the following conditions:
    (a) driving to the funeral of a mutual friend;
    (b) discussing a moving picture over a glass of beer;
    (c) telling a seven-year-old boy about a horse race.
6. Jot down in your notebook specific examples of dialogue that not only characterize but also individualize.

CHAPTER IX

Thoughts Are Things

CHARACTERIZATION THROUGH THE THOUGHTS OF A CHARACTER

THE thoughts of his characters are actualities to the fiction writer. They have weight, substance, and power; in his hands they are the tools with which he builds effects of many kinds for the reader. Their most important function is to characterize the thinker, but while characterizing him they should accomplish other functions as well. They should, for instance, give information about what has happened in the past, point out the significance of what is happening in the present, foreshadow what may happen in the future, characterize other actors, and perform still other useful duties. But since we are chiefly concerned at present with *thoughts* that *characterize*, let us direct most of our attention toward them, realizing, however, that, since no phase of writing can be considered apart from every other phase, the thoughts of our characters perform still other functions beside those of characterization.

Before we launch into the subject of thoughts as a means of characterization in fiction writing, let us clarify one purely mechanical problem that offers difficulties to many writers. This concerns the problem of when to enclose thoughts in quotation marks and when not to do so, and of the different ways of wording thoughts that are, or are not, to be enclosed in quotation marks.

The answer to this problem is quite simple, once the underlying principle is clarified in your mind.

Thoughts that are *put into words in the mind* of the thinker, just as though the words were spoken to a listener, are enclosed in quotation marks. Thoughts that are *told* to the reader by the writer are not put in

quotation marks. Thoughts that are analyzed by the writer are not enclosed in quotation marks.

Example of thoughts to be enclosed in quotation marks:

> Suddenly, walking along the graveled path toward the house, the de-
> sirable Jamison Alward by her side, Susie felt a rock in her shoe. 'Why,
> oh why,' she thought wildly, 'did I wear these silly open-toed slippers this
> morning? Now I'll have to stop, take off my shoe, and shake that rock
> out. No, I won't! This is my one chance to show Jamison Alward I'm as
> sophisticated as Judith Trent. And I can't look sophisticated shaking a
> rock out of my shoe. I'll walk on that rock — and without limping — if
> it kills me!'

This is in the first person, as if Susie were speaking.

Example of thought told to the reader by the writer — not to be put
in quotation marks:

> Suddenly, walking along the graveled path toward the house, the desir-
> able Jamison Alward by her side, Susie felt a rock in her shoe. Why, oh
> why, she thought wildly, had she worn those silly open-toed slippers this
> morning? Now she would have to stop — take her shoe off, and shake
> that rock out. No, she wouldn't! This was her one chance to show Jami-
> son Alward she was every bit as sophisticated as Judith Trent. She
> couldn't look sophisticated while shaking a rock out of her shoe. She'd
> walk on that rock — and without limping — if it killed her.

This is in the third person, as the writer tells about Susie's thoughts.

Example of thoughts analyzed by the writer and not put in quotation
marks:

> Suddenly, walking along the graveled path toward the house, the de-
> sirable Jamison Alward by her side, Susie felt a rock in her shoe. Susie's
> thoughts immediately became a jumble of wishing she hadn't worn her
> open-toed slippers that morning, and debating whether to take off her
> slipper and dispose of the rock, or disregard the pain the rock was causing
> her and so retain her assumed air of sophistication patterned after the
> lovely Judith Trent. Being determined to make an impression on Alward,
> she decided on the latter course.

This is a combination of telling about Susie's thoughts and analyzing
them.

Note carefully the difference in wording of these examples and you
will never be in doubt again about whether to use, or not to use, quotation marks when writing the thoughts of your characters.

In fiction, thoughts, as well as speech and action, must be in character. But they must do more than that. Besides characterizing, or at
least being characteristic of the actor thinking them, they must do one
or more of the following: give information, show conflict between persons, situations, or natural forces, help develop the plot, plant the means
by which the story problem will be solved, or foreshadow difficulty or
disaster. Consider Susie's thoughts, as given above. They characterize
Susie as a naïve person who wants to appear sophisticated and one who
has courage, self-control, and determination. What else is accomplished by Susie's thoughts? Immediate conflict is shown between
Susie and the situation confronting her. Suspense is built. Will Susie be
able to walk without limping? Will Susie be able to impress young
Alward? Dramatic action is foreshadowed between Susie and Judith
Trent, and between Susie and Alward. Reader-interest is roused in
what will happen next.

Important as thoughts are in fiction writing, they should be given very
little space, except in certain rare instances that will be given later. This
is explained by the fact that, while a character is thinking, the story is
standing still. Until you are very adept in presenting thoughts dramatically, do not begin a story with one actor alone on the stage, thinking.
In most cases, the thoughts of this character do nothing except give information about what has happened before the opening of the story. A
sound general rule is to begin your story with interesting dialogue and
action, to arouse curiosity in the reader as to what is going to happen and
then, having obtained his attention, interest him in what took place
before the story began. At this point only is it safe to present past completed action and, even then, with a minimum expressed in thoughts.
Of the many devices available for presenting past completed action
in an interesting way, that of giving them through an actor's thoughts
is one of the least desirable.

The reason thoughts provide such an excellent means of characterization is based on the fact that people, for the most part, think honestly
and make no attempt to deceive themselves. While, generally speaking,
this is true, very clever characterizations have been given through the
thoughts of people who are definitely not honest with themselves. To
achieve this feat, the technique is difficult, though fascinating for that
very reason. Let us see how this might be done in writing a story:

> Fat old Mrs. Anthruster sat hunched over her inlaid rosewood desk
> making out her Christmas list. 'No one can say I'm not a generous giver,'

she thought, 'especially to my poor relations. Take Annie, now, Brother Joe's wife. She has always liked nice clothes, though goodness knows she's not had many, what with the starvation wages Joe's always made. I'll send her a fur coat. If I can get a dyed and pieced one it won't cost so much, and Annie will never know the difference. Still, I don't know. A fur coat would be out of place with the rest of her clothes. Still, I do want to give her something nice. I'll get her a cloth coat with a good fur trim. But there's disadvantages to that. I haven't seen Annie for a matter of twenty years. Probably her hair is gray from taking care of all those children she and Joe had. I might get a fur that would be extremely unbecoming to her. I better not let my generous nature run away with me. I'll get Annie a plain black cloth coat — a last-year's model would do her all right — I ought to get one for about twenty-five dollars — a real good one. I wouldn't send Annie anything cheap. And goodness knows, that's being generous. Neither Annie nor Joe ever in their lives sent me a Christmas present that cost twenty-five dollars.'

Note the exact devices and words used to characterize old Mrs. Anthruster as a vastly different person from the one she thinks she is. While, in her own opinion, she is generosity itself, her thoughts characterize her as anything but that.

Again, thought characterizes by showing the motive behind the action. Sometimes motive and action correspond in their characterization; at other times, they do not. That is, the act characterizes in one way; the motive behind the act in a way entirely different. Often the easiest way of telling the reader the motive back of an act is by going into the mind of the actor himself or, in case the story is being told in the first person by a minor character, by having this minor character-narrator tell the reader what his own thoughts are concerning the motive behind the act of the main character.

By withholding the motives behind the act that characterizes in a certain way, the writer employs a valuable device by which to build a surprise. Many a short short story can attribute its surprise ending to the application of this principle.

The following is an example of an act and a motive that agree in their characterization:

'Janice, darling,' said Marian as she came into her sister's room, carrying a large gray box, 'I've brought you that red-and-white-striped formal you liked so much at Manton's yesterday. Oh, don't thank me. Of course I can afford to buy it for you. I really want you to have it.' Marian knew

> she couldn't afford to buy a dress at Manton's for herself or anyone else.
> 'But Janice must never know that,' she thought. 'It would spoil her
> pleasure in the dress, which is so becoming to her. I'll manage to pay for
> it somehow.'

Here we see a kind act prompted or motivated by love and generosity.
Now, leaving the act exactly the same, let us examine a different motive as shown by different thoughts:

> The thought of the fantastic sum she had paid for the dress didn't cause
> Marian a moment's uneasiness. She had sources of income about which
> Janice knew nothing. Her thoughts were on another matter. 'Will she
> look a fright in it! Clyde won't think she is so beautiful when he sees her
> wearing it at the Andover's party. While I — I shall be wearing that
> divine green and silver gown Cedric designed especially for me. I'm going
> to take Clyde away from Janice, and,' she told herself in triumph, 'this is
> the first step!'

This will help to impress upon you the importance of thoughts used
to disclose motives and, in this way, to characterize the actor. The
reader is often not convinced of the real nature of the character you are
portraying simply by showing him perform an act that appears to be
good or bad. It is sometimes necessary to acquaint him with the motives
as well, by exploring the actor's mind and revealing his thoughts.

This cannot always be done, especially in the case of minor characters.
Since most stories are told from the point of view of the main character,
you take the serious risk of breaking the unity of impression if you go
into the consciousness of a minor character as well. You can, however,
give the motive behind the act of a minor character. For example:

> Orlando [minor character] stood on the side porch, bowing and smiling,
> his cap in one hand, a large basket of purple figs in the other.
> 'I pick heem for you thees morning, Meester Carleton,' Orlando said,
> 'the first off my trees thees season. I hope you like heem.'
> 'Of course I shall like them, Orlando,' Mr. Carleton [major character]
> said. 'They're mighty fine-looking figs.' He held out his hand.
> 'What a thoroughly nice chap Orlando is,' Mr. Carleton thought
> warmly. 'He could have gotten a good price for those figs in the market,
> but he gives them to me instead. Orlando never thinks of himself.'

The reader likes Orlando now, because Mr. Carleton, the main character, believes Orlando's motive for his act is an admirable one.

But, suppose Mr. Carleton's thought had been as follows:

'Wonder what trouble he's in now?' thought Mr. Carleton. 'When Orlando arrives bearing gifts it's time to look out. Never knew him to bring me anything yet that he didn't want me to smooth out some mess he had gotten into by his own foolishness.'

Here we see Orlando in a very different light — because of a different motive shown through the thoughts of the major character.

In these days of streamlining everything, the art and craft of writing has not been overlooked. More and more, one paragraph, one sentence, one act, and even one word is asked to do the work of two, or of half a dozen. It is not enough, many times, for one literary device to accomplish one end. One device must accomplish several ends. This economy of words makes for shorter, more compact, more sharply dramatic stories. So the modern writer, who hopes to keep up with the trend of his times, will be wise to spend much time in learning how to achieve several ends by one device.

Thoughts, as we have seen, are valuable in characterizing the thinker. The next step is to use one thought, or a series of thoughts, to characterize both the thinker and the one thought about. Very good effects can be achieved by this means, with a minimum of words. Let us see how much characterization can be packed into a very little thought:

'Mr. Akers is sure a fine fellow, once he gets to trust you,' Muriel thought. 'I'm going to work harder than ever to show him I appreciate what he did for me today.'

Here we are told that Mr. Akers is cautious, but very generous when he feels his trust will not be abused. Muriel is appreciative and the kind of girl who wants to show her appreciation in a practical way. The reader likes both characters.

Now suppose we have a few more words at our disposal than in the last example. We want to characterize a major character, Mose, and a minor character, Mr. Snell, the villain, all this to be done in the thoughts of Mose:

'He's a mean man, that Mr. Snell,' Mose thought, polishing the headlights of the car with long, swift strokes. 'Long as I been takin' care uv this swell car uv his'n he ain't give me a tip or a praiseful word, neither. Plenty uv the other kind, though. Some garage boys I know would uv put a handful uv sand in his gas tank or forgot to check the water in his battery. But shucks, not me. I couldn't enjoy my po'k chops if I ever done a thing like that, no matter how ornery Mr. Snell's actin'.'

Mose' thoughts tell the reader that Mr. Snell is a hard man to work for. He shows no appreciation whatever and acts in a most disagreeable manner. Mose is more hurt than angry at the treatment he has received from his boss and harbors no thoughts of revenge.

It is all too easy, when characterizing by means of thought, to write that thought in an uninteresting manner. Yet because it is difficult to write thoughts that interest is no reason for your not being able to do so. *Anything that is difficult should be approached as a challenge and the difficulty overcome.* Thoughts can always be written in an entertaining way if you will take care to have them *specific* and not general, and be sure that they express *emotion* or show *clash.* When you get one or more of these characteristics into the thoughts of your actors, readers will find those thoughts interesting.

We shall examine a characterization by means of thoughts written in a boresome way, and then see how easy it is to change it so that the reader will be stirred:

Angie thought, 'Jim is a bad boy. He doesn't mind his mother and he tells lies.'

This leaves the reader cold, both toward Angie and toward Jim. But rewrite and see what a different reader-reaction you will get:

'I hate that horrid Jim Ballard!' Angie thought furiously. 'You'd think any boy would mind his mother — once in a while, anyway. But he never does. And that lie he told her this morning about where he got the apples he had in his shirt — I've a good mind to slap his face the very next time I see him!'

See what the addition of specific detail and emotion does? Now the reader is interested. He likes Angie and hopes she will keep her word about slapping Jim. The whole point is, you have succeeded in getting the reader emotionally involved — you have made him *care.* One characterization is just as good as the other, as far as essentials go, but one involves the reader emotionally and the other does not. This reader-interest makes the difference between a salable story and one that is not salable.

Pages back I promised you I would show you how to give long passages of thought in a way that would hold reader-interest. Several suggestions for doing this have already been given. Let us review them now, so that they will be clear in our minds before we consider the subject in greater detail:

1. Write thoughts in the language and phraseology that the person would naturally use if he were speaking informally.
2. Avoid generalities by having your actor thinking of specific things and specific acts.
3. Have your actor thinking under the stress of emotion.
4. If possible, get clash in his thinking. This means, don't write thoughts that are static, but write thoughts that are dynamic.

Once in a great while you will read a story that is told effectively almost altogether through the thoughts of the main actor. This is one of the most difficult feats the fiction writer can accomplish, and I do not advise the untrained writer to attempt it. However, since I know he will try and, in fact, he wouldn't be worth his salt if he didn't, I shall do my best to explain how to do it successfully. The reason I am discussing this problem here is that in such a story the actor is characterized all the way through by his thoughts. As a rule, he does nothing of any great importance, so there is no other way of characterizing him except through his thoughts. But his thoughts are important.

The basic technique of a story such as we are considering is that the writer treats the main character as two persons. That is, the story is an argument between the two sides of the character. One side thinks one course is right, the other side thinks the other course is right. Invariably — that is, in any story of this type that I have seen — the main actor is sitting alone, waiting for another actor to come. When that other actor arrives, something momentous will take place. What will occur, the main actor does not know. He is torn to pieces imagining one thing that will happen, then another. This builds a really intense suspense. The reader can hardly wait to know what actually will occur. Of course, in the end something happens that neither the actor nor the reader expected.

But it is with the characterization of the main actor by means of a long passage of thought that we are particularly concerned now, and with the technique of doing it in a way that will hold reader-attention. The following example illustrates the basic technique:

'Well, my girl,' Helen thought, as she sat waiting for Lawson to come, 'strange things have happened to other people, so why shouldn't this happen to you?' She glanced at the clock on her desk. Fifteen minutes and

Lawson would come — to tell her he was through with her. For a moment she was sure that's what he would say. But, on the other hand, she argued, why should he? She'd always been honest, said exactly what she meant. Surely he would believe her when she told him ... Suddenly she crumpled in her chair. That was the trouble. She hadn't meant what she had said to Hale — those careless words that Lawson had overheard — and so all her years of careful sincerity and honesty of word and deed with Lawson fought against her now. For a moment she felt defeated — but only for a moment. 'I'll make him see how it was,' she said, sitting up with resolution. 'I'll make him!' She glanced again at the clock. Fourteen minutes more. What would Lawson be saying — what would Lawson be doing, fourteen minutes from now? Whatever happened, she determined not to give up easily.

A careful analysis will show you clearly that in this passage where thoughts alone are given there is real action taking place, real clash. Emotion is shown in the actor and being built in the reader toward the character who is thinking. The actor is characterized by her thoughts as really fine and loyal, honest and sincere. The reader hopes she will be able to convince Lawson that this is so.

Of course, in actual writing, these different ways of characterizing by means of thoughts are not kept separate in watertight compartments. You will notice in the last example that Helen's thoughts are given directly as well as indirectly. When writing a story, told chiefly through the thoughts of the main character, thoughts will also be presented in other ways to avoid monotony. The writer, for example, will tell about some thoughts, analyze others, and present still others in the form of a brief scene, with conversation and action.

There are two simple rules for characterizing your actors by means of thoughts in an interesting way. These are:

1. Be sure your characters think naturally and logically.
2. Be sure they think specifically and with emotion.

Do this and all the rest will be added unto you.

Method of Study

1. Should characters think for long spaces of time without interruption?
2. What is the main reason thoughts are so valuable as a means of characterization?

3. When an actor does not think honestly to himself, can his thoughts still be made to characterize him?

4. Write a characterization in which you show, by the thoughts of an actor, that an act and the motive behind the act correspond.

5. Write a characterization in which you show, by the thoughts of Actor A, that the act and the motive behind the act do not correspond.

6. Choose three examples of 4 and 5 from published stories.

CHAPTER X

Action and Reaction

CHARACTERIZATION BY STIMULUS AND RESPONSE

ACTION and reaction, cause and effect, stimulus and response. These are different names for the same mental concepts, concepts that should engage the earnest attention of every writer who hopes to become a skillful craftsman in the practice of his art. Particularly should he be aware of these actions and reactions as they concern the creation of characters for presentation to the reader.

During the unimaginably long passage of centuries since man first began to think and then to reason, his thinking and his reasoning have been chiefly concerned with trying consciously to learn, and being forced by experience to learn, something of the simple yet infinitely complicated ways in which the law of cause and effect works.

There is, most people will agree, no cause without an effect and no effect without a cause. The question as to which comes first is as unanswerable as the old bromide about which comes first, the chicken or the egg. For practical purposes everyone arbitrarily selects a point where his thoughts or reasoning shall begin, and he makes no effort to go behind that. This point, the writer uses to show character as instrumental in causing an effect. Sometimes, as a device for whetting reader-curiosity, an effect will be shown first and the cause explained later. This in no way affects the principle that character is the primary cause that lies behind all drama in fiction writing. The effect shown becomes, in turn, the cause of still further effects, and this continues in a series of ascending crises to a final dramatic and conclusive effect, where the writer ends his story.

Since cause and effect are the links of the chain that hold a story together and give it strength and unity and a logical sequence, the earnest writer should learn all he can about how cause and effect work in delineating character.

Do not allow yourself to become confused about this application of the law of cause and effect to the delineation of character. It is one of those simple, fundamental, and, therefore, important laws that take many words to explain, but are in reality no more complicated than the fact that one and one make two. Nevertheless, it is upon the fact that one and one make two that the whole structure of present-day mathematics rests.

The law is this: Any cause must result in a logical effect and any effect must be the result of a logical cause.

A specific example of action and reaction, cause and effect, stimulus and response — whatever term you may wish to use — will clarify this point.

We are writing a story. At the moment the story opens, the villain slaps the hero. The reader instinctively recognizes this as an effect, the cause of which is unknown to him. The slap remains an effect only as long as it bears no result. But the moment the hero does something about it, or responds, the slap becomes likewise a cause; the cause of our hero's response. *What that response will be depends entirely on the dominant character-traits of the hero.* If we have created him in our minds as a dominant extrovert, he will knock the villain down, push him into the lake, punch his nose, or do any one of a hundred other things, depending on his individuality and on the attendant circumstances. But if our hero is an introvert, the effect of the cause, that is, the slap, is certain to be different. Our hero may reason with the villain, he may walk away in embarrassment, or he may be deeply hurt. It is this showing of the effect of this cause, the slap, on our story-character that will characterize him for the reader. In turn, whatever our hero does is an effect that in time will become a cause, as soon as it brings about action on the part of the villain, that is, action that will characterize the villain.

The stimuli to which human beings respond fall into two broad classifications: those from within and those from without. We are so accustomed to thinking that we respond only to impacts from without that we often overlook the important part played in real life and, consequently, in stories, by impacts from within.

Stimuli from without may be words, written or spoken, facial expression, gestures, and bodily actions, situations, and so on in an endless sequence. Stimuli from within may be a thought, a decision, an emotion, a dominant character-trait, a mood, a wish. People react to moods from within just as characteristically as they do to physical violence from without.

Let us select a stimulus from without and see how we can characterize by showing the reactions of different individuals to this same stimulus. Our first actor, of whom we know nothing beyond his name, Johnny McPhail, finds a billfold on the seat of a transcontinental bus when all the other passengers and the driver are having lunch. What does Johnny do? He grins, muttering, 'Atta boy!' and surreptitiously slips the billfold into his pocket. He does not report finding it. Nor does he so much as look at it again until he is locked in his hotel room that night. That is his response to the finding of the billfold. It characterizes him clearly as fundamentally and purposefully dishonest.

Now let us observe how another character, Fred Preston, behaves under the impact of the same stimulus: Fred picks up the billfold, looks inside for an address, but sees none. He looks farther and gasps when he sees six hundred-dollar bills folded neatly inside. He frowns thoughtfully a moment, then puts the billfold in his pocket. As the passengers return to the bus, after finishing their lunch, Fred asks each one, 'Pardon me, but have you lost anything?' Each passenger says, 'No.' At the next stop Fred tells the bus driver what he has found and asks him what he had better do. The bus driver looks at Fred, then looks quickly away. 'Just give the billfold to me,' he says, 'I'll turn it in. Rule of the company.' 'I'll turn it in myself,' Fred says firmly and hurries back to his seat. When the bus reaches the terminal, Fred gives the billfold to the head man in the bus office.

By Fred's reaction to the stimulus of finding the billfold we have a very good idea of Fred's honesty, caution, and good sense.

Now, instead of characterizing one person by his reaction to one stimulus, suppose we complicate matters by characterizing two people by their reaction to meeting each other:

> Perry returned to the shade of his red-and-white-striped beach umbrella, carrying an ice cream cone in one hand and a paper cup filled with something called Cherry Nectar in the other. He had to watch the Cherry Nectar because it sloshed dangerously whenever he stumbled over some apparently detached portion of human anatomy sticking out of the sand. So he didn't see the girl curled up under his umbrella until she said, 'Of all the luck! Give me that drink. I'm perishing. You can get another.'

'Oh, I'm sorry — that is, I'm glad — Sure, take it,' Perry stammered. 'And the ice cream cone, too, if you like.'

'Gimme,' said the girl, holding out both hands. 'You've a heart of gold and everything. Sure she won't mind? I'd hate to start trouble.'

'She?' repeated Perry blankly. 'Oh, no. There isn't — there wasn't — not till you came. Gosh, I mean is, I bought 'em for me.'

'Then you're sort of — by yourself,' said the girl with a break in her voice. She bit into the ice cream, looking up at him. What she saw must have pleased her, for she said with an uncertain smile, 'So'm I. What's the answer to that one, big boy?'

'Why — I guess — if you think it's all right — I'd like you to have dinner with me and dance at the Casino afterward,' Perry said, with the eyes of a spaniel that hopes he is going to get a pat on the head but wouldn't be surprised if it turned out to be a cuff.

'The head of the class for you,' the girl said, licking out the cone with the end of her pink tongue. 'Come on, let's go.'

Perry's character as shown by his response to the stimulus of meeting the girl is that of a shy, friendly, unsuspicious young man, very responsive to kindness. The reader likes him at once, feels he has had an unhappy past, hopes he will find happiness in the future, but isn't so sure about his taking up with this girl. The girl is forward, but reader-sympathy is built for her because of her evident loneliness.

Now, very quickly, let us watch the responses of two more young men to the same stimulus, though perhaps not to the same girl, to which Perry responded. We shall take the scene immediately following the girl's first speech:

'Give you nothing!' Oscar exploded angrily. 'I didn't get this cherry stuff for any girl, much less a brazen piece like you!'

'Whoosh!' said the girl. 'What does he think he is, something out of a zoo?'

'News item!' said Oscar grimly. 'This is my umbrella, not yours. I've been sitting alone under it in peace and I aim to keep on doing just that. So scram outta here, baby, and leave poppa by himself.'

Oscar's response characterizes him as an irritable and rude young man, who is completely engrossed in his own affairs.

Now let us see what a young man named Dent reveals when he responds to the stimulus of meeting a pretty girl.

'Sure, darling, take it,' Dent smiled cosily down at the girl. 'And the ice cream cone, too. Would you like a hot dog? Some salt water taffy? I never saw you before but that makes it all the more fun. How about

dinner and dancing tonight? Come, come, of course you eat. Of course
you dance. All girls do, nice or otherwise. I ought to know.'

From this response the reader knows that Dent is flirtatious, not very
discriminating in the girls he chooses to play about with, rather a preda-
tory person, and one who is probably going to turn out to be the villain
of the piece. So much for stimuli from without.

It is equally fascinating to see how a stimulus rising from within can
call forth a characteristic response from a story-actor. But it is still more
fascinating when the response to an inner stimulus, when considered
alone, gives a completely erroneous picture of your character and it is
only through understanding the reasons (motives) that underlie her responses (actions) that we know the real person.

For example, a woman named Naomi Landers, in response to a stimulus from within, kills her husband. In most cases, committing a murder
definitely characterizes an actor as violent, unrestrained, and, therefore,
unlikable. But this is not always true. Let us examine the stimulus, as
well as the response, if we are to be sure that we understand the character of this woman. The indirect stimulus in this case was the knowledge of the cruelty of the husband and father of their child, a boy of
seven. Naomi was convinced that the husband would never allow her to
take the child from him, and that if his cruel treatment continued her
son would be wrecked, physically as well as mentally, for life. So a determination to protect her son was the direct stimulus that brought
about the response of murder. In this case, from Naomi's point of view,
the stimulus characterizes her as being both brave and determined. Of
course the reader may feel that Naomi should choose some other solution to her problem or that she is a case for a good psychiatrist.

Suppose we now see how we can characterize an actor by his response
to the stimulus of a mood; the mood, we'll say, being one of sorrow. Our
story-character, Malcolm, has recently lost his wife, Helen. The
thought that he will never see Helen again rolls over him like a wave.
Malcolm buries his face in his hands for a moment, then springs up, calls
his dog, and goes for a brisk walk in the October sunshine. Or, he buries
his face in his hands and refuses to answer when his young daughter calls
him to take her for a promised ride. Or Malcolm takes a gun from the
desk drawer and shoots himself, leaving his daughter to be brought up by
distant, elderly relatives. It is unnecessary to point out how these three
different responses to the mood of dejection characterize Malcolm as
three different persons.

Stimuli from without are usually such as might happen to anyone and, therefore, characterize weakly, if at all. However, there is an exception to this, and careful writers will do well to remember it. There are people who, by their very natures, seem to attract certain types of stimuli from without and repel other types. For example, we all know the man to whom adventurous things are always happening. He is forever being in train and automobile wrecks, offered jobs in South America, starting to Bali, and on the right spot at the right moment to help the police catch a brutal murderer. Another constantly gets into odd entanglements with erratic strangers because of his tendency to offer help to anyone who appears to be in difficulty. These are the people who are characterized, partly at least, by *what happens to them*.

Stimuli from within, however, characterize an actor just as much, and sometimes more, than his response to outer stimuli.

One point to keep clearly in mind, when characterizing your story-people by means of action and reaction, is that *once you have established the characteristics*, those dominant character-traits of your actor, *both the inner stimulus and the outer response to inner and outer stimuli must correspond with and be in keeping with those dominant character-traits.* In other words, your character must never step out of character. You will not show an unselfish character suddenly acting in a selfish manner, or a kind person suddenly becoming sarcastic and cruel.

Beginning writers often do this. They will tell their reader that their main character, a bride, is gentle, sweet, and affectionate. Then her husband comes home and says he forgot to buy the chops for dinner. Instead of reacting to the stimulus of the forgotten chops as the reader has a right to expect, the bride slaps her husband. 'You mean, selfish, horrid man!' she screams spitefully. 'You never do anything I ask you to! Get out of my way. I'm going home to mother.' This surprises the reader as much as it must surprise the husband, and almost as unpleasantly.

Get a surprise element into your story if you can, but not by having your actors change their characters at a moment's notice. Because characters don't change at a moment's notice. If you show *character change* at all, have it come about very slowly, as a *matter of growth* or *development*. The play or the novel is the usual vehicle for the portrayal of character change. The short story is, as a rule, too small a canvas on which to show anything more concerning character than its consistent reaction to varying stimuli. One of the best ways to treat such material, in a short story, is to begin as near the final character-determining crisis as possible, and then go into a long flashback in which the motivation and accumulated emotional build-up of months and years is explained. In this way the reader will accept as logical and inevitable the character change that is brought about in the story's end.

The one cause, the principal motivation, that will probably appear most often in your stories is that of love for one of the opposite sex, since love stories make up the bulk of published fiction. The effect, or way in which this love shall be expressed, is one of your major problems of characterization. There are as many ways of doing this as you have story-characters, so the problem is one that must be worked out in its specific details for every love story you write. But be sure that your actor does react characteristically, not only as he is a type, but as he is individualized within the type.

Let us try working this out with three men of widely differing character-traits, each in love with the same girl. Thus the stimulus is the same for each one. We shall see the dominant character-traits of each man by his responses in action:

> Jed Carter, Ambrose Willoughby, and Flick Brough are in love with a concert pianist named Persia Sutcliff. Jed is a horsy individual who owns a racing stable and likes good food, good wine, and an easy life. His characteristic and individual way of showing Persia that he loves her is to take her to the races and feed her fancy food. He entertains her with stories of all the horses he owns and has owned. He earnestly assures her that if she marries him she shall never play another concert and he will give her Red Mackerel, the fastest horse in the world next to Seabiscuit, for a wedding present.

Well, we know Jed rather thoroughly by now and we hope a lovely, talented girl like Persia isn't going to marry such a selfish, limited, egocentric man.

> Ambrose Willoughby is artistic, writes poetry, and attends all the really worth-while teas. He shows Persia his love by presenting her with thin, limp books, privately printed, bound in purple leather ornamented with gold tooling, containing his own poems. He reads these poems to her whenever she has time to listen. This, he tells her, is a great concession on his part, as he reads his beautiful brain-children only to those who 'understand.' He is very rude to both Jed Carter and Flick Brough because, he tells Persia, he is appalled by the thought of such crudeness as they represent even touching the white garment of her soul. She is to

forget Red Mackerel. He, Ambrose Willoughby, will dedicate his next book of poems to her if she will marry him.

That is about all we can stand of Ambrose, and we sincerely hope Persia feels the same way. But what about Flick Brough?

Flick is the successful owner and manager of a wholesale hardware business. He loves Persia very much but finds that he can't tell her so, because she seems so wonderful. He asks Persia's maid what kind of flowers she likes best. The maid says, 'Talisman roses.' Flick gives the maid a five-dollar bill and every day after that sends Persia Talisman roses. When Persia thanks him, he turns red and stammers, 'Oh well — I just thought — Anyway, I'm glad you like them —'

He doesn't mind being up late, he says, so he always takes her home from her concerts, but he doesn't come in afterward or even talk to her much on the way home. He knows, he says, that she is tired. He notices Persia wears green a good deal. When he comes back from a trip to India he brings her a huge uncut emerald he persuaded a maharajah to sell him. 'Some day,' Flick says, looking at the floor when he gives the stone to Persia, 'I'd sort of like to have it cut for you, and set in a special kind of setting. One that would look well on — on the third finger of your left hand, Persia.'

'Any time you like, Flick,' Persia whispers.

And we are all glad that was her answer, because Flick showed by his response to the stimulus of the woman he loved that he is a thoroughly kind, considerate, and unselfish man.

Characterization through action and reaction requires, as do all other ways of characterizing your actors, that you know your character well before you start writing. If you don't know your actor, how can you determine what his responses will be to stimuli either from within or from without? The answer is you can't make such a person come alive. If you don't *know* your character, in one scene he will react one way, in the next still another way. The result will be that your character will appear unreal and, therefore, flat and unconvincing. Since the purpose of writing is to interest the reader, you will have failed in your purpose and wasted your time.

First, get acquainted with your characters. Don't start writing until you know each one, even the most minor character, through and through; as well as you know your best friends, even better than you probably know yourself. Nothing short of this will do. Then be sure that each story-actor acts and reacts in truly characteristic ways, both to stimuli from within and the stimuli from without.

Method of Study

1. With what do story-action and reaction begin?
2. What are the two main classifications of stimuli to which human beings respond?
3. Is it always possible to determine character accurately from a stimulus alone; or from a response alone?
4. Select a stimulus. Write a brief scene showing an extrovert responding to that stimulus. Write a brief scene showing an introvert responding to the same stimulus. Make these scenes as interesting and dramatic as you can.
5. Select a response. Write a brief scene showing the stimulus, thereby characterizing your actor as a likable person. Write a brief scene showing the same response, but with a different stimulus that characterizes your actor as unlikable.

CHAPTER XI

Those Useful Figures of Speech

HOW TO CHARACTERIZE BY THE USE OF FIGURES OF SPEECH

MOST of us, even though we use figures of speech in our writing, more or less instinctively and by accident in most cases, think of them as something listed in a rhetoric book that we studied long ago. Instead, we should think of figures of speech as important devices to be studied in the present so we can improve our stories and get better prices for them. I assure you that figures of speech, while lending themselves to the most artistic handling, can be as practical as that.

Do not confuse the image-building writing that editors want today with the flowery verbal gymnastics indulged in by certain writers of yesterday. The figurative writing of today is as modern as stratosphere flying and television.

Fresh, modern figures of speech can lift an inherently dramatic and emotional story to greater heights of drama and power than would otherwise be possible. Their use in a weak 'thin' story will often be the principal means of increasing reader-interest and reader-enjoyment so that the tale will command a high price in a top market. Read the fiction in a half dozen smooth-paper magazines and you will see that this is true.

It is well worth our while to stop a moment to see why this is so. *Figurative writing is writing that stresses and sharpens sensory appeal to the end that it helps the reader to exercise his own picture-making faculty and, thereby, involves his own imagination in image-building.* It helps him, not only to see, but to feel, to hear, to taste. This reaction, in turn, increases his own emotional reaction. In other words, figures of speech help the reader to live more fully, more intensely, as he reads. And as he lives more intensely and more fully, the reader becomes more interested in what he is reading. Since the aim of all writing is in the final analysis, to give the reader pleasure, it is folly for the writer not to learn all he can about these almost magic aids to getting reader-interest.

Before we consider specific figures of speech, we should formulate clearly their functions. In this way we shall be able to check our figures of speech with these functions to make sure the device is being used to its best advantage, namely, to appeal to the reader and rouse his emotion.

There are three of these important functions:

1. To get reader-interest.
2. To stimulate the reader's imaginative faculty.
3. To cause the reader to respond emotionally.

By no means do any and all figures of speech perform these functions even fairly well. Even those stories published in the most literary of magazines sometimes fall far short of the minimum requirement under each heading. For example, suppose you write, 'She sang like a bird.' This should not interest the most naïve reader. There is no clear picture given in these trite words, since many birds sing, and the reader can imagine no specific sound since birds sing in many different keys. Perhaps she sang like a sparrow, perhaps like a nightingale, perhaps like a guinea hen. Not knowing in what way he is expected to react emotionally, the reader of 'She sang like a bird' experiences no emotional reaction at all. But suppose you wrote, 'She sang like a missel thrush at twilight,' the whole reaction is entirely different. The reader's attention is instantly arrested because of the specific kind of bird and the specific time of day. Also, this comparison gives material from which his imagination can make a picture, a picture so pleasing that he reacts with a favorable emotion toward the singer. This is a figure of speech, the simile, reduced to its simplest form for purposes of analysis and serving its threefold purpose of arresting attention, building an image, and evoking an emotion.

Figures of speech are to fiction what grace notes are to music, what spice is to apple pie, what carefully selected jewels are to a beautiful woman. They are not absolutely necessary, though they add greatly to already existent virtues. The writer who dresses his story up with figures of speech is being generous with his readers and his readers will repay him a hundredfold by interest in his story and demands for more like it from his pen.

What I have said up to this point applies to all aspects of treatment.

description of whatever kind, exposition, narration, conversation. Now let us turn our attention to the figures of speech that lend themselves most readily to characterization and the specific ways in which to use them:

THE SIMILE

The simile is the most flexible, the most adaptable, and, as a result, the most used of any of the figures of speech. *The simile is a comparison of one thing with another.* The human race has learned everything it knows by comparing one thing with another, recognizing this likeness or unlikeness to the other and to yet other known things or experiences. Since the earliest life forms learned to compare well-being with a diminution of well-being, or comfort with discomfort, down to the infinitely complex comparisons of likeness and unlikeness of the present, consciousness has expanded and continues to expand through the recognition of likenesses and unlikenesses. One of the foremost I.Q. tests for determining a person's intelligence is based on the rapidity of his powers of recognizing similarities and differences between words, objects, and sensations.

There is no other figure of speech so deeply rooted in the human, so let us look on the simile with the respect it deserves and use it skillfully as a tool for achieving the results we desire to build in the reader. Understanding the strong appeal it has, we must learn how to use the simile with power and effectiveness to gain our ends.

While similes are based upon comparisons, all comparisons are not similes. The simile requires that the two things compared be essentially different in all but one or two qualities, and that the comparison be made on the basis of that small difference. A true comparison, on the other hand, is based on many likenesses and perhaps only one or two differences. An example or two will clarify this: You want to characterize a young girl in one of your stories by a comparison. So you say, 'Emily is like her mother.' The differences between Emily and her mother are not great, being based, we shall say, mostly on the differences between their ages.

But suppose you want to characterize Emily by a simile. You might say, 'Emily is like a clover blossom.' Emily and the clover blossom certainly have nothing in common except, possibly, a sweet unassuming simplicity, which is probably the very quality you wish to emphasize.

A simile, then, is a tool, with which the writer can carve out a more finely drawn characterization. Since we know what it is and what we can do with it. let us now find out how we can use it to best advantage in our writing.

Our first actor is named Joel. Suppose we tell the reader, 'Joel is a slow man, slow in action, slow in thought.' That is decidedly dull and undramatic. The reader neither sees Joel nor is made to care anything about him. How can we get reader-attention, help the reader imagine a picture, and make him feel some emotion about Joel? A few minutes' thought and we hastily scribble, 'Joel trudged across the campus like a thoughtful, slightly melancholy turtle.' Now, what have we accomplished with this simile? We can feel fairly sure that we have interested the reader in Joel. The reader probably sees two pictures, one of a sad-faced turtle — all turtles have particularly sad faces — slowly and laboriously pushing itself across a campus, an incongruous place for a turtle to be. The second picture is of Joel, stooped, head thrust forward, trudging, his face mournful, in a slow, ungainly fashion across a campus. That is a better effect, is it not, than the one we secured by writing, 'Joel was a slow man, slow in action, slow in thought'? In the first, we *told* the reader; in the second, the reader *sees* for himself, and, as a consequence of his seeing, *reacts*.

Sharp contrast secured by bracketing together objects that are incongruous to each other is an almost certain device for getting reader-interest. Comparing Joel to a turtle gets contrast through incongruity.

The emotion, except for the emotion of interest, roused in the reader toward Joel in this simile with no accompanying text is slight; the reader is probably just a little sorry for him, or maybe, the image amuses him. But at least the reader's attention is arrested and he *sees* a specific person in action.

Let us consider how we can characterize a very different individual, Petie by name, who is small, nervous, quick, and easily frightened. If we give the reader no more than a list of Petie's characteristics or attributes, the reader will probably not only fail to visualize anybody, but he will also be bored. So let us try presenting Petie's characteristics by means of a simile. 'Petie skittered across the grass like a small black water-bug being chased by a roistering red-and-yellow dragonfly.' Or, to avoid the use of the word 'like,' which sometimes becomes monotonous, we write with better effect, 'Petie skittered across the grass, giving a perfect imitation of a small black water-bug being chased by a roistering red-and-yellow dragonfly.'

The words that most often identify a simile are 'like' and 'as and as,' and 'so and as.' We have already used the word, 'like.' Just for the sake of practice, let us use the others:

His words of praise are as insincere as the smile of a Hallowe'en mask.

His proposal was as perfectly phrased as the commercial for a soap program.

His face was as long as a movie show on Bank Night.

The above similes characterize more arrestingly than if we had said: 'His praise is insincere'; 'His proposal was too carefully polished and couched in exaggerated terms'; and 'He looked down-hearted.'

The greatest usefulness of the simile is, perhaps, in dressing up description by making it dramatic and exact in its pictorial appeal. But this is a fascinating bypath that takes us away from our present study of characterization and cannot be followed now. To the serious writer, however, this suggestion should lead to further profitable study of the functions and uses of the similes in published stories and to the application of what is learned to his own writing.

THE METAPHOR

After the simile the metaphor is the next most important figure of speech. Important because of the opportunities it offers for dramatic, pictorial, and emotional characterization.

The metaphor differs from the simile in that where the simile says one thing is *like* another, the metaphor says one thing *is* another, which, in literal truth, it is not.

For example, you might say of a man whom you wished to characterize as mean and sneaking, 'Old Skellet is a jackal.' You do not mean this literally. You mean that old Skellet has the attributes of a jackal, and to get the effect you transfer the name of jackal to Skellet. The result is a metaphor that gets reader-attention, is pictorial, and rouses the feeling of dislike or, possibly, of fear toward old Skellet. All in four words. If you change your metaphor to say, 'Old Skellet is a sheep,' you create an entirely different set of impressions and reactions in your reader; and if you add to that, 'the last of the indomitable bighorns on this range,' you again change the pictorial and emotional pattern in the reader.

The metaphor is an effective tool in the hands of the trained writer. Practice using it as a means of characterizing your major and minor characters. Write dozens of them for one story or one character. Then select the best and weave them into your story as a tapestry-weaver brings his scarlet and gold threads to the surface where they will give his design life, beauty, contrast, variety, and meaning.

It has been said that a metaphor is a strengthened simile. This is true, since it is surely more forceful to say that something *is* something else than to say it is *like* something else. For this reason the metaphor may become more important than the simile if the present trend toward strong, decisive writing continues. To that end, it might be helpful to learn the method of strengthening similes and so converting them into metaphors.

Suppose we have an actor who has lived all his life on a vast cattle range surrounded by lonely mountains, and who does not feel at home in town. We want to tell the reader quickly what kind of man he is by means of a simile: 'Dunk McWhorter was like a wild horse that has felt the bridle and the circingle, but has never liked them.'

To change this simile to a metaphor we write, 'Dunk McWhorter was a wild horse that had been trained to the bridle and circingle, but had never liked them.'

As you see, in a simile resemblance is claimed; in a metaphor identity is claimed.

There is one grave error into which even successful writers sometimes fall, and that is the mixed metaphor. Watch carefully and when you start with one figure, continue it at least to the end of that sentence. For example, do not characterize an actor by saying, 'Life to Wellington Hunsack was a twelve-cylinder car in which he sailed a straight course to the goal posts of opportunity.' Let Wellington Hunsack drive a car, or sail a ship or play football, whatever you please, but don't let him do all three in one sentence. Perhaps you laugh and say, 'No danger that *I* shall ever write anything as absurd as that.' Perhaps not. But many a writer who publishes regularly has done so, and been eternally grateful to his editor for the blue pencil that kept the monstrosity from reaching print. Humility, and the constant thought that he may unthinkingly commit practically any blunder that can be perpetrated by means of the written word, should be with the writer in all his down-sittings and in all his uprisings, especially the down-sittings before a typewriter.

PERSONIFICATION

When you use personification you tell the reader that *an inanimate object or a force of nature possesses human attributes, emotions, or powers.*

Since a human being is already a person, he cannot, of course, be personified. Therefore, the only way personification can be used to characterize is to apply it to inanimate objects and forces of nature. Since inanimate objects and forces of nature often play really important rôles in fiction, sometimes as a villain force and sometimes as a factor for the hero's success — sometimes even the hero rôle is a storm, as in the book by that name by George R. Stewart — any device that characterizes such objects and forces in an arresting image-making and emotion-building way is highly valuable.

Personification is one of the best tools the writer has for this purpose. It is at the same time extremely effective in giving passages of description, movement and life, and in keeping a story apparently moving, when in reality it is standing still while information is being given or time-transitions effected smoothly without disturbing unity.

Do not forget that inanimate objects and natural forces require characterizing, just as do your living actors. By characterizing them you tell the reader what kind of traits your actor possesses and, in so doing, the kind of rôle he will play; hero, villain, comedy relief, or whatever it may be. While it is not always necessary to characterize inanimate objects or natural forces in the above manner, it is often very desirable to do so.

Let us see how this works out in practice: We shall begin with a simple personification of an inanimate object, our purpose being to make a smooth time-transition. Without personification it might be written this way: 'Harry and Eleanor rode down the mountain to the village.' This gets Harry and Eleanor from their starting point to their destination, but it leaves the reader cold as far as interest and emotional reaction are concerned. So let's try again, this time using personification:

> For hours Harry and Eleanor followed the trail that, coiling round the granite shoulders of the mountain, plunging down a steep ravine, then zigzagging briefly over a rocky hogback, brought them at dusk in safety to the village.

This, as you see, gives a sense of life, movement to the trail, and makes the time and space transition smooth so that the reader arrives at the village with Harry and Eleanor with no sense of having been jerked there. For the reader, too, time has passed. This is personification with very slight characterization, since all we know about the effect the trail had on Harry and Eleanor is that it brought them *safely* to their destination. The trail was, then to that extent, characterized as friendly.

Now let us examine another use of personification when the attributes of the inanimate object are more clearly revealed as they affect the fortunes of the characters in the story.

The facts are:

> The travelers walked across the side of the mountain. Once in a while there was a small avalanche.

This is dull reading, because it does not characterize the mountain as a threat, or villain force. We turn to personification for help:

> The mountain frowned grimly at the travelers, and sent down small avalanches to show it could crush the whole party in a moment if it thought the effort worth while.

The result is more pictorial, arresting, and stronger in emotional effect.

Personification is often useful to establish and sustain a mood. Suppose you want to establish a mood of sustained sorrow for a scene. A brief, effective way of accomplishing your end is to personify and at the same time characterize an inanimate object. Suppose you have already written, 'Rain dripped all day from the locust tree just outside May's window.' You want to inject into the sentence emotion and a feeling of something about to happen. So you rewrite:

> The locust tree, outside May's window, wept through the dreary afternoon.

Examine the following:

> The tawny desert crouched, waiting to pounce on them the moment their strength began to fail.
> The storm fell upon them, growling and hissing.
> The car horn chuckled, or laughed, or screamed raucously, as its master wished.

In your own reading, watch for countless uses and advantages of personification; then give them your most careful attention in your own writing.

THE USE OF SARCASM

This is another useful tool and one that is often wrongly labeled by the writer. I say 'labeled' advisedly, because the writer nearly always follows what he thinks is an example of sarcasm by the words, 'he said sarcastically.' It is almost the only form that the writer feels he must label for the reader.

A sarcastic speech is one that is bitterly reproachful, often taunting in its implications. But not all reproachful or taunting speeches are sarcasm. Sarcasm is one in which the literal meaning of the words is exactly the opposite from the meaning intended to be conveyed by them. For example, 'You have been cruel to me, but you must know by now that you are even more stupid than you are cruel,' is a reproachful and taunting remark, but it is not sarcasm. Yet we can turn it into sarcasm by writing:

'How kind and affectionate you have been! And clever, too. No doubt you have discovered by now how astonishingly clever you are!'

Well-written sarcasm characterizes the person speaking and the person spoken to, and the writer should remember that it is not only a two-edged sword — to use a time-worn metaphor — but a very sharp one as well. Consequently, never have your hero use sarcasm unless it is completely justified and used toward a villain character. When the villain uses sarcasm toward the hero or toward a likable minor character, he characterizes himself still further as a villain and rouses pity for the likable character.

For example, do not allow your nice young hero to say to his wife as he throws the breakfast biscuits in the sink, 'Mother never made such thoroughly delightful biscuits as these. She didn't have your skill. You're certainly a prize wife!' Don't do it, because it characterizes your hero as cruel, and petty. Even if the biscuits were uneatable, this response to the stimulus of bad biscuits is not one the reader can admire.

On the other hand, this would be a fine speech to put in the mouth of your villain character, since it would show him speaking in a way that would rouse the indignation of the reader against him.

If you use real sarcasm you rarely have to tell the reader you are doing so. The text preceding the speech and the speech itself should make clear the inference to the reader.

Often, beginning writers sprinkle their pages with this sort of thing:

'Oh, yeah,' he said sarcastically.
'Going far?' he said sarcastically.
'I see you don't like candy,' she said sarcastically.

Whenever you find yourself writing, 'he said sarcastically,' check your work carefully to see if he really did speak sarcastically and, if so, whether you need to label the speech for the reader. No speech, if really sarcastic, needs to be labeled as such.

IRONY

Irony is so closely akin to sarcasm that it is often difficult to classify the borderline cases with absolute accuracy. They differ in degree rather than in kind. Like sarcasm, irony is a speech in which *the implication is the opposite of the literal meaning of the words.* The difference between the two lies in the fact that sarcasm is biting, caustic, bitter; while irony is gentle, only mildly reproachful, sometimes even witty.

As an illustration, let us state a situation in literal language and then in ironical language:

> Tommy comes into the house covered with mud. Grandfather says, 'Tommy, you are a very dirty boy. I'm afraid your mother is going to be unpleasantly surprised when she sees you.'

This characterizes Grandfather as a kindly old gentleman who states facts, but has no desire to hurt Tommy's feelings. Let us keep this characterization, but see if we can't do it a bit more entertainingly by the use of irony:

> Grandfather says, 'Tommy, I don't know when I've seen a more tidy boy. Your mother is surely going to be pleasantly surprised when she sees you.'

Tommy knows what Grandfather means and so does the reader, though the words have been changed. Grandfather is characterized just as he was before, but with an added touch of whimsicality and humor that causes the reader to like him even better than when he spoke literally.

An ironical situation is one in which the externals of that situation remain as expected, but an *unexpected* factor has entered, changing the emotional effect on the actor. The following is an example of an ironical situation:

> Binkie had always hoped he and Sue would have several children. Well, Binkie thought, he had them. And how! Sheer panic gripped him. Triplets, the nurse had said.

Binkie wanted children and he had children, but having three arrive at once changed things considerably, and the consequent situation was ironic.

METONYMY

Metonymy is putting one word in place of another, as 'The White House is silent on the subject.' What we really mean is, 'The President is silent on the subject.' Or we might say, 'The airplane was a faint speck in the blue.' Here the word 'blue' takes the place of the word 'sky.' Or, 'The stage opposes the idea,' when what we really mean is that actors and other people directly connected with the theater oppose the idea. *Metonymy*, as you see from these examples, *intensifies an idea and expresses it pictorially*.

Metonymy is, with one exception that we shall examine later, the least known by name of any form of figurative language in general use. Yet it is seen frequently in every type of writing, from the crisp news items of the press — 'the press' being an example of metonymy, by the way — to the most formal writing in the highest type of literary story or novel.

Its greatest value lies in its brevity, pungency, and image-making effect. It is flexible, versatile, and adaptable to almost any style or purpose and, therefore, to almost every writer. In fact, it is difficult to think of any writer to whom it would not be useful.

Metonymy is especially adaptable to characterization, where a minimum of words must exert a maximum of effect on the reader. Suppose one of your characters is entering your story for the first time. It has not been possible previously to characterize him in any way. He enters in a scene where tense action is going forward and you must characterize him as fully as possible in as few words as possible, without stopping, or even slowing, the action of that scene. Turn to metonymy and see how it can serve you. After a moment's thought concerning the dominant character traits of your actor you write:

> The next moment there was a roaring, mane-shaking lion in the room. 'Father!' implored Anne, 'Calm yourself! Remember your blood pressure!'

You have substituted 'roaring, mane-shaking lion' for 'Anne's father' and have arrested reader-attention by an incongruous idea — a lion in a room. You have given the reader a clear-cut picture of Father, with movement and sound, and characterized Father by attributing to him some of the well-known qualities of a lion, such as a dangerous temper easily roused, with an implication of courage and pride. This is a good deal to accomplish in one brief sentence, but it illustrates the usefulness of metonymy as a working tool of the writer.

Of course you have often used metonymy in your writing, perhaps without consciously thinking about it. Train yourself to use it *consciously*. Practice writing metonymy until you are skilled in the infinite variety of its uses. I cannot recommend it too highly to writers who want to give their work that extra power, extra dramatic and emotional effect that will lift it from the commonplace and trite to heights of originality and exciting interest that readers avidly read and for which editors gladly pay top prices.

HYPERBOLE

Hyperbole is exaggeration so excessive that it arrests reader-attention. While always leaving him aware of the exaggeration, it creates a sharper, more arresting impression than might otherwise be possible. Sometimes useful, it should be used sparingly, except in humorous stories that are more or less fantastic.

Here is the method of developing a simple, bare statement of fact into the figure of speech called *hyperbole* and using it to characterize a story-actor. First, we state the simple fact: 'Paul's mood changes frequently.' A correct characterization probably, but presented in a way that lacks everything to interest the reader. We try again: 'Paul's mood changes every five minutes.' This is exaggeration, but to such a slight degree that the statement has all the disadvantages of the first one with the added disadvantage of not being quite true. We try once more and this time we are determined to produce an example of true hyperbole. We write, 'Paul's moods changed with every tick of the clock.' The reader knows this isn't literally true, yet it gives him a truer *impression* of Paul than either of the preceding statements that were nearer the literal truth. Such is the magic of figures of speech.

PARADOX

A paradox is a statement that is nonsense, or contradictory, if taken at its face value, but which has a deeper meaning that is readily apparent. It is not often used, perhaps because of the difficulty of devising striking paradoxes. However, some very good effects can be secured by the use of paradoxes, provided you have the type of mind and patience required to think of them.

The following examples of the paradox used to characterize will make clear what a paradox is and how to use it:

Marie was a girl who worked hard to keep from working.

Jack always said that Mal was wider awake when he was asleep than he ever was walking around with his eyes open.

Someone should tell Harry Altmont that no one is important unless he is unimportant.

ONOMATOPOEIA

The figure of speech with this terrifying name is as simple and as commonly used as metonymy. Neither is talked about very much, probably because no one could possibly feel on familiar terms with anything called either metonymy or onomatopoeia. The latter is often spoken of as the 'Bowwow Theory.'

Onomatopoeia is nothing more than *fitting the sound* of the word to its sense. It is seldom used in characterization, because it is limited to sounds. Though in descriptive bits and in poetry it often appears, giving a very charming effect. However, it can be used in characterization, especially of animals, machinery, and forces of nature, and every writer should be thoroughly familiar with its possibilities as well as its limitations.

Examples of onomatopoeia follow:

Characterizing a person:

Aunt Hat's scolding words clacked and clattered in Trudie's ears.

Characterizing machinery as a menace or villain force:

The great flywheel threatened her with its merciless hum and whirr.

Characterizing an animal:

When the door opened, the captive rattlesnake rustled with the sound of a thousand hula dancers swishing grass skirts on a heat-stilled evening.

One highly important quality of the figures of speech that will help you to write effectively is that of suitability of choice: that is, choosing figures of speech that are suitable to the story-setting and locale, to the time, to the type of characters you are using. This is often overlooked, with disastrous results to the unified and artistic effect of the story and to its convincingness.

For example, don't write a sea story filled with figures of speech concerning life on a farm, in a mining camp, or on the desert. Be sure that those you choose have to do with the sea. If your character is a woman leading a life of ease and pleasure in the city, use figures of speech having to do with city life as she knows it. Don't, for instance, say, 'Her laugh was like the faint tinkle of distant cowbells in a summer evening.' Instead say something like this, 'Her laugh was like a muted saxophone, sobbing faintly beneath the brasses of the night club orchestra.'

Figures of speech suited to the setting or locale of your story, or to the types of characters you are using, will help immeasurably in *unifying* your story and giving it a thoroughly professional touch. Many a trite plot and mediocre story has been lifted to freshness and charm and originality by the author's careful attention to the figures of speech he chose and used and his hard work to gain the requisite skill and ease in writing them.

Arresting, effective figures of speech are not written by chance or by inspiration, except on very rare occasions. They are thought out carefully, planned carefully, for their suitability, their interest-getting qualities, their pictorial effect, and for their emotional stimulus to the reader. *Keep a notebook in which you jot down choice and original figures of speech when they come to you.* Such a notebook will be a rich source on which to draw when you are in search of the right image or comparison.

Method of Study

1. What is the figure of speech most often used by writers? Why?
2. What are the three chief functions of figures of speech?
3. What is the difference between a simile and a metaphor? Between satire and irony?
4. Write original examples of each of the figures of speech given in this chapter.
5. Create a story character and characterize him by using four different types of figures of speech concerning him.

CHAPTER XII

Motives Make the Man Go

THE REASON THAT LIES BEHIND ACTION

A COMMON weakness of the beginning writer is that his story-characters do strange and inconsistent things not at all in keeping with the kind of persons they individually are. Such stories come back from editors with the comment, 'Not convincing,' or the reader of a published story exclaims, 'I don't believe it!' When convincingness is lacking, it means that the fiction characters do not act as people in real life act. How can you overcome this weakness in your stories? This can be done in 6 ways:

1. By making your characters *live* — every chapter thus far has helped you in this.
2. By giving your character a *problem* of *importance* to solve, a problem in keeping with the type of person he is.
3. By putting your character in a *situation* in which he would *logically* find himself, or by building that situation into one acceptably probable to the reader.
4. By *endowing* your character with certain qualities and dominant traits that will plausibly and inevitably find expression in a certain course of action.
5. By *setting* at the beginning of the story the *mood* and the emotion that will put the reader in the frame of mind to *accept* what happens to the characters.
6. By giving your character a *reason* for wanting to do what he does; that is, a logical reason in keeping with that dominant character-trait of his and dominant emotion.

When a story is logically motivated, even though your character does the most outlandish things, your reader will accept such actions and say,

'Of course, he would do that. It is absolutely in keeping with the type of man he is.'

It is this problem of motivation that we shall consider in detail in this chapter. Repeatedly I find stories among my student-writers' manuscripts wherein there is 'too much ado about nothing.' That is to say, the story-characters frantically tear across the landscape or hate each other for no *apparent reason* whatsoever. I keep asking myself, '*Why* do they *want* to do this? What *reason* lies behind their actions?' I find either there is too much action for too little reason, or not sufficient action for so much reason. Usually the former.

Webster defines motivation as '*to supply with a reason; to move.*' This is exactly the sense in which the writer should interpret motivation and use it toward his own ends. *Characters in a story must act as the result of a motive and the story must move.*

When the reader *knows* the motives of a character, then he will realize the significance of certain actions in the working out of the actor's story problem, and why it is so *necessary* that he *solve* that problem.

Motivation is the springboard of all action; it is the engine that makes the car go. If the writer will but seriously consider this matter, he will find his whole story taking on a basic pattern that is the pattern of all life: motivation + dominant character-trait + dominant emotion = problem and action. Or, interpreted, *why* (motivation) + *who* (dominant character-trait + dominant emotion) = *what* (problem) and *how* (action). This really becomes a chart against which to check for the logical build-up of your plot material. Each one of these is a result of and an outgrowth of the other, and all are in keeping each with the other and the whole. Of course, this sounds very involved, but it isn't. Just remember that *what* you want to do (problem) and *how* you will do it (action) are the direct result of *why* you want to do it (motivation) and *who* you are in terms of traits and emotions. Or, conversely, *why* you want to do it and *who* you fundamentally are foreordain *what* you want to do and *how* you will do it. It is important that you, the writer, carefully consider this, because it is the foundation of the whole problem of *how to build a story around a character* (Chapter XVI). When you fully understand these essential principles, you will no longer wonder why one person can want to and does do so many apparently contradictory things. Likewise, you will understand that a change of emotion with another dominant trait uppermost, and the same person will not only find himself, as a result, confronted by different problems, but he will go through entirely different actions in solving the same old original problem. Such is the diversity of human nature; an inexhaustible mine of story-material for the writer who sees below the surface into the cause (motivation) that lies behind the result (action).

So, behind every act we perform, there lies a reason, whether conscious or unconscious. This urge that lies behind all action is the most compelling force in the world. It is responsible for all the changes in the lives of individuals and all the upheavals of history. Psychologists in their scientific approach to the subject have used such terms and classifications for our urges as:

1. The life urge: self-preservation — hunger, fear for safety, self-defense.
2. The sex urge: love in all its forms — pity, loyalty, the desire to reproduce.
3. The worship urge: gratitude, awe, altruism, remorse, standards of right and wrong.
4. The power urge — with all of its ramifications from the expression of the constructive instinct to the will to become a dictator.
5. The social urge — from the gregarious herd instinct through all its social manifestations, play and humor.

Whatever way you tabulate these urges, they are the roots of all activity. Sometimes we have simple reasons for our actions and sometimes very complex ones, but in all cases, whether evident or not, there is an instinctive urge that is a relentless driving force. Because it is usually guided by emotion rather than the cold logic of the mind, it is all-powerful and often ruthless in its action. For example, Scarlett O'Hara's prime motivating force was her great love for Ashley Wilkes (sex urge); to be sure, as a result of the war, she had to make a living and, due to the fact that she was capable, did so (life urge); there were other times when the power urge and the social caused her to act accordingly. Rhett Butler was dominated by the love urge (sex), although his desire to make money (power urge) and his determination to establish himself in the community for Bonnie (social urge) were important directing forces in his life. Every action of Melanie's whole life seemed the result of her love for others (sex urge) and her kindly spirit that was compounded of the social and worship urges. Ashley Wilkes was activated by the love urge but influenced most by what he considered was 'the right thing to do' (social urge). Or, to cite Shakespeare, Macbeth himself, determined to be king, was driven by the power urge; Lady Macbeth, because of her love for her husband (sex urge), committed murder so that he could be king; Malcolm, Donaldbain, and Macduff, whose loved ones had been so ruthlessly murdered by Macbeth, revenged themselves on him (self-preservation). And so it is possible to go on endlessly analyzing and assigning the *cause* behind any story-character's behavior; the *why* behind the *what*.

Thus we see that the raw materials to be used by the fiction writer are those revelations of character as deduced from actions. But the writer must not concentrate on those outward revelations or manifestations of behavior that he observes and, consequently, fail to realize the importance of his work, which is the setting forth of the emotions and the convictions and the wishes that, in turn, stir up desires in his story-characters and *cause* them to do what they do. To consider in detail the importance of all this to the writer:

Often the motive behind the act is more significant as a means of characterizing a fictional character than the act itself. The motive behind the *purpose* of the main character for the story is more packed with implications regarding character than the purpose itself. That is the reason that you, as writer, must be sure that you have given your story-characters strong, logical, and significant motives. These motives may be bad, or good, depending on your characters and the necessities of your plot, but never allow these motives to be trivial, weak, or of small importance. Much more than the characterization of your actors depends on this. Reader-interest in your story depends on it. Without strong motives that impel your characters to act as they do, you cannot build suspense, drama, emotion, and climax. The reason for all of this is fundamental. If your hero's motive is weak, he will not care greatly whether he succeeds or fails. The same is true of your villain, and of all the other characters. If your characters are unconcerned over the outcome of their story, you cannot expect the reader to care. And the moment the reader doesn't care, he stops reading.

One of the commonest faults of writers who have not yet attained professional status, and sometimes of those who have, is that they do not give strong motives to *both* their main characters, that is, to the hero and the villain as well. This has many effects on a story other than that of reducing characterization to the vanishing-point, but since all that is 'another story,' not directly related to characterization, we shall, except for the preceding observation, ignore it and return to our subject, which is motivation as an aid to characterization.

Don't be stingy with your motivation. Motive to a story-character is what gasoline is to a car. It gives the character vitality and the ability to go places under his own power. The best, the most powerful motives are none too good for the characters of that next story of yours. If you give your character a strong motive you characterize him as a strong character, one in whom the reader can take an active interest. If you give him a weak motive, you characterize him as a vague, illogical being who will not only with certainty bore the reader, but whom the reader will, in all probability, reject in disgust as being not true to life. Therefore, weak or strong, behind every act lies a reason and a logical one in keeping with the kind of person we are.

If you put high-test gasoline in your car it climbs the hills in high, without faltering or hesitation, reaching its destination at the appointed time. If you put cheap gasoline in your gas tank your car will jerk and splutter up the hills and will arrive at its destination certainly late and perhaps never.

If you put no gasoline in your car it won't even start. You may be able to push it around the block, but as for getting anywhere with it, that is impossible. You don't even try.

Exactly the same is true of motive and your story-characters. Give your actor, whether hero, villain, or minor character, a sound, strong motive and watch him travel. He will move swiftly and purposefully forward. Nothing will be too hard for him to accomplish in the end. And if he is the hero, he will arrive at his destination successfully and dramatically. If he is a villain he will come to conclusive and decisive defeat.

But give any story-character a weak motive and watch his erratic, creeping progress toward a weak, undramatic end.

If you fail to give your characters any motive at all, your story will never start. Oh, you may write five thousand words or so *about* those characters, but the result will not be a story that the reader enjoys. Always remember that *to make a character live, he must move under his own power*.

Suppose we illustrate the way in which strong motives and weak motives change the characterization of an actor, and strengthen or weaken a story:

We write an outline of a story about a girl named Mary Andrews. Mary's purpose for this story is to win the attention, approbation, and love of, and finally marry, Bob Thorndyke, Oakdale's most eligible bachelor. This is perfectly satisfactory as a story-purpose, since it is important, familiar and, unless shown to be otherwise, laudable. But what about motive? We examine our outline carefully and we discover with horror that Mary's motive is to show the other Oakdale girls that she is smarter than they are. If we use this motive our story will limp and splutter and never get anywhere. The motive is not only intrinsically weak, but it characterizes our main character, whom the reader must like if he is to feel interest in what she does, as a selfish, scheming bit of fluff, not worth the reader's attention. We have put cheap gasoline in our car and the result, if we start out with it, will be disappointing. As characterized by her motives, Mary would do for the villain or a minor character accomplice of the villain, but not for the heroine.

Let's put some standard-grade gasoline in the tank of our story and note the result. Change Mary's motive back of her purpose of marrying Bob to that of achieving lifelong happiness for herself, making Bob happy and thus insuring a normal, useful life for both of them. That is better. The story will move along very well now, but we still shall have to coax it up the hills and, with clever conversation, divert the reader from the thumping that's going on inside somewhere, threatening to wreck us at any moment. However, the story gets to its destination at last, without anyone, except ourselves, knowing how hard we had to work to get it there. The majority of stories, especially love stories that are published, are like this. The writer has to do skillful coaxing, but they do arrive in the end.

But suppose we put high-grade gasoline into the tank of this story of ours, what will happen? Let's try it to see. Now Mary's motive for marrying Bob is, of course, first of all, her deep love for him, but it is more than that. There is a siren on his trail, determined to marry Bob for his money. Mary not only wants to marry Bob because she loves him, but because she wants to protect Bob from the siren, who will ruin his life if she succeeds in her purpose. The motive, an unselfish desire to protect Bob, added to Mary's original motive has helped tremendously both to characterize Mary as a thoroughly likable girl, and also as a driving force behind all she does in our story.

Editors get literally thousands of stories each month without adequate motivation and consequently without adequate characterization. Of course it takes more than motive to characterize, but *motivation is an indispensable ingredient of characterization.* For example, this is one of the favorites. Editors know it as a 'want-a-dress' story, even though the object wanted is not a dress, but a ring, a car, a house, a lot, and so on indefinitely. Alfreda, or Alyce, or Mehitabel, as the case may be, wants a new dress. For no particular reason that the story discloses. In other words, she has no strong motive for wanting or trying to get a new dress. She just wants one. The desire is understandable enough, even to men, because a large percentage of men write this kind of story. But, since the motive of any one of these girls for getting a new dress is no more important than a wish to dazzle her contemporaries or enjoy a mild esthetic pleasure from viewing her own reflections in a mirror, nothing much is accomplished that adds to the drama of the story or characterizes the girl.

But why does she want the dress? There is most certainly a reason that lies behind the desire for the dress. Now look what happens when we add a real motive. Let's go back to Mary and Bob, two people we already know. We decide to write one of those 'want-a-dress' stories, but with a difference. The story opens with Mary wanting a dress, a very special dress, for a very special party. The dress is to be the most beautiful dress in the world, and as different as possible from the sophisticated gown the siren will wear at this party. Mary wants the dress to help her show Bob that she, Mary, is the girl to make him happy, not that black-satin-and-orchids-bedecked 'other woman.'

But what is the difference? We have given Mary a strong, important motive for wanting a new dress, and we have characterized Mary by doing so.

When you are planning your stories be sure to give at least as much thought to the motives of your characters as to the clothes they wear.

Which is more important as a means of characterizing your actors, the clothes they wear, or the motives that cause them to act as they do? Of course, you answer that motives are far more important than clothing in this respect. Remember this when you *plan* your next story. It is a curious fact that the beginning writer rarely *dresses* his actor 'out of character,' but he thinks nothing of having his actor impelled to action by motives altogether foreign to the character he has led the reader to believe the actor possesses. He will have his hero motivated by revenge, or his villain motivated by pity at the drop of a hat, when nothing would induce him to put a checked suit on a minister, or a frock coat on a gambler. The motive of revenge characterizes your hero as mean and despicable, while the motive of pity characterizes your villain as kind and sympathetic. Mixed motives are even worse than mixed metaphors, because they confuse the reader as to the true character of your actor.

To be sure, in life mixed motives appear to exist. Upon careful examina tion, however, there is found to be one dominating real motive that *underlies* all the others.

Take the next story-actor you meet who seems to be impelled by many motives in conflict, explore the man and his actions, go behind *what* he does and *how* he does it until you reach the important *why* he does it — and you will find that under all these seeming reasons is the one basic reason that is the *why*.

No discussion of characterization by means of motives is complete without definitely establishing what constitutes 'good' and what constitutes 'bad' motives. This is particularly important since here exists a wide and honest divergence of opinion on the subject.

In writing a story, a book, a radio play, a movie, or a stage production, the author abides by the generally accepted moral code in selecting his 'good' and 'bad' motives. This code is made up of our laws and of that vague, yet very concrete, thing known as 'public opinion.'

In this connection the writer should never forget that the reader, as such, is much more moral than when actually going about his everyday life. Motives that he might readily condone in himself, or even in a friend, will completely alienate his sympathy from the hero of a story he is reading. In novels for adults and in stage plays, this rule is relaxed to some extent for reasons that will be discussed when we come to consider characterization in these literary forms. But in the short story, the moving picture, the radio play, the juvenile and adolescent story or book, the motives of your hero must be 'good' and the motives of your villain 'bad,' with the 'good' motives always triumphing in the end.

Should your hero happen to be assailed by a wrong motive, he will discard it immediately and sadly regret having entertained it for a moment. If, however, he so far forgets himself as to allow this wrong motive, such as revenge or spite, to carry him into action, he will rue the day and make all amends possible.

With your villain, the case for motivation is reversed. The strength of your villain as an opposing force to your hero is in direct ratio to the degree of danger he represents. Therefore, anything that weakens him as a villain, weakens the drama and suspense of your story that you are trying with every means available to you to build and to intensify. Any good motive held by the villain for more than an instant will lessen the effect of uncompromising opposition and menace to your hero, weaken the characterization of your villain and the drama of your story.

This does not mean that your hero must never do anything that a sweet, maiden-lady, Sunday-School teacher would not do. I am speaking of *motive* now, not action. Your hero may transgress all legal, moral, and ethical codes, even to committing murder — except in radio plays, moving pictures, and juvenile fiction — and go unpunished by God or man, *provided his motive for the act was clearly and decisively 'good'*; that is, unselfish; and that the act springing from that motive was for the protection of someone other than himself who is weak and defenseless.

In other words, if the hero commits an act generally accepted as 'bad,' his motive for the act must be 'good' enough to *justify* him in the eyes of the reader. His 'good' motive characterizes him as an admirable character and so nullifies the 'bad' act he committed, insofar as reader-liking and reader-sympathy is concerned.

The knowledge of how to use motive as a means of spotlighting likable character-traits, thus throwing unlikable character-traits into deep shadow, is of great importance to the writer. This allows him to use as the hero of his story, a character that would neither appeal to nor interest the reader were it not for the careful spotlighting of likable character-traits seen through the hero's motive that lies behind the action that makes up the story.

All of us have read stories that were variations on the theme of the drunken derelict, a thoroughly good-for-nothing scamp as far as his life up to the moment the story opens allows anyone to judge. But in the story he saves the lives of hundreds of people at great risk of his own by warning the villagers that the dam has broken. This may be the only good deed the tramp ever performed in the course of his life, yet he is good hero-material. Why? Because the motive back of his actions during the time-lapse of the story is 'good'; that is, unselfish, and for the protection of others. This motive spotlighted the one good character-trait the tramp possessed and, while the reader is dimly aware of his many 'bad' motives that impelled him to action in the past, those motives are thrown into deep shadow for the duration of the story and serve by contrast to heighten the effect of the present 'good' motivation.

In consequence, do not think for a moment that all or even most of your story-heroes must be pure as distilled water or the snowflake on an apple blossom. You may cast any type of person you please in the rôle of hero, if you but give him a *good motive* for his action in the story.

Because — and I repeat this for it is of the utmost importance to every writer — a good motive will spotlight the desirable character-traits of the hero, and effect a partial blackout of the undersirable character-traits that you do not want the reader to see, except dimly. And because the reader is dimly aware of those undesirable traits, he will all the more rejoice at the victory of 'virtue' in the end.

Like every other rule, the rule that the main character of a story must be characterized by a good motive has its exceptions. We shall consider those exceptions now.

The first exception is in a type of story that is fairly common; one that you will doubtless want to write many times. The plot form that is known as the Biter Bit. In it Actor A, the main character, is not a hero, but a villain. Consequently, the motive used to characterize him is as bad as it can possibly be made. In the end he himself brings about his own defeat and is properly punished; that is, the biter gets bitten, the admirable, and in this case minor, character, being left happy and triumphant, although through no great effort of his own. Many short shorts are of this type.

The second exception is very rarely seen, but you should be able to identify it when occasionally you see it in a magazine or other published form. The main character in this type of story is intrinsically weak, so he never appears as a main character in the longer forms of fiction. He is neither a true villain nor a true hero, but a whimsical person whose motives are intrinsically selfish, but who harms no one very much and no likable character at all. He is most often a lovable scamp who outwits real scoundrels at their own game. Stories of this type are difficult to write because of the necessarily weak motivation, and editors seldom buy them. When well written, they are fairly entertaining, however.

HOW TO MOTIVATE

There are innumerable ways of showing motive that characterizes, but the methods used most often are as follows:

1. By the acts of the character.
2. By speech:
   (a) speech of the actor who is being characterized by motive,
   (b) speech of a minor character.
3. By thoughts of the major character.

These thoughts may be given directly, indirectly or analyzed by the writer. The thoughts of a minor character cannot be used to give motive unless you are using the omniscient viewpoint, a viewpoint that is suited only to certain material and one that is difficult to handle successfully.

4. By a statement of the writer's.

First we shall see how a *characterizing motive can be shown by an act.* Our main character, a young fellow named Walter Curtis, hears that his friend, Ben Skidmore, is seriously ill in a hospital. Walter is making a large salary, whereas Ben was just getting along. Walter goes at once to Ben's home and tells Lillian, Ben's wife, not to worry, from now on he is taking over the financial responsibility of the family until Ben is well enough to go back to work. Unless we clearly show the reader to the contrary, he will believe, from this act, that Walter's motive was a strong desire to be helpful to Ben and Lillian.

This same motive can be presented to the reader *by means of a speech* of Walter's. He may tell his father, 'I am going to help Ben, he's got a tough break.' To make the motive still more clear to the reader or to clear up a possible misunderstanding about Walter's motive, his father, a *minor character*, can say, 'Son, you are certainly a good friend of Ben's, helping him out this way. He'll appreciate it.'

Or Walter *may think*, 'Gosh, it's little enough to do for Ben. He's a good old scout and I'd be a rotter not to help him out.'

Or *the writer may say*, 'Walter was a good-hearted chap, never missing a chance to help a friend. Ben was suddenly stricken with pneumonia, good old Walt went right out to Ben's house and told Ben's wife not to worry.'

Sometimes the writer has a more difficult problem in showing motivation than in any of the examples given above. This occurs when the act, or the speech, does not show the *real* motive behind the act. Let us assume that the motive back of Walter's act of helping Ben financially was not a 'good' motive, but a 'bad' motive. His motive is to give himself an opportunity to see a good deal of Ben's wife so he can win her away from Ben. The act remains the same and, unless the motive behind the act is made clear, the reader will think Walter a fine fellow. How can the reader be shown the true motive so that he will understand Walter's real character and dislike him, instead of admiring him? Remember what we said before: *the act does not always correctly characterize, but the motive does.*

In this case, Walter may reveal his real motive by means of speech to his friend, Lewis. Let's listen to Walter, who is about to characterize himself as a villain, even though he has just done what appears to be a highly meritorious act:

> 'Sure,' Walter said, putting his feet on Lewis' desk and lighting a cigarette. 'I told Ben's wife — Lillian's her name — that everything was jake. She didn't need to worry about money. You know, there'll be things to talk over and decide. And when there isn't anything, I'll be there anyway, just in case.' He winked knowingly. 'Ben's too slow for her.' Again he winked. 'And once Ben's out of the running...'

The *speech of a minor character* can be equally useful in revealing motive that characterizes differently from the act. Suppose Walter has just told his father, *a minor character*, of offering to shoulder Ben's financial burdens. Walter's father looks at him and says:

> 'Son, I've known for a long time you were no good, but I didn't think you'd sunk to where you'd use your money to disguise yourself as a lamb so you could play the rôle of wolf. I'm no fool. You're planning to take Lillian away from Ben under cover of helping him.'

The *thoughts of the major character* are still another excellent means of revealing motive. To return to Walter. He is just driving away from Ben's house after making his offer of financial help to Lillian. He is thinking:

> 'It's going to be a pushover. What with Ben broke and in the hospital, he won't suspect a thing until too late for him to do anything about it. Lillian always did like me, and with this set-up she's going to like me a lot more — enough to leave Ben and marry me, or my name isn't Walter Curtis.'

Or the *writer can make a plain statement* of Walter's motive, though this method is the least artistic and the least effective of any means of revealing motive that is open to the writer. But if you use this method, do your best to think of some way of presenting that plain statement in an unusual and entertaining way.

Instead of saying, 'Walter Curtis was planning to take Ben's wife away from him under the guise of helping Ben financially,' you might phrase it:

> Walter Curtis was one of those fellows that if you saw him putting a nickel into a beggar's cup you knew it was just a blind for taking out a dime, or a quarter — more likely. So when he offered to take care of everything for Ben and Lillian, you didn't have to be clairvoyant to know what he was scheming.

Motivation must be shown, in order to characterize your story-actors convincingly and accurately, but more than that it is a necessary ingredient in a salable story.

Method of Study

1. Which is more important in characterization: the act, or the motive behind the act?
2. What is the fiction writer's definition of a 'good' motive? Of a 'bad' motive?
3. What are the two types of short stories in which the main character may be impelled to action by motives that are 'bad'?
4. By using each of the four ways of showing motivation, characterize an original fiction character, making the motive correspond to the act.
5. By using the four ways of showing motivation, characterize an original fiction character, making the motive at variance with the act.

CHAPTER XIII

Simple and Complex Characterization

MAJOR AND MINOR CHARACTERS AND HOW TO INDIVIDUALIZE THEM

It is with the specific procedures of selecting and portraying character-traits of story-actors in their rôles of major and minor characters, and with ways and means of individualizing these characters, that we shall concern ourselves in this chapter.

Few people who belong to what we are pleased to call the highly civilized races have simple characters. They have, in the vast majority of cases, highly complex characters, with many character-traits, some admirable, some far from admirable, and of these some will be strong, others weak.

Think of someone you know very well and with whom you have been associated a long time. With approximately their relative importance, make a list of all the character-traits you have seen this person display in the years you have known him. Unless your perceptive faculties are blinded by some strong emotion you feel toward this person, such as love, or hate, or fear, or pity, you will be amazed at the number of character-traits you have listed and by the wide divergence between the best and the worst. This little exercise in listing the character-traits of an individual will make clear to you the impossibility of putting anyone in a book exactly as he is. To attempt to bring out all these character-traits in a short story would be the height of absurdity. Your aim as a creative writer is not to reproduce a character in the form of a scientific chart, but to present him so that he gives the *impression* of living, moving reality.

This person whose character-traits you have listed does not demonstrate all his character-traits simultaneously. Some of them are fairly constant in their manifestations, others appear only under special circumstances, provocations, or stresses. Therefore, if you want to give a true picture of this man, or of a character of your own creation, you will select one, two, or, at the most, three strong character-traits and you will stress those in your story, not showing the others at all, or at most letting one or two appear dimly, merely to enrich and round out your character-portrayal.

Fictional characters may be divided, for our present purposes, into five types: Simple, Complex, Flat, Round, and Background. The first step in analyzing these types is to agree on a definition for each, so that we may clearly understand the explanation:

Type 1. *The Simple character is an actor who shows one dominant character-trait throughout the fictional form in which he appears.* This does not mean that this dominant character-trait is the only character-trait this actor is shown to possess. The Simple character is shown to possess other character-traits that are in accordance with the dominant character-trait and reinforce or complement it. They are not unduly stressed, they are, on the contrary, subordinated. The Simple character should be both characterized and individualized and he is usually a major character.

Type II. *The Complex character is one who has two or more strong, contradictory or conflicting character-traits, not of equal strength, but of almost equal strength.* He, like the Simple character, has other character-traits in the background that serve to reinforce his dominant character-traits. He should be both characterized and individualized. He is always a major character and usually the hero of the psychological character-conflict story.

Type III. *The Flat character is one who is without any dominating character-trait,* or has one, with no supplementary character-traits that either reinforce or contradict the dominant character-trait. Whether or not a Flat character is given a dominant character-trait, he should be individualized. He is invariably a minor character.

Type IV. *The Round character may be either Simple or Complex. This term designates a character that is three-dimensional,* as distinguished from a one-dimensional, or Flat character. In other words, a Round character is one that is sufficiently characterized and individualized so that the reader feels, while he is reading, at any rate, that the character is a real person. He is always a major character.

All of the above character-types should be given a name in keeping with their dominant traits and personalities (see Chapter III), as suitable names help to characterize as well as individualize.

Type V. *The Background character is one who has nothing important to do with the plot unfoldment*, but is necessary to drive a car, open a door, deliver a message, or perform some such service. His service is purely functional. He should not, except in rare cases, be either named, characterized, or individualized, because when you do any of these things for a character-actor you give him importance in the eyes of the reader. No character who does not play a vital part in the plot unfoldment should be made important; to do so upsets the emphasis and hence the balance of your story.

This listing of the types of fictional characters is not a mere academic classification. It has a practical purpose and can be of real help to the writer who is striving to make his first sale, as well as to the writer who wants to increase his sales, or sell his stories in a higher market than he is now publishing.

As I have said many times, and shall repeat many times more, it is characters that sell stories. Hence, any device that will help you to discover *when* your actors are not sufficiently characterized and *why*, is a valuable help, if you will only take advantage of it. Here is the measuring-rod to determine these facts concerning your fictional characters: Are they Flat or Round, Simple or Complex? Are they properly characterized for the rôles to which you have assigned them? A check with the definitions given here will give you the answer. Such a check will save your story from the common weakness of a Flat character assigned to a major rôle and, thereby, being incompletely characterized.

Now that we have our characters clearly classified as to types, the next step is to ascertain the type of story best suited to the Round, or Simple, or Complex character, in the leading rôle.

The Simple character cast in a major rôle is suited to the story of Purpose; that is, the story in which the main character has a Purpose for the story, a Purpose which he either achieves, fails to achieve, or abandons. In the story of Purpose, the main actor strives to accomplish his Purpose from the end of the story-beginning, to the Climax that introduces the story's end. He does not deviate from his Purpose in any way. Therefore, this type of story demands a Simple character as the main actor; an actor who has one *dominant* character-trait that drives him to the accomplishment of his Purpose. He would possess other character-

traits, to be sure, but they should merely complement his
acter-trait and not contradict it. For if he has a contradicto
trait, he will waver in his Purpose and the story will be p
weakened. *Since the great majority of stories published are stories*
pose, the Simple character will be the one you will most often use.

Now let us plan a story of our own, a story of Purpose, in which the
character is, of course, a Simple character, with one dominant character-
trait and supplementary or reinforcing character-traits that are in harmony with it.

Our Actor A is a young woman named Christine Brian. Her dominant
character-trait is moral courage, with reinforcing minor traits of determination and ingenuity. Her Purpose for the story is to achieve success
as a designer of homes and also as a homemaker in the capacity of wife
to Ed Blake, a young man to whom she is engaged. But in the archi-
tect's office where she is working, she has to compete with men who
have had more training than she has, and Ed is against the idea of
Christine's achieving any success except as a homemaker for him.

So we show our heroine, Christine, working her way up at the office
with courage and ingenuity against overwhelming odds, until she has a
job designing homes. She doesn't get a very good salary as yet, and she
makes no headway at all in overcoming Ed's objections to her continuing
to work after she marries him.

Finally Christine achieves the status of a real career-woman when she
attracts a wealthy client to her firm by an especially clever house-plan
she has designed. She is given a large bonus and an increase in salary.
(We will check back here to be sure we have shown her achieving this
Purpose by her dominant character-trait, moral courage, aided by the
reinforcing character-traits, determination and ingenuity.)

Christine yet has Ed to cope with. So, still possessed of courage and
using first her determination, and second her ingenuity, she takes the
money she received as a bonus, plus her savings, and builds the dream-
house she has designed for herself and Ed. When it is finished she moves
in, invites him out one evening, cooks and serves him a model dinner,
and so proves to Ed that she can succeed, both in a career and as a homemaker. Ed, of course, capitulates and we have the traditional happy
ending.

The Complex character cast in the major rôle is suited to the psychological character-conflict story that is usually the literary story, or to the
story of Decision; that is, the story in which the chief character is forced

to decide between two courses of action. In either story the hero sways between two courses of action, motivated by contradictory character-traits, one of which impels him in one direction, the other character-trait impelling him in the opposite direction. The story of Decision is more difficult to write than the story of Purpose because it is a story of conflict *within* the main actor, instead of conflict between the main actor and outward obstacles or opposing forces or persons, as is the case with the story of Purpose. The Complex character should rarely, if at all, be cast in a minor rôle, even in a novel or play. Wherever he is, he is dominant.

The two dominant character-traits of almost equal strength that oppose each other in the story of Decision are fundamentally impulse and restraint, though they are very often made more specific than this. A certain published story will serve to illustrate:

The major actor, a Complex character since the story is one of Decision, sways between love of a likable but selfish and thoughtless husband and the desire to be free to follow a career of her own. The impulse, in this case, was to leave her husband, and the restraint was her feeling that both her duty and her happiness lay in staying with him. The two dominant character-traits that battled for supremacy were loyalty on the one hand and ambition on the other. The character-trait of loyalty was reinforced by minor character-traits of unselfishness and capacity for affection. The character-trait of ambition was reinforced by the minor trait of pride. The character was shown as swaying four times between staying with her husband and leaving him for a career. Each time two dominant character-traits were clearly and definitely shown; each time those traits battled with each other. At last, as is usually the case in Decision stories, restraint won. The wife realized her husband's great need of her, so loyalty conquered ambition.

Your task, as writer, is to fix in the reader's mind the dominant character-trait of the Simple character cast in the major rôle, or the contradictory dominant character-traits of the Complex character cast in a major rôle. The way to do this is by repetition. *Remember, you cannot characterize any actor, and especially your major actor, once and for all. You must keep on characterizing him up to and including the end of your story.* That is to say, your principal actor is constantly being characterized as the story unfolds. *Your most important means of characterizing him is through his dominant character-trait or traits.* So, call the reader's attention to them and, over and over, remind him of them. This is done through the use of words, acts, thoughts, and the many other means that have previously been explained for characterizing actors.

The value of repetition in this regard cannot be overestimated. In a recently published story of Purpose, the main character was an old woman whose dominant trait was determined courage. She showed courage and determination in almost every act and speech. The writer told the reader five times that she knitted 'resolutely,' six times that she acted in a 'determined' way. Her thoughts were determined and courageous. She was in great danger, and she faced different phases of that danger with courage. No single contradictory trait was shown, though complementary and reinforcing traits were revealed, such as unselfishness, kindness, ingenuity. Therefore, at the end of the story, when she performed an outstandingly courageous act that required great determination to accomplish, the reader was convinced that she possessed the character-traits from which her final conclusive act logically sprang. Thus, the major character was not only characterized convincingly, but the whole story, up to and including the final act of courage, was logical and convincing. *The means used was the selection of one dominant character-trait impressed upon the reader through repetition.*

The Flat character is easy to characterize, since he should almost never be given more than one clearly evident character-trait. More characterization than that draws reader-attention to him, and away from the main character and the character next in importance to the main character. These two carry the main thread of the story, hence anything that distracts reader-attention from them breaks the effect of unity for which every writer should strive. Let us go back to the story of the old woman whose dominant character-trait was determined courage for an illustration of how to characterize a Flat character. The old woman had a daughter-in-law, and it was this daughter-in-law and her newborn baby that the old woman was protecting. So far as the reader was aware, the only character-trait the daughter-in-law had was cowardice. She was afraid. She cried and whined and demanded attention. Of course the reader will say she was justified. Nevertheless her fear was absolutely all the reader knew about her. She was a typical and well drawn Flat character.

Since Background characters should not be characterized at all, we need not speak of them further, until we come to examine ways of individualizing characters as distinguished from characterizing them.

Individualizing the character, whether he be Simple, Complex,

Round, Flat, or Background, is of tremendous importance in making him 'come alive' for the reader. It is self-evident that characterization also individualizes, particularly when deftly done and carried to the point where the actor emerges from the type. But the *character-actor can be still further individualized in ways that do not characterize him at all.* And it is these ways of individualizing your characters that we shall consider now:

Suppose we have a man in one of our stories, the father of our heroine, whom we have characterized as a good man, kind, considerate, thoughtful. But he refuses to come alive and there is likelihood of the reader's confusing him with the heroine's uncle, this man's brother, who is in and out of the scenes in our story all the time. What shall we do? The answer is, individualize this man and individualize his brother. But, the question is, how? Suppose we give father a mole on the left side of his face near his nose and assign him the habit of yelling, 'Where is everybody?' at intervals, and of rattling his newspaper when he is angry. *This has not changed his characterization at all, but it certainly has individualized him.* Now, he is a real person, someone the reader can *see* and *hear*.

But what about the brother? We had better do something for him too, though, since he is not so important as Father, we shall individualize him in only one way — by his walk. He walks like a crane, slowly, stiffly, and he steps over all low objects such as footstools, or sprawled legs, rather than walk around them as most people do. Brother may be a saint or a devil; we have not characterized him at all, but we have made him an individual. So, at suitable intervals throughout our story, the reader will see Father's mole, hear him yell and rattle his newspaper. And Brother will stalk through the rooms like a crane and step over this and that. Both men now are much more real than if we had not added these little *individualizing* touches.

The value of individualizing characters is recognized by the trained writer, and the more professional the writer is, the more you will observe the clever ways in which he individualizes his characters and the *frequency* with which he does so. Methods of individualizing characters are countless. A brief survey of a few will be helpful as reminders and as models for your imagination to follow:

Details of dress, ornaments, or accessories worn are excellent means by which to individualize a story-character. Suppose one of the women in your story never wears an evening dress of any color except white. Or one whose gloves always need mending. Or one who likes red slippers. Or another who collects Cambodian jewelry.

Mannerisms, too, individualize a character. One man may draw faces on every stray piece of paper that comes to hand. Another may scratch his left ear when he is puzzled. Another may lay his right hand palm down on his desk before issuing an order.

If a girl has unusually beautiful hair, or a woman villain a pock-marked face, frequent mention of either fact will individualize the characters. *Your first step in learning to individualize your story-actors is to observe how people in real life show that they are individuals and not merely types.* Everyone is an individual in some way and expresses that individuality by *some specific outward manifestation.* You don't have to travel to a distant place or move in a social stratum different from your own to observe these manifestations of individuality. The next time you get on a bus look at the driver. What about that tiny mustache he wears? How he badgers his passengers, the way he starts and stops his bus? Watch the young man at the soda fountain, the milliner who tries on your hat, the banker who holds the mortgage on your home. Each one is an individual, not a type. It is your business, as a writer, to observe *wherein* and in *what* he is shown to be an individual and in this way learn how to individualize your story-characters, whether they be Major, Minor, or Background. By knowing how to make of your story-characters living individuals, you have laid another important stone in the foundation of your successful writing career, for there can be little sustained interest if the reader can't 'see' the character and doesn't care about what he does.

Next to *direct observation of real life-characters,* the best method of learning to individualize characters is by *analyzing published stories* by professional writers to see how they characterize their story-actors. In a recent story by a famous writer the major character, a man, was individualized by telling the reader over and over that the actor's clothes were tight, that the actor himself had to squeeze into the cockpit of his airplane. In another story, a girl is individualized by her lovely eyes, which have nothing to do with her character. *Read carefully for individualizing bits and make notes as you read.*

In your own writing, if the passages that individualize at the same time perform the function of characterizing, all the better.

Method of Study

1. What is the difference between characterizing an individual and individualizing him?
2. What are the five types of fictional characters considered in this chapter? Define each.
3. What kind of story is suitable to the Simple character? What kind to the Complex character?
4. Write a characterization of a Simple character, showing the major character-trait and the reinforcing character-traits of each.
5. Write three examples of individualizing a character and characterizing him at the same time. Write three examples of individualizing a character without characterizing him.
6. Choose three examples from published stories of all the types discussed in this chapter.

CHAPTER XIV

Intensifying Character-Effects by Contrast

THE IMPORTANCE OF CONTRAST AND HOW TO USE IT

CONTRAST is so much a part of our everyday life, so completely inherent in everything we know or experience that for the greater part of our lives we forget that it exists, and we almost never think of it, or even begin to realize its importance for us. Yet the effects brought about by contrast are in our consciousness every waking moment.

Contrast is the intangible ingredient, the catalyst that makes life exciting. The human mind rejects monotony even to the point of destroying itself in madness, when monotony is forced upon it for too long. The higher the mental development, the greater the need for contrast. For example, the intelligent man imprisoned in solitary confinement, the sensitive woman on an isolated farm following a treadmill of identical tasks for months and years, often lose their reason because of the deadly, continued impact of monotony, which is nothing more than lack of contrast.

Contrast gives variety and interest, whether it be in the universe as a whole with its light and darkness, its ceaseless motion and constant change, its creation of worlds and destruction of others; a simple landscape of valley, stream and mountain; or a dinner with its foods of different flavors, consistencies, and colors.

The need of the human mind for contrast has its roots in the mind's age-old habit of looking for differences and likenesses. When the mind can find no differences and no likenesses, as is the case when monotony is present, it restlessly, then resentfully, and at last frantically seeks for contrast that it may again busy itself with observing differences and likenesses. The mind, or consciousness, feels itself more alive the more differences and likenesses it can observe, and less alive as the observable number of differences and likenesses decrease. When there are no differences or likenesses, absolute monotony is present and with it absolute boredom.

Contrast serves another purpose besides that of breaking monotony and thus keeping the mind interested. *Contrast intensifies effects.* And it is with this function of contrast that we shall chiefly concern ourselves as we observe its manifold uses in characterization.

It is important that you understand clearly what is meant by the statement that contrast intensifies effects. For the moment, let us turn our attention for illustrations of this to fields other than that of writing. If you will allow a lump of sugar to melt in your mouth and then drink the juice of a lemon, you will never again doubt that contrast intensifies an effect. The sweetness of the sugar will intensify the acidity of the lemon juice to an almost unbearable degree.

Just for a moment, turn your attention to the art of painting and see how the painter uses contrast to intensify his effects. You are no doubt familiar with Rembrandt's use of brilliant flesh tones against a dark background. The darkness of the background intensifies the high coloring in the faces of the people whose portraits he painted. The same is true of the paintings of the masters of the old Dutch school, where so often the delicacy and whiteness of lace ruffs is intensified by contrast with the somber, thick clothing of the wearers.

In present-day movies contrast is used more than in any other medium of entertainment the world has ever known. The movie producer avoids monotony by every means in his power. He will show a scene, no longer than five minutes' duration, from half a dozen different angles and, in addition, intersperse it with a scattering of close-ups of the main actors. He will take his audience, in an instant of time, from the interior of a cathedral to the bottom of the sea. He will build a scene of tremendous emotional intensity, then contrast it sharply by a comedy shot of two cats fighting over a bone in a dirty alley, or he will contrast a battle scene with two happy people strolling beside a quiet lake. *For sharp contrast and the avoidance of the slightest suggestion of monotony, the writer will do well to study the technique of the movie producer.*

From this brief survey we see that the human mind demands contrast, that nature is continually striving for contrast, that *contrast plays a vital part in every craft*, from making movies to manufacturing automobiles and the designing of neon signs.

Contrast is present in every kind of fine and applied art. Since it is their cornerstone, the logical conclusion is that the writer should understand the reasons for and the uses of contrast, that contrast is necessary in any art that is done with the hope of interesting a reader or an audience. Valuable as contrast is in strengthening characterization, it has yet still further uses in connection with writing. It helps build suspense and drama when danger is contrasted with security. It stimulates interest in the reader by rousing him emotionally when, for example, problems of old age are contrasted with those of youth. These and hundreds of other effects can be secured through the careful and intelligent use of contrast. However, we must turn away from these, for the present, and concentrate our attention on the ways in which contrast can be used as a help in characterization.

Strictly speaking, contrast does not characterize. What it does do, however — and the importance of this cannot be overestimated — is to *heighten the effects of characterization*. A brief example will make this clear.

Suppose that the main character in your story is an old man, rapacious, licentious, and wealthy. The character next in importance to him is an old woman who is cruel, greedy, and even richer than the old man. We stop and think about this. We see at once that we have almost no contrast between these characters and that, unless other means are definitely planned to overcome it, our story will tend toward monotony. Also, neither character will be as effectively characterized as it would be if intensified by contrast.

The way to overcome this is simple. We take the old woman out of this story and save her for another we shall write later. Into her rôle of secondary character, we shall put a young and beautiful girl with a thoroughly nice disposition and no money at all. The old man's villainy is immediately intensified in the reader's mind; he appears even blacker than before though, in reality, he has not been changed in any way. What we have done, however, is to heighten the effects of characterization by contrast.

Now what shall we do with the old woman, who is a perfectly good character if given the right running-mate? Since she is already a thoroughgoing villain, we shall leave her that way and select a hero who by his sterling qualities, will show her up properly. We shall create a very rich young man who wants to use his money for medical research and to endow hospitals. The old woman plots and plans to take the young man's money away from him and buy a steamship line and a half-dozen banks with it, all for herself. By contrasting her with the altruistic young man, we have intensified the effect of her character-traits in the reader's mind, and increased his interest in our story.

If for no other reason than that of adding contrast to your stories and thereby avoiding monotony, you should be very careful to have all your characters as different as possible. *Assign them different character-traits, different physical attributes, different ways of acting and speaking, and give them names that in no way resemble each other.*

Don't, for example, have three friends, named Don and John and Joseph, twenty-three years old, slender, dark-haired, enterprising, and aggressive. Instead, have two of them antagonists, one named Don and one named Hubert, and have Joseph a minor character. Don is twenty years old, Hubert thirty-five. Don is tall, has dark hair, a face like a hawk, and a determination to get the best of everybody around him. He despises Hubert. Hubert is fair, short, timid, blushes easily, is always glad to help friends and strangers alike, and he admires Don and Don's success, never suspecting that Don is planning to take his, Hubert's, savings away from him. Thus you get contrast in your story and contrast is a magnifying glass through which your reader sees the character-traits of your actors enlarged and, therefore, interest-compelling.

Theory is a necessary foundation for a clear and thorough understanding of the fundamentals of any art, but unless theory is applied in a practical way, it is of no value. Let us then proceed to apply the theory that contrast heightens character-effects by study of specific and practical examples. Since almost the first service we must do for a character after we have created him is to name him, we shall start with a name. In doing this, we shall not only show contrast between the name of one character and that of another, as with Don and Hubert, but with the name itself and the character bearing the name, his appearance, personality, or character-trait.

For example, suppose we have a character who is six feet two, weighs two hundred and fifty pounds, and is a star on a football team. We want to intensify, by contrast, his size, strength, masculinity, and love of physical activity of the more violent kinds. An obvious way to do this would be to call him Tiny Something-or-other, but, of course, we want to avoid the obvious and the trite, so we discard 'Tiny' as a name for our character. Instead we name our hero, Deedee Epp, and our purpose is accomplished.

In this story our character next in importance to Deedee is a very small man, timid and retiring, but exceedingly smart in thinking his way out of difficulties. We shall assign him a name in keeping with his appearance and character-traits, but we are not looking for harmony now, we are looking for contrast. So we name him J. Throckmorton Mackinnon, and the impression of his small size and timidity is intensified by contrast with his long, pompous name.

Contrasting characters with their environment or setting is a common device used by professional writers for intensifying the effect of character-traits. For example, a young, prim, unsophisticated school-teacher in a simple, small-town environment is only mildly interesting. But put this same girl in a New York night club, seated at a table with a diplomat, a famous actress, and a movie producer, and bring on a floor show featuring a strip-tease artist, and the girl's character-traits and her interest to the reader are intensified many times, though you have not changed the girl herself in any way. You have done exactly what Rembrandt did in his pictures; you have given her a highly contrasted background, thereby making the reader more sharply aware of her fundamental character-traits and of her as an individual.

But suppose we have a character who is already intrinsically interesting, a beautiful and, of course, blonde movie star. She is highly temperamental and unpredictable; no one knows what she will do next. She is in her natural environment, Hollywood. The reader is probably interested, but in a half-hearted way, since the types of stimuli and this character's logical response to them are, after all, somewhat limited and stereotyped. How can we intensify the effect of this girl's character-traits and so step up reader-interest by giving her a contrasting environment? There are, of course, many ways. Let us try the first one that comes to mind. We take her far from the luxury, the crowds, noise, personal service, and adulation that surround her, and place her in the shack of a bad-tempered old prospector in a rocky canyon of a Nevada mountain a hundred miles from the railroad. It is safe to say that this environment will cause the reader to be more acutely aware of our heroine's character-traits than before, and much more interested in seeing how they will manifest themselves.

One arresting way of spotlighting the character of an actor is to *confront him with a highly contrasted problem, or situation.* Suppose you take as your main character a wealthy young bachelor who lives in a penthouse in New York. He has never known what it was to perform any personal service for himself or anyone else. When your story opens this young man has just returned to his penthouse at three o'clock in the morning to find his servant gone and a tiny, wailing babe lying in the middle of his bed. The reader is immediately aware of all the character-traits possessed by this young man and of their suitability or unsuitability for solving the problem confronting him. This will not need to be stressed by the writer. The contrast between the young man and his problem will be adequately brought out without further emphasis.

Or suppose that one of your story-characters, a wealthy society matron, starts to get into her limousine after having attended a performance of grand opera. She finds a strange Pekinese on the seat of the car. There is no contrast in this situation, since a Pekinese, a society matron, and a limousine are usually thought of as belonging together. The normal character-traits of a society matron may be expected to appear but are not stressed. But change one detail of the picture and see what happens: instead of a Pekinese on the back seat she finds an enormous more-or-less sheep dog lying there, wet, muddy, cold, hungry, and with a bloody paw that is leaving marks all over the doeskin upholstery. Whatever individual character-traits this woman has will be brought out sharply by this situation and by the way she meets it.

The contrast between motive and action gives the writer, who is awake to the inherent possibilities, many opportunities for stressing character-traits.

A father goes secretly at night and sinks his son's powerboat, that the son had paid for out of money he had earned by hard work. This is, on the face of it, a very wrong act. But let us examine the dominant character-trait of the father and the motive behind the act. The father's dominant character-trait for the story is affection for his son. His motive is to save his son from becoming an innocent accomplice to a band of smugglers who have hired him to meet them before daylight next morning with his boat to land some contraband cargo. The father knows that the G-men will capture the smugglers next morning and his son with them, if the son carries out his plans. In spite of being warned by his father that the men who offered him such a high price for his boat are criminals, the son still refuses to give in.

So the father commits an intrinsically 'wrong' act, but from a good motive. *The good motive is so strongly contrasted with the act* that the father is made to seem more noble than perhaps he really is. However, this should be remembered, in this case the father's love for the son

would undoubtedly add to the inner struggle of the father as he decides
to destroy his son's boat, and so increase the drama of the story.

The method works equally well when the motive is 'bad' and the
action 'good.' It is the use of sharp contrast that is so effective and
arresting.

Contrasting emotion with action is one of the most widely useful ways of
stressing character-traits by contrast. Susie Phipps is timid, afraid of
almost everything and, especially, of the dark and of thunderstorms.
You have been careful throughout the story to show Susie, by her acts,
to be a cowardly character, yet the story is monotonous and unconvincing. If, however, you show Susie, no less afraid than she has always
been, making a long journey alone at night through a raging electrical
storm, in order to get a seriously injured child or favorite dog to a doctor,
you have contrasted the emotion of fear with an act of courage. Let us
look carefully, in order to understand clearly what you have accomplished by this use of contrast. You have stressed Susie's dominant
emotion of fear; shown it to be exceedingly strong as Susie, almost over-
whelmed by the emotion, pushes on through the night and the storm.
By this intensifying of the effect of Susie's fear, you have roused several
strong emotions in the reader toward her. You have roused pity for
Susie's suffering, and admiration for Susie's unselfish purpose of saving
the life of the injured child. Neither of these emotions would have been
aroused in the reader if Susie had been only slightly afraid, or if she had
not been afraid at all but had gone quite calmly about the business of
getting the injured child to the hospital. Never forget that the reader
wants to *feel*; that his concern with any character in any story is determined by the strength of the emotion or emotions he feels toward the
actor or actors in their relation to the story-action. In this case, Susie's
dominant emotion of fear is strongly intensified in the mind of the reader
because her fear has been contrasted with her courageous action.

Contrasted character-traits within the actor himself will help to give the
intensification that adds so much to variety and, consequently, to
reader-entertainment. Suppose we assign the single character-trait of
impulsiveness to Annette, the heroine of our story. Annette is very
much in love with a young man of attractive appearance and manners,
whom she met only a week before our story opens, and she is determined
to marry him. Annette's father tries to persuade her not to marry Preston because, in the father's judgment, the young man is so selfish and
self-centered that he will make Annette very unhappy in his rôle of

husband. Annette, however, does not swerve from her impulsive determination to marry Preston. Unless contrast is secured in some other way, perhaps by stressing her father's caution and ability to judge character, Annette's character-trait of impulsiveness will not be highlighted. But let us give her a widely contrasted character-trait, that of caution, inherited from her father. Now, these two opposing character-traits will highlight each other, as first one gains supremacy in Annette's mind, then the other. Therefore, the character of Annette will excite more interest because of the intensification of her original character-trait, that of impulsiveness.

Contrast, to the writer who masters its use, is a magic wand that he can wave over any character, major or minor, good or bad, sympathetic or unsympathetic, and change him in an instant from a dull character into a living, individual one. With equal ease he can change an already fairly interesting character into one that is intensely so. Surely, it is worth any writer's while to learn all the ways of using this magic wand.

Method of Study

1. Does contrast, in itself, characterize?
2. What effect does contrast have on characterization?
3. What is the fundamental, universal function of contrast?
4. Write two scenes in which a character is contrasted with environment.
5. Write a scene in which an act is contrasted with the motive behind the act. Write a scene in which contrast is shown between character-traits in the same person.

CHAPTER XV

Doing It the Hard Way

CHARACTERIZATION BY NARRATION, EXPOSITION, OR ANALYSIS

WHEN you use narration, exposition, or analysis to characterize your fiction people, you are, if you accomplish your end, doing it the hard way. 'But,' I can hear you say, 'it is much easier for me to write narration, exposition, and analysis concerning the character-traits of my actors than it is for me to write scenes in which character is shown by action, thought, and speech.' We are not speaking of the ease or difficulty of writing narration, exposition, and analysis, but of the ease or difficulty of *characterizing* your story-actors by these means. It requires far more skill, thought, and hard work to characterize actors by these means *because you are attempting to make a character live by describing him from without*; whereas if you write your *characterization from within*, you present your actor to the reader in a scene in which *he* tells and acts out his own story. *Never forget that your success in making your character live is in due proportion to your ability to identify yourself with that character; to become* him. That is one of the cardinal principles of good acting, as it is of good fiction writing. And your following this rule will affect your whole story: your characters, because they live, will be actively attempting to solve problems that are of vital importance to them; they will have logical reasons (motives) that cause them so to struggle toward a solution; and you, the reader, will want them to succeed or fail since *you* are emotionally involved in their whole story because the characters are *real* to you. This does not mean that the writer should never use other means to characterize his actors. It does mean, however, that the writer must understand the relative importance of the various devices that serve his creative purposes.

The writer should not think of the readers of his stories as passively absorbing the entertainment offered. That is a wrong conception of the writer-reader relationship. Since it is a wrong conception it is almost certain to lead to disastrous results, results more disastrous to the writer than to the reader. Why disastrous to the writer? The reader can always stop reading if he is bored. And the reader is bored because the writer left nothing for him to do; but the writer who does all the work in a story will never know, provided, of course, he gets his story published, that he failed to give the reader what the reader wanted. Readers want to *enter* into and be engrossed by the stories they read. That literally is the meaning of entertainment: The reader *lives* the story with the character-actors.

Fictional characters exist in only two places, neither of which is on the printed page. They exist, first, in the mind of the writer and, second, in the mind of the reader. The writer must create the character in his own mind — but he cannot create it in the mind of the reader. The reader must do that. That is his *active participation*. But he can create characters only from suggestions given him by the writer and the use of his own imagination. The reader enjoys doing this. The writer who tells the reader everything there is to know about a character, and so deprives him of the opportunity to use his imaginative faculty freely, soon finds himself without a reader. Unless narration, exposition, and analysis are handled with skill and specific knowledge of their limitations, as well as of their requirements, the reader is almost sure to be deprived of the opportunity to use his imagination.

Before we go any further in this discussion of narration, exposition, and analysis, we should agree on a definition of each in its relationship to characterization.

When we use *narration* to characterize, we bring out the character of the actor by *telling the reader* about something the actor did or about something that happened to him. Perhaps we say that 'Zeke Peters was a bad-tempered man. When he came home in one of his rages, he often kicked his hound, Old Turk, and sometimes he even struck Elvie, his wife. Zeke had been like that ever since he was eleven years old, when his father had almost beaten him to death.' In the foregoing, we have given the reader an account or recital concerning Zeke.

When we use *exposition we explain about a character*. For example, we rewrite the above to explain or interpret the cause of Zeke's ill temper:

> Zeke Peters was a mean, ill-tempered man, probably because his father had almost beaten him to death when Zeke was about eleven years old.

We use *analysis* when we analyze or *diagnose* or examine, as it were, *component parts of a character* for the reader. To analyze Zeke:

> Zeke Peters was easily angered, but you couldn't blame him for that. He was a sensitive boy of eleven when his father almost beat him to death. He was a sensitive man now, hiding his vulnerability behind blustering, threatening rages.

There is nothing actually wrong with the use of any of these means, and where brevity is necessary or in the case of characterizing a minor character, they are effective. But if any one of these forms of characterization were employed very long, unless specific steps were taken to make the presentation interesting, it would become boresome indeed, to the reader. Why? Because each *tells* the reader too much, and leaves too little to his own imagination.

Now let us characterize Zeke in a scene, and see what result we get when we leave the reader something to imagine:

> Zeke Peters lurched through the door, kicking old Turk out of his way. Elvie came running at the sound of Zeke's stomping feet and Turk's yelp of protest. She took one look at Zeke's black scowl, and at the end of Turk's tail disappearing under the sagging bed. 'Land sakes! You mad again?' she exclaimed. 'Well, nothin' new about that. My goodness, Zeke, I believe you been mad ever since that time your pappy whipped you with a blacksnake.'

You will see at once that in this scene the writer tells nothing, explains nothing, analyzes nothing. He *shows* an angry man in action. *The reader constructs the scene,* in his imagination, that is merely suggested, not described. The only descriptive detail is the 'sagging bed.' The reader is made conscious of Zeke's character from what Zeke does and from what Elvie says; not from anything the writer says. The reader is left with the happy delusion that he has ascertained Zeke's character from direct observation of the man in action, and the reader likes that feeling. It is possible to attain this desirable result by means of narration, exposition, and analysis, but it is by no means so easy as by using the scene, which, more easily, furnishes suggestions from which the reader's imaginative faculty can work.

In an earlier chapter we went into the subject of characterization by action and thoughts. Here again we have used a scene to show how much easier it is to characterize an actor by means of the suggestions offered by a scene, than by specific facts offered in the form of narration, exposition, and analysis.

The way to characterize vividly and convincingly by means of narration, exposition, and analysis is to be specific in your choice of words and phrases that are *suggestive;* that is, words and phrases that start the imagination of the reader to working, and keep it working. On the contrary, if you *tell* the reader all there is to know about a character, you leave him nothing to imagine.

Make your writing pictorial. Choose image-building words. Appeal to the reader's senses of sight, hearing, taste, touch, and smell. Use fresh and vivid figures of speech. Use contrast. In fact, when characterizing by means of narration, exposition, or analysis or by any combination of them, you will need every device you have learned that is helpful in getting and holding reader-interest.

Before we go into further details regarding how to characterize successfully by the three means under discussion, it might be helpful to consider two 'don'ts':

1. Don't make a list of character-traits.
2. Don't tell the reader too much.

Suppose we decide to characterize by narration the heroine of our story, Penny Aldrich, a beautiful young debutante, and we do so by cataloguing her character-traits:

> Penny liked to play tennis and handball better than to go to parties. She was good-tempered, friendly to everyone, and not at all snobbish or conceited. Though she was gay and happy most of the time there was a serious side to her nature, too.

Dull reading, isn't it? Not much chance for the reader to use his imagination here. In fact, this is terrible. It is dull enough to justify any reader in throwing our story across the room. Yet beginning writers turn out this sort of bad writing all the time, and professional writers do it far too often. Such writing is a sign in the writer of one or all of the following weaknesses: ignorance, laziness, or lack of writing ability. When perpetrated by a professional writer, it is inexcusable.

Let us hasten to improve this pale gray passage in our story. After covering several pages of paper with 'experimental' writing, and throw-

ing them, one by one, into the wastepaper basket with a combined feeling of despair and nausea — remember, I said this was the 'hard way' to
characterize — we arrive at the following:

> Penny romped through tennis and handball games with the abandon
> of a puppy — and won most — but she patted more yawns at a party
> than a bored hostess. She flirted with everybody, from the bishop, who
> had baptized her, to the policeman on the corner. But always with a
> little air of, 'Isn't this fun — but of course I don't mean it, and neither
> do you.' You would have thought life was no more serious to Penny than
> to an hour-old butterfly on a bright summer morning, if you had not heard
> the long conversations between her and Jim, the head gardener, on the
> subject of selecting a suitable career for Penny.

Well, the above will not get the Nobel Prize for literature, but the
reader will certainly find this characterization of Penny more arresting
and more satisfactory than the first one. Let us see exactly why this is
so: The first example, we have agreed, offers no material to the imagination of the reader. He has an accurate blueprint of Penny, but he still
doesn't 'see' her, or 'know' her. She doesn't *live*. In the second, pictures of Penny in action are suggested, with a minimum of detail; the
action, in turn, suggesting character-traits. The reader imagines Penny
playing games, patting yawns, flirting with the bishop and the policeman, and talking with the gardener. The reader fills in the details of
these pictures out of his experiences and memories. Thereby he is enabled to *create for himself* the character of Penny, in a very close approximation to the character we created in our minds and called Penny
Aldrich. And in addition to seeing Penny, each reader individually has
put her in a certain setting, wearing certain play-suits, attired in certain
formals. Their stylish mode, color, even Penny's own coloring, mannerisms, and gestures, we are not *told* specifically. They don't matter. To
every reader, she is a different Penny, a real living Penny of his own imagination; and, what is more, he likes her.

Now let us look at an example of *telling* the reader too much:

> Milt Lassiter was one of Petroleum Consolidated's bright young ex
> ecutives who had made his way by an education achieved at Harvard,
> plus brains, hard work, and ability. Milt watched every detail of any
> job he was on, but he saw Petroleum Consolidated's plans for expansion
> as a whole and meant to have a part in them. He made friends easily
> and got along with his superiors as well as those who worked under him.
> All these things made Milt's success seem certain.

This tells us a great many things about Milt — probably more than the reader needs to be told — and in an uninteresting way. Let us try to present this bit of narration more briefly, and more effectively, while leaving out no essential idea. Because of the position Milt holds, the reader will take for granted his education, hard work, brains, and ability, unless told he does not possess these qualities. So they can be omitted. Other things can be stated more briefly, as follows:

> Milt Lassiter was one of Petroleum Consolidated's bright young executives. He combined a warm friendliness for all his associates with a realistic attitude toward the plans of Petroleum Consolidated for expansion that meant he was definitely on his way to success, even in the New York meaning of the word.

As narration, exposition, and analysis definitely have their places in writing, let us examine in detail six definite ways of using them to characterize briefly, yet vividly:

1. Suggestive words and phrases.
2. Pictorial writing.
3. Appeals to the senses.
4. Figures of speech.
5. Contrast.
6. The evoking of memory-images and sensations.

In each of these the imagination of the reader is called upon to play an active part.

Let us see how valuable each of these means is in the actual characterization of a story-actor:

1. *Suggested words and phrases that are specific in their detail*

First, let us write a characterization without aid of the above and examine the result, using analysis this time:

> No one could understand old Rob Hogan's insatiable desire for money. It was as strong now that he possessed millions as it had been when he first went to work for a pittance. But his associates would have wondered no longer if they could have seen the poverty-stricken home in which he had spent his formative years. It was a fear of poverty implanted in his boyhood, of which he himself was now unconscious, that drove Rob Hogan to ever greater and greater financial conquests.

Now we shall rewrite this, using the most suggestive words and phrases that we can devise. Observe how specific is the selected detail:

No one could understand old Rob Hogan's implacable determination to own more banks, get control of one more railroad, buy one more airplane factory, when he cared nothing for power and already had more money than he could ever spend, or even comfortably give away. But if his associates could have seen the bare shack in which Rob was born, and in which, at the age of nine, he had seen his mother die because there wasn't food enough to go round and she had given most of hers to Rob, her only child, the matter of Rob Hogan's desire for money would have been an enigma no longer. The horror and fear of poverty that had tortured him through the long agony of his childhood had sunk below Rob's level of conscious thought now, but it ran on and on, like a dynamo of exhaustless power, in his subconscious mind. It was this that drove old Rob Hogan to greater and more far-reaching business enterprises, each one pouring a flood of gold into his already overweighted hands.

Go through this carefully and look for the words and phrases that suggest specific pictures, specific mental states and emotions to the mind of the reader. Remember, these do not describe, they merely suggest, and suggestions, providing they are the right ones, are all the reader needs.

2. *Pictorial writing*

First, we shall merely tell the reader the kind of person Miss Lucy is, with no attempt to make our effort interesting:

Miss Lucy approached us. She was sixty years old and dressed very queerly. Her clothing showed she was eccentric.

This is made up of generalizations that offer very little material to the reader's imagination. So we rewrite:

Miss Lucy was definitely in a state of agitation as she came down the garden path. Her rusty black dolman hung askew and her hat of the vintage of 1900 dipped unexpectedly over one wild blue eye. She made me think of nothing so much as a moulting sparrow that had just escaped from the claws of Omar, my lordly orange Persian.

This is like one of those pictures that used to be so popular in which you were urged to find as many faces as you could, more or less concealed in the lines of the drawing. Look in this for the picture-making words, by means of which the reader vividly imagines the appearance of Miss Lucy, and through that appearance, her character.

3. *Appeals to the senses*

Since Number 2 is necessarily an appeal to the sense of sight, we shall stress in this example appeals to senses other than that of sight; specifically, those of touch, sound, and smell.

> Mrs. Marchmont was a kind, unselfish woman and very careful how she spent her husband's money; except for one extravagance. No matter through what financial stress she and Ed might pass, she always found the money somehow to fill the perfume bottle that stood on her dresser with Night in Shalimar, which cost sixteen dollars an ounce.

But this has very little imagination-evoking power and almost no appeal to the senses. Let us see what we can do by working it over:

> Mrs. Marchmont came into the bedroom, careful that her slippered feet should make no more than a whispering sound on the blue carpet. (Sound.) She did not want to disturb the strange young man she had put to bed in her guest room after the doctor had bandaged his arm. She would have to pay the doctor, but that was all right. She could save the money out of her allowance. Softly Mrs. Marchmont laid her hand on the head of the sleeping young man. The feel of the resilient waves of his blond hair suddenly made her very tender toward him. (Touch.) The sweet, delicate scent of Night in Shalimar, the expensive perfume she so dearly loved, floated in the air. (Smell.) The young man must have smelled it. He stirred.

4. *Figures of speech*

Let us first characterize Freddie by plain narrative:

> Freddie was very absent-minded and rarely kept appointments on time. He would forget to do things he should and sometimes lost packages or picked up bundles that did not belong to him.

That was easy to write and covers Freddie's character-traits in the mind of the writer, but it isn't of much help to the reader in creating Freddie as a living, active individual. We try again, this time using specific detail and figures of speech:

> Freddie was as undependable as an electric clock in a thunderstorm, and as unpredictable as a swarm of bees. Sometimes he kept an appointment on time, and sometimes he was two hours late. He'd ask Elise to go to a show with him and then forget to buy tickets. One time he started home with a bag of hard rolls for dinner, and arrived with a parcel containing a pair of pale blue knitted bootees. That night Elise

was so angry that she pecked at him all evening like a little black-and-white magpie. She told him he was a pack rat, an absent-minded professor, and a ridiculous, irresponsible infant, all rolled into one.

5. *Contrast*

Contrast, as was said before, is a valuable device for throwing character-traits into high relief. Let us see how well it works when we are using narration, the hard way to characterize:

Adelbert Mountjoy was a mild young man who had never been angry in his life. But then Adelbert Mountjoy had led a sheltered existence. Nothing much had ever happened to him. Though some people had been known to say that they had seen vague stirrings of resentment under his calm exterior.

This is a flat, colorless picture of Adelbert, without highlights or contrasts. What can be done to improve matters, from the standpoint of the reader?

Adelbert Mountjoy was a mild-mannered young man who had never been really angry in his life until the night of that big party Loretta Alden gave. It all started when Adelbert didn't fight Hunk Randall. When Hunk knocked a glass of punch out of Loretta's hand and walked away without apologizing, Loretta, who is pure and unadulterated brimstone when she is mad, turned on Adelbert. She snatched a blue ribbon from her own hair and tied it in Adelbert's brown wave. Then she called him her itsy-bitsy girlsie. In the next sixty seconds Adelbert had slapped Loretta, smashed a tray of cocktail glasses that happened to be in his way, and knocked Hunk Randall out cold.

Now, because Adelbert's opposing character-traits of calmness and a capacity for strong emotional direct action have been sharply contrasted, he is much more sharply characterized than before.

6. *The evoking of memory images and sensations*

The reader likes to remember. When you cause him to recollect some past experience, he not only remembers the moment you recall to him, but also the richness and overtones heightened by many associated memories. For example, if one of your story-characters causes the reader to remember what a good cook his Aunt Martha was, how delectable her ginger cookies were, once more he feels the love, as his memory revives these sensations, that as a child he felt for Aunt Martha. Consequently, he transfers all this wealth of pleasant feeling or emotion to your story-character. As a result of this remembering, your story-character is much more alive to the reader than would otherwise be the case.

Let us see what we can do to strengthen and add emotion to a characterization by exposition through evoking a memory:

> Uncle Dave never had any children of his own. But he liked kids, especially boys. Whenever they came to see him, as they often did, he would carefully show them, as all the Uncle Daves of this world have always done, how to carve a basket from a peach pit and make a willow whistle.

It is unlikely that the reader ever had an Uncle Dave, but it is almost certain that at some time in his life he has known an old bachelor who liked boys. All the pleasant attributes of that personality immediately come to life, even to details of physical appearance, and are transferred to Uncle Dave, the character in our story, with the result that he is much more alive for the reader than he would be otherwise.

Do not fall into the error of thinking, because the examples given here of characterizing the hard way (by narration, exposition, and analysis) are fairly long, that they must be long in order to be effective. Words were used generously here in order to illustrate fully the points covered. Just to prove that you do not have to use many words, suppose we write a few examples, none longer than one sentence, to show how arresting these methods of characterization can be made by the uses of such devices as specific detail, pictorial imagery, and figures of speech:

Narration alone:

> John, when he heard Jim and Adele were married, was very angry and immediately began to lay plans to harm them.

Narration with figure of speech:

> When John heard Jim and Adele were married, his thoughts were as swift, as cruel, and as dangerous as the sword of Damocles.

Narration alone:

> Lou was a stupid woman, and so never really happy or really sad.

Narration with emphasis upon imagery:

> Lou was wrapped in her stupidity as a silkworm lay wrapped in its cocoon, shut softly away from all poignancy, whether of pain or ecstasy.

In writing characterization by narration, exposition, or analysis, and thereby trying to stir the reader imaginatively so he will do his part of the characterization and do it with pleasure, remember always to write simply. Never seem to strive for an effect. No matter how hard you may work over a pictorial phrase, or an effective figure of speech, be sure the result appears to be spontaneous, as though you have only that moment thought of it. Never forget that your character is in your mind and, if you are a skilled craftsman, in the mind of your reader; he is never on the printed page. After all, words are only symbols that evoke memory images and sensations in the mind of the reader.

Method of Study

1. What is the true writer-reader relationship?
2. In what two places do fictional characters exist?
3. What is the definition of narration when used to characterize? Of exposition? Of analysis?
4. Choose three examples from published stories of each of the above ways of characterization.
5. Write an example of each of the above ways of characterization, writing it the 'easy' way. Then rewrite each one the 'hard' way.
6. Write an example of each of the six ways given in this chapter of improving your characterizations by narration, exposition, and analysis.

CHAPTER XVI

Characters Are Plots

DEVELOPING A PLOT FROM A CHARACTER

STORY-IDEAS may spring from countless sources, such as a crisis, a situation, a theme, a bit of dialogue, a setting, and hundreds of others — important, unimportant, trivial, or significant. But a plot cannot begin without a character, because *plot is character in action.*

Since we want to write successful stories, that is, stories that editors will pay for and publish, the first logical step toward that desirable end is to find out what kinds of characters editors want and what types they do not want. When we say 'editors' in this case, what we really mean is 'readers.' The editor is a business man and his customers are the readers. Like any good business man, he carefully studies the tastes and likes and dislikes of his customers and does his best to please the people who buy his output. Once in a while he may make a mistake — as what business man does not? — but most of the time you can depend on it that the editor knows what his readers want. All of the time he knows better than you do, because buying stories to sell at a profit is his business.

Readers as a whole have very well defined demands as to what story-characters shall be like and what they shall do and not do. Before we can create a character from which to build a plot, we should learn all we can about these likes and dislikes of the great majority of readers, and, therefore, of editors, to whom we shall, in due time, offer our story for sale. There are certain facts that we shall consider, and first of these is, whom shall we choose as our chief or major character?

1. *The character* you choose *must* be *interesting*, not merely to you, but *to the group of readers for whom you are writing the story*. This is such a

self-evident qualification of a fictional character that, if I did not know better, there would seem no reason to state it. But, as editors and critics all over the country will testify, hundreds, perhaps thousands, of stories are written every month around a main character so uninteresting that no one except his proud creator cares what he does or what happens to him. He may go through fire and flood and rescue the heroine after the most dangerous adventures, but still the reader will not care. Why? The poor thing was never a character at all, in the real sense of the word, having neither been characterized nor individualized, but allowed to remain a puppet of wood and of strings, a complete nonentity.

The story-character, to be successful, must be not only intrinsically interesting, but interesting to the group of readers for whom you are writing your story. For example, gangsters and the rougher sort of criminals are not of particular interest to most women. So you would be showing poor judgment if you cast a racketeer, even though he had a heart of gold and loved his mother, in the rôle of chief actor in a story you intended to send to the *Ladies' Home Journal*. Nor should you, when plotting a story for the adventure pulp magazines, give the major rôle to a sweet, gentle woman, or any woman at all, for that matter. Maybe you think no one ever made so obvious a mistake as this. You're wrong. I have seen innumerable examples of similarly incorrect character-casting in stories mailed to me for criticism or handed in by my students. If I were not fully aware of the prevalence of this error, I would not discuss it at such length here. Having been duly warned, let us hope you escape making this general blunder by creating characters of interest to the group for which you are writing. If the group is very well defined, as in the case of the women's magazines, you will exercise especial care. Where the group is large and somewhat heterogeneous, as in the case of *The Saturday Evening Post, Collier's,* or *Cosmopolitan,* your problem is to select a character that will interest the largest possible number of people, both men and women, and of all ages from the post-adolescent on to grandfather and grandmother sitting by the fire — or radiator, as the case may be. Whatever your field, it is of paramount importance that you select a character of interest to the group for which you are writing, a group based, to a large extent, on reader age, background, and education.

2. *Select a character that is pleasant to read about.* People, as a rule, read for entertainment and excitement, not to have their feelings harrowed, their hearts torn, or to contemplate the disagreeable aspects of

life. For this reason, select characters, especially for major rôles, who are normal, mentally and physically, who do not suffer from incurable, painful, or crippling diseases, and who do not die in the end. Readers do not like to lose their fictional friends by death. These stipulations apply particularly to the 'popular' magazine field. In the 'literary' story, far more leeway is allowed. Also, under exceptional circumstances, the writer, who has at his command unusual skill, ability, and knowledge, may be able to override these limitations. In the vast majority of cases, however, it is wise to remember that the reader likes to be shielded from the dreadful things in fictional life. The precedent for this is as old as Greek tragedy. Villains, who may wound or kill with the greatest of abandon, must soft-pedal their acts of brutality. A surgical operation should not be shown in its gruesome entirety. Study movie technique and note how the scene is laid, the action suggested and gruesome details left to the imagination of the spectator. The audience sees an operating room, surgeons, nurses, and, now and then, an instrument. It sees no incision; is spared participation in the actual experience. The camera angle takes care of that. Get the camera angle in your story, show the nurses, doctors, and even the instruments if you must; but never the incision or the actual surgical process. To gain the ability of writing by implication and thus allowing the reader free rein of his imagination is an important and valuable goal toward which a writer should steer.

3. *Select a character who is familiar to the reader.* The reader likes to read stories about people similar to the ones he knows. In order to impress this on your mind, let us present an extreme example. Do not, for instance, select a Hottentot warrior for your hero in a story you hope to sell to a newspaper syndicate. There is no common ground on which he and your reader can meet. If, on the contrary, you select for your main character a man who works hard in the office all day, rides miles on a crowded streetcar to get home, and likes to play rummy, half your battle of getting reader-interest is already won. There is, however, a device for making the unfamiliar familiar that is extremely useful in bridging this gap between the reader and a character the reader does not know. It is this: give the unfamiliar character familiar emotions, or tastes, or ideas, or put him in familiar surroundings. Even the Hottentot warrior might possibly work out all right if you put him in an automat restaurant, gave him a love for hot cakes and coffee, made him homesick for his wife and impatient to go hunting with the boys of the next village.

.

The principle is, of course, to *establish a common ground of understanding and sympathy between your reader and the unfamiliar character*.

4. *Use*, with very rare exceptions, if you expect to publish your story in this country, *an American for your chief actor*. Do not have a villain who is a member of any nation friendly to the United States. Do not have your villain a member of any church or religious organization, lodge, fraternal organization, political party, or racial group within the United States. This may hamper the writer considerably, but the editor cannot afford to make enemies of any group who might advertise in his publication or subscribe to it or buy it at a newsstand. The editor will appreciate your cooperation in this respect and in others that will be discussed under the subject of 'editorial taboos' in Chapter XVII.

5. *Give real thought to deciding on the age of your main character.* Magazines should be studied for their editorial leanings in this matter. Even within an age limitation, different treatment is expected by different editors. In two magazines, for instance, which deal with stories of adolescent boys, an entirely different treatment is required. One magazine wants stories with a farming or pioneering background in which boys must undergo all sorts of dangers and hardships. The other wants stories of boys of today, usually with a small-town background, in which very little actually happens, but which are packed with character delineation and psychological significance.

One way to find out the best-liked age for characters in a certain magazine is to get a file of copies for the preceding year. Go through the stories in each issue — noting the approximate age of the major character and the minor characters. When you have finished, you won't need to guess any more about the age that editor wants most of his characters to be — you'll know. You will also know exactly how much chance you have of selling that editor a story about a seventy-year-old woman after you have discovered that he published, during the year, twenty-six stories about young women, fifteen about middle-aged women, and three about women of seventy years of age. In order to get around this editorial prejudice against publishing stories about old people, a valuable device is to inject into your story a strong subplot concerning the problem of two young people, introducing some love interest, preferably. This will increase your chances of selling your story by at least fifty per cent. Consult the statistics you gathered while analyzing the year's magazines and you will see that the above figures are very nearly right.

All this may sound complicated, but it is not so in reality. The entire subject of character-selection can be mastered by careful thought and the application of commonsense, together with a thorough study and analysis of the magazines for which you want to write. In this way you will reach the stage where you will automatically discard characters and character-traits unsuited to fictional use, or to the market you have in mind. Moreover, you will naturally select characters suitable for the readers to whom you wish to appeal. You will, thereby, have made an important step toward writing a salable story.

Now that we know the kind of character we must have for our story, where shall we find him? Naturally, we can find him anywhere. More specifically, however, characters for your stories may be discovered from among your friends, acquaintances, strangers, in your own imagination, or by combining imagination with an actual person known or seen. Every person is a potential fiction-character.

6. *Against who or what shall our hero struggle?* In other words, what shall we have for villains or villain forces? All the problems of the world grow out of man's clash:

With man
With environment
With social forces
With economic forces
With himself (psychological character conflict)
With death, disease, fate.

Now that we know what kind of characters to select, where to find them, and against what they will struggle, we can go on to the actual creation of a story-character and the plotting of a story from that character. Let us start with an imaginative character, remembering that he must be familiar to every reader, young and old, man and woman, and one who, because of that familiarity and of pleasant memory-associations, is agreeable and potentially interesting to a wide field of readers and suitable to appear in a major rôle in many magazines.

Without making things too deliberately easy for ourselves, let us take the first eligible character that comes to mind. It happens to be a woman of about fifty. This is too bad, since a story about a young girl would have been more readily salable. However, here our character is, and we must do the best we can with her. We know at once that we had better add a love story to this, so we present our character — who is not really a character at all yet, only an idea for a character — with a daughter of twenty-two. Our actor, we go on thinking, is a widow living in a small country town. That gives her a setting. The next step is to individualize her. What does she do? She likes to raise and arrange flowers; in fact, she makes quite a hobby of it. The item about the flowers is a good idea, since practically everybody is fond of flowers, and everyone is familiar with them. Still, the woman hasn't come alive. All we have at present is a widow, who grows and arranges flowers, and is possessed of one daughter. In other words, we have merely a 'flat' character, not a 'round.' The next step is to name her. We must find something suitable. We write down Mehitabel Johnson, Rachel Ellington, Connie Burke, and Amelia Moorhead. We choose Rachel Burke as best for our character because it is simple. Rachel is suitable to the old-fashioned small-town environment, the last name is short, and ends with the sharp, decisive sound of K, and we hope our character is going to turn out strong and reliable.

7. With what *dominant character-trait* shall we now endow her? You already know how important to the story-actor and to the story this is. Out of many traits, such as independence and resourcefulness, that a woman like Rachel, as far as we have characterized her, might logically possess, we shall select the one of devotion to her daughter. This is one of the important turning-points in our story, though we have not yet begun to plot it. Yet the action of our plot will certainly be very largely governed by the dominant character-trait of the main actor. Obviously, if we give Rachel a dominant character-trait other than that of devotion to her daughter, as, for example, ambition to become president of the national D.A.R. or even of the Village Improvement Association, we shall have a very different story. This illustrates how different plots and, therefore, different stories can be developed from the same character by changing either the dominant character-trait or the Purpose of the actor for the story.

8. What is the *natural purpose* of a woman like Rachel Burke with a dominant character-trait of devotion to her daughter? You will agree that her purpose will be to help that daughter to achieve a successful marriage. It might also be to give her daughter a college education, or any one of dozens of other purposes. Again, our selection of a Purpose for Rachel dictates the general direction of our story. But the first one seems most promising, so we keep it.

9. Now let us *select secondary characteristics* for Rachel. What must she have to succeed in the Purpose assigned her? She must obviously have determination and ingenuity to carry out her plans to the end.

Perhaps others, also, but these, certainly, since she can scarcely hope to succeed without them. Now *what of her motives?* It is her mother love that wants her daughter to find happiness, security, and protection in marriage.

We have now reached the stage when a few details are needed to fill in the picture. Rachel's slim means fail entirely to support her and her simple home without the financial help of her daughter, who works in San Francisco, sixty miles away, and comes home to the village of Las Floritas most week-ends to be with her mother. We won't take time now to characterize the daughter, or attempt to individualize her, beyond the fact that she is a pretty, normal, charming girl, since we are concentrating at the moment on developing a plot from one character.

Now we have the character-actor of Rachel Burke developed in our minds as well as her Purpose for the story: to help her daughter achieve a happy marriage. We know that Rachel Burke must solve her problem through the exercise of her character-traits of determination and ingenuity working with and through her special capacity for raising and arranging flowers. Since we gave Rachel that hobby, she must use it in the plot development. We are now ready to begin the actual plotting of a 'commercial' story from a character, having chosen a character, decided upon her dominant character-trait, dominant emotion, and given her a motive and a problem that would be the logical outcome of such a combination. Now, what actions will Rachel Burke go through in solving her problem? They, inevitably, must be in keeping with the kind of woman Rachel Burke is. That is to say, she must be in character. Of all the actions she may go through, which shall we select?

We know that here is another crucial point in our thinking, and that with a character, a set of circumstances, and a setting, dozens of different, interesting, and original stories could be plotted. After following several germ-ideas and discarding them as not offering sufficient promise of originality of treatment, of drama, suspense, or intrinsically interesting as scenes, we hit on an idea and, after considerable thought, developed the following Plot Outline and summary:

Title: ORDER ME AN ORCHID
> *Actor A:* Rachel Burke (we already know Rachel and also her character-trait, motivation, etc.)
> *Minor characters in the order of their importance:*
> Maida — Rachel's daughter.

Jim Atwater, Maida's young man in the city, who, with his father, owns the city's finest flower shop. He is of wealthy family and, Maida feels, very sophisticated.

Lillian, an old, cantankerous, but heart-of-gold maid-of-all-work of Rachel's. She is highly contrasted in appearance and character with her name. Serves the purpose of giving the opportunity of presenting the opening situation and the story-purpose by dialogue and of helping Rachel accomplish her Purpose. She gives contrast and a touch of humor.

Actor B (Villain or Villain Force): Rachel's feeling of inferiority because of her small-town background and her old-fashioned ideas.

Problem: Rachel wants to help Maida marry Jim.

The story begins with Maida returning to her home in Las Floritas late one Saturday afternoon. In the dialogue between Rachel and Lillian it is revealed that Maida had written a letter to Rachel earlier in the week telling her mother that Jim Atwater has accepted an invitation to come to dinner Saturday night and then take Maida on later to Del Monte for dancing. Jim will be driving into Las Floritas from the Valley, where he is making arrangements for shipments of peach blossoms for a spring display in his shop. This is the first time for Maida to entertain Jim and, since she is already in love with him, she is deeply concerned over first impressions. In her letter she has asked her mother to spare no expense in regard to flowers and to make Jim's coming an occasion. She ended by saying, 'Order me an orchid.' Rachel and Lillian think all this about flowers is a joke, particularly since Maida often says 'Order me an orchid' when she feels pleased about something she has done.

But Maida was serious this time and, upon her arrival, is chagrined at the simple arrangement of old-fashioned flowers from the garden, which she finds in the hall, the living-room, and the dining-room. The unsophisticated corsage of lilies-of-the-valley and Cecil Bruner roses that her mother has arranged for her has disappointed her tremendously. However, she tries to hide the extent of her disappointment so as not to hurt her mother. But Rachel sees and fears that she probably has ruined Maida's chance of attracting Jim Atwater. Rachel can get no other flowers except those from her garden, as the only florist shop in Las Floritas is always sold out by Saturday afternoon.

She sends Maida to dress and calls Lillian, who comes grumbling because she is busy with the dinner. Rachel, with Lillian's help, is finding containers and bringing water. She takes the simple, old-fashioned flowers and arranges them in modern ways: three sprays of Bridal Wreath, with one full-blown Talisman rose at their base, in a tall aquamarine bottle that had once held Japanese saki; spikes of deep blue delphinium rising from a low mound of mignonette in a great curved pink shell Rachel's father had brought home from the South Seas fifty years before. Swiftly Rachel evolves a half-dozen arrangements, each startlingly different and beautiful.

For Maida's corsage, she arranges a flat, formalized effect that resembles the jeweled decoration on the turban of a maharaja, its highly contrasted colors centering around a single blood-red fuchsia glowing like a great ruby.

Maida sees the beauty of what her mother has done, but is fearful it will appear homemade to Jim. So as not to hurt her mother, she smiles and pins on the corsage, fully convinced that Jim will never again be interested in her. Rachel, aware how Maida feels, is miserable to think she has failed her daughter.

Jim comes. They notice his surprised glances at Maida's corsage. His brief comments appear constrained. After the nightmare of dinner is over, Jim and Maida go. Maida says, 'Don't wait up for me, Mother,' and Rachel answering, 'All right, darling,' knows she will as she always does. The hours, filled with fear and worry, finally pass.

Maida finally comes running up the stairs to her mother's room. Rachel must put on a dressing-gown and come downstairs — Jim wants to see her. She goes. Jim tells her he has never seen anything like the results she has achieved with simple, old-fashioned flowers in the way of modern, sophisticated effects — just what he wants to feature in his shop. Will she come to San Francisco three days a week and arrange table decorations and corsages for him? He will pay her well. Rachel is dazed, thinking more of Maida than herself. Suddenly, something Jim says and the look on Maida's face makes her know that their romance is developing swiftly. So she has helped Maida and not ruined her happiness, after all! And the way is opened for Rachel to make money, keep Lillian and her home and garden — and her independence — when Maida marries. So all ends happily, as it should. The story closes with Maida, in her pride and happiness, saying, 'Order me an orchid, Mother,' and Rachel nodding and smiling in understanding.

So we have a plot developed from a character, a plot that may be developed in a light, semi-humorous style. Or it may be presented as a story of deep emotional and psychological significance, just as the writer wishes, depending on whether the writer emphasizes what Rachel does or what she thinks. *It is a plot that is inherent in the character and in the situation as it affects that character.*

Now, to exercise our mental and imaginative muscles, let us set ourselves a more difficult task.

Let us select a character and develop from that character an off-pattern story with a theme and, if possible, a build-up of pity and admiration on the part of the reader for one of the major characters. If we can manage to add timeliness and social significance, so much the better.

Since we have decided to dispense with the aid of a plot pattern in this proposed story, we shall select a strong theme to aid us in giving our work unity and cohesion. A theme is an abstract principle or idea interpreted concretely by means of the story. It adds such significance to a story that a theme story is often defined as a 'story with a message.' These then are our requirements: a worth-while theme, a build-up of emotion, timeliness, and social significance. What kind of character will fit our requirements? If we are to have the elements of timeliness and social significance we must necessarily select as our main character a person who is facing today's problems and, preferably, one who has a well-defined philosophy of life. We think of him as a young married man, working in a men's clothing factory. He is in a routine job, with small pay and almost no chance for advancement, as far as he can see, in spite of the fact that he is well-educated and intelligent. He and his wife live in a shabby two-room apartment, their lives cramped and frustrated. The young man is hard, bitter, realistic, seeing himself in a treadmill for the rest of his life. He prides himself on facing facts and is convinced that all facts are unpleasant. He hates what he calls the 'silly dreams' of people of his own social status, who are foolish enough to think they can ever pull themselves out of the harsh round of living that appears to be all they can hope for in the present. But he has a grim courage and is likable. Out of the little he earns, the two of them are saving for a home some day.

Our character-actor is beginning to take form now, so what shall we name him? Something simple and uncompromising like himself — Milt Hancock. His wife we shall call Alice. She has shy longings and hopes for a home of their own, but represses them because she thinks Milt is just wonderful and always right.

Now that we have our main character fairly clear in our minds, we must create a character that is highly contrasted to Milt and put them in opposition to each other. We think of a frail, scholarly old man who runs an elevator in the factory where Milt works. One night Milt brings the old man, named Joe Pruit, home to supper. Joe does not live in and for 'facts' as Milt does, but in and for his dreams. Let's tentatively name the story here, either 'No Words Can Tell' or 'Dream It True.'

Joe Pruit's dream is to save enough money from his tiny wages to go to Arizona and find one of the fabulous lost mines in the Superstition Mountains. He has a map, drawn by an Indian, he tells them, painted on a round flat stone in mineral colors, supposedly dating from the days of the Spaniards. This map is his most treasured possession. His eyes shine when he talks about the lost mine, the Plata de Oro. He will go into those fabled mountains some day and find that mine. It is the dream of adventure and romance that holds him, not the lure of money, as such. He tells all this to Milt and Alice. They like Joe Pruit, so they oppose his plan and try to make him see sense, as they think. Milt tells him the map is probably a fake, that he is too old, and, anyway, he knows nothing about the desert or mines. But Joe holds to his dream. (Here two philosophies of life are objectified and opposed to each other in the persons of Milt and Joe.) And Milt and Alice begin to admire him for it. They see much of Joe and become very fond of him.

Spring comes, and Joe must leave, as this is the most favorable season of the year for going into the Superstition Mountains. He hasn't quite money enough. Milt and Alice fear that Joe will not live to another spring. Secretly Milt gives him money they really need, so the old man may go. Milt abuses himself roundly for this and is ashamed that he isn't as hard and realistic as he thought. He becomes harder and more realistic in other ways to compensate for this lapse.

Joe is grateful but, being proud, the only condition on which he will take the money is for him to make out a paper in which he gives Milt the stone map. If anything happens to him, the map is to be Milt's, though of course Joe takes it with him.

Joe Pruit goes, his face illuminated and transformed by happiness. After a time lapse, the stone map comes addressed to Milt. Alice opens it in their dingy, cramped apartment, and reads the brief note from Joe, written before his death, on a scrap of paper at the high moment of satisfaction and achievement when he felt he had found the Plata de Oro. Alice is proud that Milt has helped Joe and tells her husband so when he comes home from work.

Milt looks at the stone map and at Joe Pruit's note. He remembers all the things Joe said about dreaming things true, that no words could tell the happiness that comes with the fulfillment of a dream; and that a dream is more real than its physical counterpart. Milt sees that Joe's dream about the Plata de Oro had brought Joe more happiness than years of 'facing facts' had brought to him. Joe had said that if you dreamed long enough and hard enough, your dream would come true. Joe had been right. Joe had dreamed the Plata de Oro true, as true as Joe ever wanted it to be.

Milt calls Alice, gets some paper out of the drawer of the wobbly table, and together they begin to draw plans for the little home that Milt was so sure would never materialize, but that he now determines to 'dream true.'

The theme of this plot might be stated as 'Dreams are necessary to happiness.' The story is timely and has social significance, in that it concerns the problems of independence and homemaking that many young people face today. It is a strong build-up of admiration and pity for Joe Pruit, and of a warm liking for and understanding of both Milt and Alice.

Suppose, by way of contrast, we don't like this ending after all, and want the story we develop from the character of Milt Hancock to take a completely different turn. Suppose we ourselves have a philosophy of life that approximates that of Milt in the beginning of the story we have just plotted. In that case, a different ending will be the logical outcome of our story-building. How can this be done?

The story can travel approximately along the same lines it did in the previous example, up to the point where the stone map comes back to Milt and Alice following Joe Pruit's death. Milt sees in Joe's death the proof of all his theories, and of the rightness of his own philosophy that dreams only betray the dreamer and it is better to face 'facts.' Milt's regard for Joe Pruit strengthens his emotion and his resolve never to allow himself to dream. So he and Alice go down to the docks, taking the stone map with them. To them it has come to be the symbol of the futility of all dreams and hopes and longings for adventure, color, and romance. To them, it represents Joe's dream, which had betrayed him to his death. They hurl it into the murky water, as far from shore as they can, and return to their dingy apartment, accepting their fate.

Our final decision with regard to the development of the story will dictate various subtle, but important, differences in characterization.

The Milt and Alice who would finally see the beauty and worth of Joe Pruit's dream, as in the first ending, are not the same Milt and Alice who would take the stone map and throw it into the water. Moreover, the basic theme, 'Dreams are necessary to happiness,' that strongly influenced the story in its original form, must be substituted for 'Dreams are worthless self-deceptions' in its second adaptation. The reader-emotion of admiration and pity toward Joe would remain unchanged, while that entertained for Milt and Alice would be admiration for their kindness to Joe and pity for their early disillusionment. In the final analysis, the exact kind and degree of reader-emotion would depend on the presentation.

In both of the above stories, I have stressed the *plot* that is built from a character, but what about the story that is almost plotless, where the emphasis is laid on the character himself, either in his conflict with all that makes up his environment or his conflict *within*?

The literary story, either the pure character story or the psychological-character-conflict story wherein two or more dominant character-traits clash in their struggle for the ascendancy, is *always built around a central character and dominated by that character*. Such a story usually emerges from a real-life personality, who is possessed of certain definite traits or, occasionally, such a story has its germinal idea in a theme. Having the theme in the mind, the writer chooses a certain person as the 'living' or concrete character to *work out* or interpret the significant universal idea that is embodied in that abstract theme. Edna Ferber's story, 'The Gay Old Dog,' illustrates my point. Miss Ferber could have started with the theme that is set forth specifically in the story as a thesis: 'Deathbed promises should be broken as lightly as they are seriously made. The dead have no right to lay their clammy fingers upon the living.' Or, rephrased, 'Is it a woman's right to bind a man to a way of life that must go on when she is gone?' On the other hand, Miss Ferber could as well have started with a person, Joe Hertz, whose life ended in complete frustration and futility because, endowed with the dominant character-trait of sincerity added to an exaggerated sense of filial duty, and handicapped in young manhood by a lack of money, he did not learn until it was too late that one's first duty is to himself.

In the literary story, the author's chief concern is the development of the qualities *within the material itself* with an honesty of presentation and an examination of the character-actors' motives and philosophies of life.

Again let me remind you of the basic pattern of the character story:

motivation + dominant character-trait + dominant emotion = problem and action (in connection with this, review Chapter XII).

Thus we have seen that any well-defined character is a potential source of many plots, that the general trend of the plot-development depends on the situation, the problem, or the decision that confronts that character. If you learn how to create characters and gain facility in so doing through practice, you need never be at a loss for a significant and an emotionally appealing plot. And you will, also, know what are the ingredients, if well presented, of a successful literary story.

Method of Study

1. What is the first qualification necessary for a story-character?
2. What device will make it possible for you to use a main character who is unfamiliar to your readers?
3. Why do general readers dislike stories that stress abnormal states of mind, serious illness, physical disability, or death of the main or likable characters?
4. Select a group of three characters who would be of interest to the women's magazines; to an adventure magazine; to a magazine aimed to interest both men and women.
5. Plot a story from the main character of each of these three groups, being sure it is a story that could happen to no one else except this particular character, in his particular situation and setting.
6. What is a theme story?
7. Wherein does a 'literary' story differ from a 'commercial' story?
8. Plan two major characters, a hero and a villain, and check your characters against the following list of questions:
   What does he wear?
   What are his food preferences?
   What is the exact state of his health?
   Has he any hobbies? What are they?
   What work does he do? Does he like it?
   What are his chief pleasures?
   His peculiar habits?
   What about his family?
   Does he smoke? If so, what?
   Does he drink? How much?
   Is he athletic? In what sports is he interested?

What about his sex life?

Has he any complexes, or problems?

What are his dreams, hopes, ambitions, fears?

How has he been educated?

How much money has he?

Where does he live? What sort of home?

Who are his friends?

What are his attitudes toward books, music, flowers, culture?

What is his race or nationality? His religion?

Has he any philosophy of life?

Has he any political or social opinions?

How much traveling has he done?

What are his peculiar reactions to:

    tears   treachery   heat   sarcasm?

CHAPTER XVII

Emotion and Characterization

EVERY living thing is constantly striving to increase its sense of being alive, and any important decrease in that sense of being alive brings the most intense suffering of which that particular organism is capable. Most people who read magazines and books, go to plays, and listen to the radio achieve a more intense consciousness of being alive *through their emotions* than they do either through mere physical sensations or through purely mental activities and conceptions. They have, in most cases, the ability to rise above physical sensations, provided those sensations are not too insistent, as in the case of extreme hunger or extreme pain, but they cannot yet, to any great extent, rise above and control their emotions, either good or bad. How often have we heard people say, 'Well, I can't help how I feel, can I?' To most of us, *the world of emotions is the world in which we live most vitally and most completely.*

For this reason, people avidly seek emotional expression because it makes them *feel* more intensely alive. They want to experience love, anger, fear, hope, suspense, curiosity, even sorrow. The conditions of their lives do not give them nearly all the emotion they want, so they turn to the writer to fill their need. The writer is successful in this in direct ratio to the desirability and strength of the emotions which he makes his reader feel, and the desirability and strength of the emotions he shows his characters as feeling.

As you can readily see from this, the writer does not concern himself with one main stream of emotion, but with two such streams. The emotion felt by the character-actor in the story and the emotion that is simultaneously felt by the reader may resemble each other, or they may be diametrically opposed; they never are exactly the same. For example, an actor in a story may be feeling the emotion of joy at having succeeded in injuring the hero. The reader certainly does not feel the emotion of joy. He probably feels sorrow for the hero and hatred for the villain. On the other hand, the hero may be feeling love, confidence, and admiration for his fiancée, and the reader may be feeling similar emotions. But, even here, the emotions are not the same; they are only *approximately* the same.

While it is undoubtedly true that the writer must use all his ability and skill in creating and carrying forward both these streams of emotion, with all their cross-currents, whirlpools, and eddies, he should never forget that his *main objective is the creation of emotion in the reader*. The emotions of his characters are a means to an end, not an end in themselves. And those emotions of the characters toward each other are important to the reader only in their *accumulative* effect on him. Nevertheless, from the point of view of the writer, how the hero regards the villain and *vice versa* is of vital importance in that *the emotion characters feel for each other is the foundation of all story-clash* and, hence, of story-drama.

Then, to return to the reader, the *basis* of all his story-interest lies in the feelings entertained by the characters for one another. Think of reader emotional reaction in terms of his interest in the following:

> Mary is in love with David, but he is the fiancé of Helen. What Mary will do about her unrequited love is dependent upon her dominant character-trait and the dominant emotion most characteristic of her. If she is a philosophical person she will probably accept the fact and, if altruistically inclined or, possibly, an older woman, may sublimate her affection for David by working for his success or by turning her emotion into channels of labor for causes. On the other hand, if her dominant emotion is jealousy, she may do anything from kidnapping David to shooting Helen.

All of this is very far-fetched and, perhaps, even ridiculous, but have I made it clear, first, that the emotion the characters feel toward each other not only affects reader-interest but, second, that taking the same character-actor and changing his dominant emotion toward another character will change the entire plot? That is to say, you will have another story. (Re-read Chapter XVI.) When you fully understand the importance of both the foregoing facts, you will realize the infinite plot variations, and hence stories, you can build around any complex character.

But what of the emotional reactions of the reader toward Mary and David and Helen? Did not your own feelings change as Mary's dominant emotion changed toward David and, hence, toward Helen? Of course they did, and this question is answered.

Therefore, the writer should decide, before he begins his story, the emotions he intends, first, to create *in his characters toward each other* and, second, to create in his *readers toward* each of *the characters*. Since this emotion that the reader shall feel is primarily dependent on the dominant character-traits of each actor, it is at once apparent how necessary it is for the writer to be able sharply to characterize his actors. No fuzzy thinking is allowable, if you are to create the full emotional effect of the character on the reader. After the dominant character-traits of the story-actors are selected, the next task is to devise incidents and situations that allow the character-traits and their corresponding emotions full scope for expression. We already know that character-traits indicate to a great extent the emotions your actors will feel, and the emotions they feel are highly indicative of their characters. For example, you can characterize a villain by showing him feeling the emotion of hatred, or desire for revenge. You can characterize your hero by showing him feeling the emotion of courage, or a desire to protect someone weaker than himself. It is highly important that you do not show your hero as feeling the emotion of hatred or desire for revenge, and that you do not weaken the character of your villain by showing him as feeling the emotion of courage or the desire to protect someone weaker than himself. This is wrong characterization by means of emotion, and is a frequent weakness in the stories of untrained writers.

Since, as we have seen, the emotion of any actor in a story and its expression is a *means* the writer uses to rouse emotions in the reader, we shall focus our attention on the second aspect; that is, on reader-emotion and how to create it. *Before writing any story, the writer should know clearly and specifically the dominant emotion he wants the reader to feel toward every character* in that story. Especially toward the main character, whether a villain or a hero. This is so necessary that no writer can afford to be vague about it. Never leave the choice of the emotional effect you want to build in the mind of the reader to chance or to hasty thinking. *Decide on the specific emotion and write it down opposite the name of the character*. If there is a combination of emotions you want your reader to feel toward the character, write them down. For example, you may want your reader to feel both fear and anger toward your villain. These two emotions are usually so closely related that it is often difficult to create them separately. Affection and admiration are also nearly always bracketed together. Amusement and tolerance is a good combination for a minor character. Pity and admiration for the hero is a combination of emotions often used with good effect, especially in a story that does not end happily for the hero.

There is always the principal reader-emotion the writer must aim for regarding the story as a whole, and that is the emotion of satisfaction. Even if the story ends unhappily for the chief actor, still the reader must feel the emotion of *satisfaction*. This is by no means the impossibility that it sounds. It is done by having the ending, unfortunate though it may be in regard to the desires of the main character for the story, inevitable and the best that could be hoped for under the circumstances. Although the reader may weep, she will say, 'It couldn't have been otherwise,' and be content.

A feeling of inevitability, of complete plausibility, of convincingness, is the first requisite of any piece of fiction writing. It takes precedent, even, over the reader's almost universal desire for a happy ending. Do not believe it when people tell you that readers invariably demand the happy ending. They do not. They demand the *plausible ending*. Under all circumstances it must be inevitable. Writers nearly always choose the circumstances and the opening situation that make a happy ending plausible and they are wise in doing this: first, because such a story is many times easier to write than a story that ends in sorrow and frustration for the hero and, second, because it is easier to sell. Pure tragedy and pure comedy require the master hand to present them convincingly. It is in the broad and fertile field that lies between these two extremes wherein success is most easily achieved. Generally speaking, give the reader a hero whom he can like and a villain whom he will correspondingly dislike, and you can depend upon it that in the story's end the reader will feel satisfaction.

Now let us see the kind of incidents, situations, and characters that are useful in rousing the feelings and emotions of anger, fear, sorrow, hope, hate, and joy in the reader; remembering as we select them that it takes two characters, or a character and an opposing force, to rouse the reader emotionally, and that the reader isn't going to feel very strongly toward a villain who is neither thinking nor acting in a villainous manner. If we saw the most notorious criminal in the United States passing along the street and we knew that he was going to the corner grocery to get a bottle of milk for his baby, the strongest emotion we would probably feel for him, provided we shut out of our consciousness the knowledge of what he had done in the past, would be one of curiosity. But if we saw this same criminal aiming a gun at our blameless and defenseless friend, our emotions would be of the most violent kinds. We should feel fear, both for our friend and for ourselves, and a boiling hatred. So don't expect your reader to feel an emotion, if you characterize your villain merely by *saying* that he is bad. *Select an incident in which the villain shows himself to be bad and cast it in a dramatic scene.* Only then can you be sure that you have roused your reader emotionally. The same is equally true for your hero and for every character in your story.

The emotion of a reader toward a story-actor is not built all at once, but is built cumulatively and as a byproduct of characterizing. Incident after incident, action after action, are used to keep the reader reminded of the character of the actor toward whom the emotion is being carefully and consciously built. Suitable character-traits, whether admirable or despicable, that are necessary to the rousing of the emotion are stressed.

Suppose your Actor A, for whom you are building the emotion of strong liking, with the hope that he will succeed in his purpose, is brave, determined, and has almost no means at his command for overcoming the strength and menace of the villain force. You show that character acting in a brave, determined manner, in small as well as important crises. For example, he may be shown walking to open a door with courage in his heart and a determined step. It sometimes takes as much courage and determination to open a door as it does to face a revolver in the hands of a determined enemy. By characterizing your actor through *showing* him moved by the emotions of courage and determination in the face of danger, you rouse in your reader feelings of hope, fear, suspense, liking, and admiration. While if you had merely said, 'George walked to the door and opened it,' you would not have characterized George, and your reader would have felt nothing. You would have forever lost your chance to cause your reader to react emotionally toward your character. *To be moved emotionally is the reader's chief, though unconscious, reason for reading your story.* You can see at once that you cannot afford to lose even one opportunity to characterize your actor.

There are five ways in which you may reveal the emotions of your actors to the reader, thus characterizing your actors and rousing the reader emotionally toward those characters, as follows:

1. By the writer's telling the reader the emotion the actor feels.
2. By going into the thoughts of the actor.
3. By the speech of the actor.
4. By the speech of a minor character.
5. By the action of the main character.

In other chapters of this book these means have been discussed from various aspects, so we shall be brief here, but sufficiently specific for our present purpose. In these examples we shall aim to characterize Beth, Actor A, as a sensitive, affectionate wife who meets complete disaster with self-control. We shall aim to make the reader feel admiration and pity for Beth. These same facts we shall present in five different ways:

1. *By the writer's telling the reader what emotion the actor feels*

Generally speaking, this is the least convincing way of building emotion, yet, in some cases, it is effective and useful, particularly where brevity is necessary. For example, in writing a short short, where every word must count, you might say of your main character:

> Beth's despair when Percy left her was so great that she felt she could not go on living.

This acquaints the reader with the emotional state of Beth, and the reader probably feels a slight emotion of pity for her.

2. *By going into the thoughts of the actor*

> 'Percy has left me...' The thought was like a white-hot iron rod drawn quickly across Beth's mind, searing a mark that would never heal. 'Why? Why? But the reason makes no difference, really. The only thing that matters is that he is gone, because he wanted to go. Oh, I can't live without you, Percy! I can't!'

This expresses Beth's emotion more vividly and brings it one step nearer the reader; consequently, the reader is likely to be more moved by it than by the first example, and to feel pity for Beth more strongly.

3. *By the speech of the actor*

This means is, on the whole, more difficult than number 2, because speech calls for greater restraint than thought. The reader excuses a certain lack of restraint in thought that he neither likes, nor excuses, in speech or action. So watch the speech of your likable characters carefully to see that it does not lack restraint.

'Ju-ju,' Beth said, coming in quietly, 'Percy has left me. No, I don't know why. I don't even care why — particularly. Oh, maybe I shall — later. But now the only thing that seems to matter is that he is gone. Did you ever feel that you couldn't bear to live another minute, Ju-ju? It's a horrible feeling ——'

Imagine that Beth spoke her thought, as given under number 2, aloud. Compare it with the speech given above and you will see how much more effective a result may be obtained by the use of restraint in speech, as compared with even the small amount of restraint with which her thoughts were expressed.

4. *By the speech of a minor character*

Sometimes the speech of a minor character is very effective in expressing the emotion of the main character, and so arousing emotion in the reader. Let us see one way in which it might be done:

'For heaven's sake!' Ju-ju cried, pushing Beth gently into a chair. 'Don't stare like that. Cry. Scream. Do anything, except look like the end of the world had come. Yes, I know that Percy has left you and that you don't know why. Though his reasons for doing this aren't the main thing that is worrying you now. You're wondering how you're going to live without him. I can see it in your eyes.'

By this means the reader is given a picture of Beth acting with restraint under severe emotional stress, and so reader-sympathy is won for her.

5. *By the action of the main character*

This is the most difficult, the most artistic, and, when well done, the most effective way of showing character through emotion, and for rousing reader-emotion toward the character. The reason is that you show to the reader what happens and permit him to draw his own conclusions, with no apparent help from the writer. The writer furnishes the material for the effect, and the reader creates the effect within himself, by the fullest use of his imaginative powers.

Knowing the difficulties of the device we are about to use, expressing character and emotion through action, let us see what we can do:

> Beth opened the note Percy had left on her dressing-table. She read in one glance the words it contained. 'I have left you and I am never coming back.' It was seconds before Beth moved. Then she let the note flutter from her limp fingers into the wastepaper basket, her expressionless eyes following its wavering descent. Slowly she walked toward the window, one hand pressed against her stiff lips. The window-pane felt cold as Beth leaned her forehead against it. Like a slow-motion picture, she crumpled to her knees, then slipped sideways until she lay in an awkward, twisted heap on the floor. Unconscious.

Some specific features of Beth's emotion cannot be expressed by this means, such as her lack of interest in why Percy left her. On the other hand, the reader probably feels Beth's despair and lack of interest in going on living even more fully in this presentation than in any other, because the reader has been given more to do of the actual creating of the emotion.

Let it be noted here that when you wish to characterize an actor so that the reader will feel pity and admiration, *never allow that character to feel self-pity*. It is a psychological fact that the moment a story-character, or a person in real life, is sorry for himself, that moment he forfeits the sympathy of other people. I cannot emphasize this too strongly. When you aim to rouse in the reader the combined emotion of pity and admiration, or even pity alone, toward a story-actor, though you can hardly imagine being sorry for someone you did not admire at least to some extent, characterize that actor as courageous, cheerful, always making excuses for people who have harmed him and who are planning to harm him further. Do not show him as indulging in that most unattractive of all emotions, self-pity.

EDITORIAL TABOOS

Another aspect of reader emotional reaction, one never analyzed by the reader and, probably, never recognized by him, is what we call editorial taboos. Of course, in truth, the editor hasn't one thing to do with these taboos, they are of the reader's own making, but because publishing is a business and magazines are published to be sold to readers, the wise editor doesn't print stories that come under this heading. These taboos also apply to the screen and to the radio, but they do not apply to the non-fiction field, the novel, and the play. In that these taboos are so important to editors and censors, it is well for the writer to know them and to act accordingly. To that end, it is every bit as important to know what *not* to write as it is to know what the editors, in reality the readers, want. So let us see *what editors do not want*. Many an otherwise good story is made unsalable because an editorial taboo has been woven into it so that the taboo cannot be removed without destroying the story. This fact makes this particular information of great importance. You will be saved much wasted effort if you will remember these taboos. Do not be disturbed, however, if, at rare intervals, you should happen to come across one or more of these taboos in print. Any writing rule, except the one that has to do with writing interestingly, can be broken if the writer is skillful enough and if he can find an editor who thinks the story has sufficient appeal to overcome the bad effect of the taboo. Usually such stories are written by writers who are 'big names' and, as a rule, they appear only in 'literary' magazines. But those two 'ifs' place an almost insurmountable obstacle in the path of the beginning writer. Why unnecessarily handicap yourself? To do so is not good everyday business sense.

The following are the major taboos:

1. *Racial intermarriage*

Don't write stories about marriage between or the intermixing of races. Readers find the idea so unpleasant that editors *very rarely* buy stories into which miscegenation enters.

2. *Sexual perversion or a too realistic presentation of sex*

These, too, are subjects from which most readers shrink in disgust and repulsion. The wise writer avoids them.

3. *Controversial questions*

In fiction, keep away from subjects on which public opinion is sharply divided. Make no attempt to use fiction as a means for propaganda, because the result will be both poor propaganda and poor fiction. The one function of fiction is to entertain, and such propaganda stories as you occasionally read are written on consignment by big names.

4. *Religion*

Religion as sectarianism or a strongly religious subject can rarely be used in fiction for the general-circulation magazine. In general, people feel strongly about religion, and their ideas on the subject differ too widely to make it good material for the student-writer. Even the professional writer seldom attempts to use it, and when he does, presents it in a way so general as to be utterly inoffensive.

5. *Choice of villains*

Do not make the citizen of a *friendly* foreign nation a villain. Never make a member of any specific lodge, club, church, or other well-known organization a villain. Even in selecting as a villain the member of any one profession, such as a doctor, be careful to make clear that you are using him as an *individual* and *not* as representative of his profession.

6. *Choice of heroes*

In nearly all stories published in this country, the hero is an American. This is not because readers do not like people of other nationalities, but because readers are more interested in, and better understand, their own nationals than those of other countries. When the *setting* is foreign, it is *especially necessary* to have an American hero.

7. *Excessive suffering*

Never include *detailed descriptions* of excessive suffering. Such descriptions, if well done, cause the reader to suffer, and no reader is willing to suffer except slightly. If you make him suffer too much, he will put your story down and never read another that you write. Use restraint when you must indicate suffering. Give no more details than necessary to allow the reader to imagine as much as he wishes and no more.

8. *Victory of the villain or showing him as successful to the end in wrong-doing*

The nearest approach to an absolute taboo is a story that lets the villain triumph in the end. The reading public demands that the villain be defeated and, in some way, punished because of his misdeeds. Otherwise, the reader is not satisfied with the ending. Another unwritten law is to omit details in the performance of a crime; that is, never *show* the reader *how* specifically to go about wrongdoing. For example: While editors would close their eyes to a few details in the story of a man murdering another by the use of quick-drying cement on the basis that almost everyone knows about quick-drying cement and how it works, they would frown on a detailed description of a man trying to blow up a safe. Why? Because, in the first example, the information imparted is not harmful because it is known; in the second, to give this specific knowledge to the reader constitutes education in crime. Watch this point very carefully when writing stories in which crime appears.

9. *Deaths (of likable characters), funerals, serious illnesses, the morbid and gruesome, prostitutes, drug addicts, insane persons, drunkards, sordid characters in general*

Do not write about these at length. Remember that the average reader regards fiction reading as a pleasure and people have troubles enough without having anxiety, unpleasantness, sorrow, and unmitigated tragedy spring at them from the pages of a magazine.

10. *The supernatural*

Don't use supernatural happenings in your stories. General-circulation magazines rarely publish stories of this kind. There is, however, a small market for them in the pulps and in the literary magazines. All superphysical happenings and subject-matter must be handled so carefully and with such consummate skill that the beginning writer is wise not to attempt their use.

When the superphysical is published in a wide circulation weekly, almost without exception it is written by a well-known writer; in other words, by a man whose following will read with interest anything he writes.

11. *Disrespect for motherhood*

Never speak of motherhood slightingly or with levity. Only very rarely is a mother used as an unsympathetic character, and then by a skilled, professional writer. In the popular magazines, motherhood must always be mentioned with reverence or, at least, respect. Life may reveal mother-offspring conflicts, but story writers must not tell.

12. *Criticism of Big Business*

Never suggest in your stories that there is anything wrong with Big Business. There are two reasons for this:

(1) It verges on the controversial and so has no place in fiction in the general-circulation magazines.

(2) The great general-circulation magazines, paying the highest prices to authors for fiction, are supported by their advertising. This means

that they are supported by Big Business. Consequently, the editors, who are level-headed business men, refuse to publish anything derogatory to Big Business.

13. *Disrespect for authorities*

Don't ridicule people in authority. Do not belittle law or law enforcement. Do not speak disrespectfully of courts or judges. A little friendly ragging is allowed toward policemen, but use discretion even there.

14. *Accident and coincidence*

These may be used in *bringing about* your story Problem, that is, in the Beginning of the story, but neither one must appear in the Body of the story or in the solution of the Problem. *Never forget this.* It is impossible for me to be too emphatic about this taboo. Accidents and coincidences in the solution of the story are too easy for the writer and completely unconvincing to the reader.

NOTE: As said earlier, many of the subjects that are taboo in the short story can be used in the article and the novel. If, for instance, you want to attack a certain social condition, your medium should be that of the article, the novel, or the legitimate play.

SPECIFIC TABOOS AFFECTING SPECIAL PUBLICATIONS AND GROUPS OF PUBLICATIONS

To discover special taboos that affect special publications is not so difficult a task as might be imagined. Select a number of consecutive issues of any given magazine, and read them carefully for choice of material and treatment.

Take, for example, the very large group of *religious and semi-religious magazines* that form such a fine proving-ground and stepping-stone to the ambitious young writer. Naturally, vou will find that they have a larger and more rigid set of taboos than a big sophisticated general-circulation magazine that appeals to both men and women. In the religious and semi-religious fields, the writer will not write of, or mention, crime, or lethal weapons. He will steer clear of sex, of violence, of divorce, and none of his characters may drink, smoke, or, in many instances, dance.

Stories for this group will deal, for the most part, with character-building and with the triumph of Right over Wrong through *strength of character.*

GENERAL

When you are in doubt as to the specific taboos of any magazine or group of magazines, begin by analyzing the advertisements, then the stories, and you will readily discover the material *taboos* as well as the *requirements* of that particular magazine group.

In considering the subject of editorial requirements and taboos, never forget that the reader of any or all groups of publications that print and pay for fiction, except the quality or 'literary' group, reads to be pleasantly entertained and to escape from the boredom and the unpleasant aspects of his life. The ordinary reader wants to see life, not as it is, *but as he would like it to be*, yet the story must, while he is reading it, make him feel that it is a true picture of life. In other words, it will be *convincing*, it will have the *aspect* of reality.

And, finally, remember that the reader, generally speaking, is far more *moral* in his reading than he is in *real life*. All professional writers understand this and take it into account. In other words, the average reader strives for the attainment of his *ideals* in his reading and gains satisfaction in seeing those ideals materialize into a *seeming reality*. The reader uses fiction to lift himself spiritually by his bootstraps till he makes his escape from the mundane world and, for a time at least, becomes a citizen of one more to his liking. Whatever the *reason* may be, the writer will do well to remember that the reader's moral sense and his sense of propriety and good taste must not be offended but, rather, satisfied and upheld.

Method of Study

1. Why do readers like to read stories in which primary and secondary emotions are roused strongly within them?
2. How are story-actors characterized through their emotions?
3. What are the five ways of communicating the emotion of an actor to the reader?
4. Write examples of each of these five ways.
5. Characterize a villain through showing his emotion. Characterize a likable character by showing his emotion.

CHAPTER XVIII

Characterization in the Short Short Story
WHEREIN YOUR CHARACTERS DIFFER

WHILE characterization of the short short story may be achieved according to any of the rules laid down in previous chapters, restrictions of the short short form almost appear to exact a separate technique in the matter of characterization. The ever-increasing popularity of the short short story makes this subject one of importance to the writer who approaches his work from the professional standpoint.

In the many types of short short stories that are published, there are, of course, many kinds and degrees of characterization. Of these, there are certain qualities that must be included in every type. Let us examine them first:

1. *In the short short, because of space-limitations, the characters are 'flat' as contrasted to the 'round' characters of longer stories.* That is, the writer rarely attempts to show more than *one dominant character-trait,* even in the major actors. The short short writer uses type-characters, who are often presented with little or no individualization. Better results, however, are obtained when the writer has been successful in covering his story-character with a cloak of individuality.

2. *The two major characters of a short short are either both 'good' or both 'bad,' or one is 'good' and the other 'bad.'* If they are both 'good,' then it is necessary to introduce a villain force. This villain force may be a misunderstanding that threatens their happiness, a condition, a situation, or a natural force, such as a storm. There is no time in a short short for subtle characterization, or for a plot arising from complicated characterization. The action of a short short is necessarily swift, unified, and tending to a single effect.

3. *Because of the word limit of a short short, characterization must be done boldly*, in swift strokes, serving the double purpose of giving the reader necessary information and carrying forward the story action. The words chosen to characterize the actors of a short short must accomplish their task swiftly and clearly. *At the same time* they must picture action, necessary to advance the story, disclose motivation, or achieve a combination of any or all of these things. Often this is effected within the limits of two or three sentences. When your skill is equal to that task, you are approaching or have already arrived at the status of a professional writer.

Short shorts are by no means alike in their demands for characterization. The 1000-word story, published by *Liberty*, may characterize merely by placing the hero on the 'right' side and the villain on the 'wrong' side. By this, I do not mean that all short shorts published in magazines such as *Liberty* and *Collier's* limit themselves to this type of characterization. Examples of sharply clear and convincing characterization appear frequently in the short short stories of those magazines. The point is, short short stories differ in their characterization requirements. Some demand no more than a mere classification of the actors as 'hero' and 'villain'; others need specific treatment. The material and the desired effect dictate the type and amount of characterization necessary in any given case.

The characters that appear in short shorts published by the better class of magazines do not require more characterization than those that appear in the popular magazines, newspaper syndicates, et cetera, *but they do require more individualization*, as a rule. More than one dominant character-trait is rarely shown, but by individualizing the major characters they are made to seem more lifelike than would otherwise be the case. In the wide overlapping of types of short shorts published in the various magazine groups, the main difference is often a matter of polish and presentation.

For example, in a recently published short short that appeared in one of the top magazines, the writer depended entirely on plot to hold reader-interest and the only characterization made of either the 'hero' or the 'villain' was that the 'hero' was on the 'right' side, and the 'villain' on the 'wrong' side. Beyond that, the reader knew none of the characteristics of either man. The story concerned an almost helpless cripple, a derelict of the First World War. By an interesting sequence of happenings, he came into the possession of a rifle and of the proof that a man he had known for a long time was the spy of an enemy country. The cripple was able to shoot the spy at the moment the spy was handing important documents to an officer in the army of the enemy.

The cripple may have been bad-tempered, dishonest, cruel. Or he may have been brave, generous, and kind to animals. But the reader was not told. The spy may have been a sneak, a bully, and a thief; or he may have been patient, philosophical, and studious. The reader was left in profound ignorance. This was the correct treatment for this story. The plot did not depend in any way on the character-traits of either actor. It depended solely on the fact that each served his country in the way that seemed best to him. So in such a story as this characterization could be reduced practically to zero and with no loss of reader-interest, since the sympathy of any reader is automatically against a spy, unless that spy is a member of the intelligence bureau of the reader's own country. The actors in this particular story were individualized by contrasting their physical appearance, but they could not be said to have been characterized.

Another short short of a very different type characterized the main actor very clearly by stressing over and over his dominant character-trait, that of courage. Actor A was an old Civil War soldier. When the story opened, he was contemplating suicide by using the gun that he had used with such great courage in the early sixties. He was feeble, and suffering great pain. He felt he had a right to free himself from a situation that could never be any better, but could only become worse. In any event, the end for him could not be far distant. But his character-trait of courage would not let him commit the cowardly act of taking his own life, even under these tragic circumstances. He decided that he must submit to destiny — there might be something left for him to do. He laid the old gun on the table before him and fell asleep. Later he was wakened by the sound of furtive footsteps downstairs. He grasped his gun and started down the staircase. He met a desperate criminal coming up, intent on kidnapping the old man's granddaughter. Though struck by an instinctive fear of the criminal, the old man never faltered. The bullet he had put in the gun to kill himself, killed the kidnapper. Not before, however, the kidnapper had shot the old man, inflicting a serious but not in itself fatal wound. The shock of the wound and the excitement brought about the old man's death. So he won his release from suffering by his dominant character-trait of courage. Therefore, it was necessary to stress this trait over and over again.

When in doubt as to what character-trait to stress and how much to stress it, ask yourself these two questions: The first is, what character-trait is necessary to your story, and how necessary is it? The second is, which is more important in your story, character-trait or plot?

Only the most direct ways of characterization can be used in a short short. Reader-attention should be focused on the one character-trait that has most influence on the action of the story, whether that trait belongs to the hero, or the villain; or focused on the most obviously threatening aspect of the villain force or situation, in case no personal villain is used.

For purposes of study, short short stories may be broadly classified under four headings, though it must be remembered that no sharp line of demarcation exists between them and that there is occasional overlapping. In spite of this, some classification will be of real help to the writer in his making the right decision concerning the amount and kind of characterization that will be most effective with the material he has in mind. These classifications are:

1. *The short short that depends for its interest on a clever, tricky plot and not on the dominant trait or traits of the actors.*

2. *The short short that depends for its interest on a combination of plot and characterization.*

3. *The short short that depends for its interest on the dominant character-trait of the main actor, and which has little or no plot; perhaps only a situation that, in combination with character, causes the reader to react emotionally.* These stories achieve a unified effect by a strong build-up of emotion, usually pity and admiration, toward the main character.

4. *The short short that depends for its interest on the psychological reaction of the main character, this reaction being objectified in dramatic and emotionally moving action.*

Now let us examine each one of these types. Since we know what the characterization problem is in each one, let us see how we can best solve it. The first step in the solution of any problem is to analyze that problem and thus clearly to understand it.

1. The short short story that depends for its interest on a clever, tricky plot and not on the dominant character-trait of the main actor:

In this case, no more than the character-type should be indicated, since dominant character-traits are not used in the story. All the reader must know is whether the characters are 'good' or 'bad.' The reader will fill in the details of the type from imagination and memory. Let us write an opening paragraph and see how nearly we can accomplish what we have set out to do, in a few words, with no extraneous material:

> Hiram was just getting ready to close his garage for the night when the big flashy yellow car rolled in and stopped with a jerk. Standing in the door of the cubbyhole, he called his office, he watched the man climb out. A short, swarthy man, fat in the wrong places and with a head too small for his body. Hiram noticed a bulge in the man's coat-pocket and wondered whether it was caused by a bottle or a gun.

In this opening paragraph the name 'Hiram' helps to type the main character as 'good.' 'Hiram' is no name for a villain character. He owns a garage, and that types him as industrious, and as belonging to the lower middle class. His office is a cubbyhole, so the reader knows he has a small garage and the reader, if left alone, is always instinctively 'for' the small worker and business man. The other character is promptly typed as a villain by the details of his appearance. We have not shown a dominant character-trait in either case. So, in reading this paragraph, the analytical reader will know at once that he is reading a story in which the interest will center in a clever plot, a plot that might be acted out by any characters of the general type of those we have introduced in our first paragraph. These are flat characters representing types, and are suitable to this kind of short short. The main actor in this type of story may be either 'good' or 'bad,' depending on the material.

2. The short short that depends for its interest on a clever plot plus characterization by the use of one dominant character-trait of the main character and possibly of the minor as well: Sometimes this type of short short has for its main character a hero with one good dominant character-trait; sometimes, a villain with one bad dominant character-trait. Sometimes the secondary characters are similarly endowed or are merely 'good' or 'bad' characters, depending on the demands of the material and the plot.

Let us see how we might begin to write a short short that is dependent for its interest on character as well as plot, and in which we intend to use a 'good' character with a dominant character-trait as the main actor:

> When Joshua Ennis was sixty he announced he had bought a plane and was learning to fly it. His friends and even his enemies shook their heads solemnly. That is, all except Del, his son, who knew his father better than anyone else. 'Dad'll make out,' was his quiet reply to all who prophesied

for Joshua disaster, ranging from a nervous breakdown to sudden death.

Tonight, ten years later, Joshua was driving his plane through the crashing thunder of an electrical storm over Nevada on his way to the Pacific coast. It did not occur to him to go around the storm, or to set his plane down until it had passed. That wasn't Joshua's way. He had always taken the quickest, the most direct route to what he wanted. That he should change merely because he was almost seventy and using a comparatively new means of transportation simply didn't enter his mind. Anyway, he had no time now to think of such trifles as caution and personal safety. Del, his only son, had that morning been arrested in San Francisco on a charge of murder. Well, he'd be there in a few hours now, and then the fellows who'd framed Del had better look out. Joshua set his lips in a grim line.

We have characterized Joshua as having a high degree of courage and determination, two qualities that almost always appear together. We have indicated that he will use both these qualities in our story-plot that concerns his flight to have Del freed from a charge of murder. We have done this, not by telling the reader he is courageous and determined, but by *showing* Joshua acting in a determined and courageous way. Since we did this in two ways, first when he, already an old man, bought and learned to fly a plane; and second, when ten years later he flies through a dangerous storm, Joshua must be going to use these characteristics to solve his problem. All the way through the story we shall show our hero acting in a determined and courageous manner to solve his problem by means of these characteristics.

Now let us see how we can characterize a villain-character that we intend to use as the main character of our short short. It will be a story that depends on both plot and character for its reader-interest. A villain is used as the main character more often in a short short than in a long short. No matter what the length of the story, in the end the villain must not only be defeated, but he must defeat himself by some oversight or some act that he performs in his effort to harm the likable character. Such a plot is known technically as the Biter-Bit.

'And that,' said Jake Orton, tapping the nicked edge of the golden-oak dresser with his pencil, 'is where we move in. You take the wheel of the bank car and I slip in the back where they keep the cash.'

'But, Jake,' Ollie protested weakly, 'it's too much of a gamble. Suppose the guard won't play ball? Lots of 'em won't. Then what?' The night was cool, but beads of sweat on Ollie's bald head glistened in the light of the single electric bulb that hung from the ceiling.

'I never gamble,' Jake said flatly. 'Not on nothin'. This is a sure thing. If the guard listens to reason, we cut him in. There'll be plenty for all three of us. If he won't listen to reason, I bump him off. Either way, we don't have no trouble. It's a sure thing, I tell you.'

The villain's dominant character-trait is obviously ruthlessness motivated by acquisitiveness. Murder means nothing to him, and he believes implicitly in his ability to outwit the other fellow.

Ollie, the minor character, is characterized as timid and weak. That our story will have a plot is indicated by the fact that Jake has a plan that he intends to carry through. The dominant character-traits that we have assigned to Jake and Ollie will, of course, play important parts in the plot unfoldment and plot solution, or we would not have assigned them to these characters.

3. The short short that depends for its interest on character plus situation:

This is a type of short short that is increasing in popularity. A high degree of skill and sensitivity is required to write it successfully. There is rarely much action in these stories, though a great deal of action that has taken place in the past, or that will take place in the future, may be implied. This action is usually left largely to the imagination of the reader. No more complicated characterization is demanded than in other types of short shorts, since usually only one character-trait is stressed, but that character-trait is shown in such a way that it has very high emotional values. Since these emotional values are not developed until the last line of the story, it is not possible to show how the characterization is done or even well begun in an opening paragraph. To that end, we shall try to write a summary of the story in order *to see the characterization as a whole.* For this story we shall choose as the dominant emotion to be roused in the reader, a mixture of admiration and pity, since that is the emotion most often roused in published stories of this type:

Actor A — Mary Arden, mother of Lolita Arden.

Her dominant character-traits are courage and self-control, motivated by her love for Lolita.

Summary:

The story opens in the evening, with a scene between Mary Arden and the doctor, wherein the reader is told that Lolita would have been graduated from high school in a few days had she not suddenly been taken seriously ill. She is now near death. The doctor tells Mary she will die between three and five in the morning when human vitality is at its lowest. During her brief illness, Lolita has been completely obsessed by the thought of her graduation and graduation dress, which has become a symbol. She still believes she will graduate with her class. Her one idea is to see the dress finished. After the doctor leaves, Mary Arden, who has not had much time to work on it during Lolita's illness, sews all night to finish the dress she knows Lolita will never wear. Just before three o'clock Mary finishes the dress to the last ruffle and the last tuck. She takes it in to Lolita, who looks at the dress and is completely happy. The reader sees Mary's satisfaction in Lolita's joy. Lolita's death follows, as the doctor said it would, but it is implied, not actually shown. (The writer must guard against building unhappy emotions by a too realistic presentation.)

If we write a story from this summary we shall, of course, stress Mary Arden's character-traits of courage and self-control by what she does, and make clear the motivation of her love for Lolita, in order to build in the reader the strongest possible emotion of admiration and pity toward Mary.

4. The short short that depends for its interest on the psychological reaction of the main character, this reaction being objectified in dramatic and emotionally moving action:

The psychological short short is rarely seen, perhaps because of the difficulty of externalizing psychological states in dramatic action. However, a well-thought-out and well-presented psychological short short is very salable. Here again, as was the case with the short short that is a build-up of emotion, the story must be examined as a whole to give any useful idea of the way characterization should be done.

Let us see what we can do in a brief summary of such a story:

Actor A — Shule Adler, a boy of eighteen, who has never been accepted on equal terms by the self-reliant and rather rowdy boys of the village. He is abnormally sensitive, apparently timid, even cowardly, and easily influenced. The boys of the village, and some of the men as well, have terrorized Shule for years. When the story opens, all his characteristics of a weakling have been intensified to the point where his psychological reactions are no longer normal.

A new young man, Brad Newton, comes to the village. He sympathizes with Shule and tells him that he should be brave, fight back. That is all that will be necessary to free him from the tyranny of the other boys and make them respect and accept him as one of them. Shule listens doubtfully, then eagerly, but still fears he can never do as Brad tells him to do.

But he promises Brad he will think it over. That night, as Shule returns to his home through a dark patch of woodland, the hoodlums set upon him as they have many times before. Their purpose has never been to harm Shule, but always to frighten him. But now, instead of whimpering and begging to be let off, as was always previously the case, Shule brings out the gun he has stolen from Brad, and shoots one of the boys. The shot does not kill the boy, but renders him helpless. Shule threatens to kill anyone who goes to the injured boy's assistance. He now has the boys in his power for the first time, and the situation causes him to lose what little sense he ever had. The other boys decide to send one of their number for Brad who, as they know, has been friendly to Shule. Brad arrives, speaks sharply to Shule, and goes to help the wounded boy. When Brad stoops over to lift the boy, Shule shoots Brad and kills him.

This story is a psychological study of the way in which abnormal fear can, and sometimes does, influence character and action. Drama is achieved by the importance and significance of the action, in which Shule, unreasoningly following the advice of his one friend, shoots and kills that friend.

GENERAL

The popularity of the short short story is certainly increasing, and most editors complain they cannot get as many good ones as they would like to print. Hence, any short short based on a sound original idea has an excellent chance for sale, even though it is only reasonably well presented. Skill, however, must be used in depicting the actors even though, for a short short story, they are necessarily of the 'flat' type. This demands clear-cut thinking on the part of the writer *before* he begins to put his story on paper. A reasonable ratio between thinking about the writing a short short is seventy-five per cent thinking and twenty-five per cent writing. For example, if it takes you two hours to write and revise and polish your short short, you should have spent at least six hours of intensive thinking about it. With many professional writers the ratio of thought to actual writing is much larger than this.

Of course, no definite rule can be made. Sometimes a story, especially a short short, will spring into the mind of a writer practically all of a piece, and be written in almost its finished form at white heat. However, this happens so rarely that it isn't safe to count on its happening to you, very often at any rate. The surest way to turn out a salable short short is to think about it a great deal and write it slowly and carefully.

Method of Study

1. As compared with long short stories, what kind of characters are used in the short short story?
2. How many character-traits of the major characters should be stressed in a short short?
3. Write in your own words a definition for each of the four main types of short short stories with reference to their characterization.
4. From published short shorts, select one of each type and analyze it according to the classification in this chapter.
5. Write an original opening paragraph for each of the first two types that will definitely indicate the type of story that is to follow this opening paragraph.
6. Write brief original summaries for stories of the two second types of short shorts, summaries that definitely indicate the type.

CHAPTER XIX

Characterization on the Kilocycles

HOW TO CHARACTERIZE FOR RADIO

CHARACTERIZATION in radio dramas is hedged about by more restrictions and limitations than in any other form of writing or acting. Yet, as everyone knows, remarkably interesting and artistic characterization is being accomplished in radio dramas. Real artists regard restrictions and limitations in any particular field not as handicaps but as challenges; often as opportunities. The biographies of all artists, from that of Benvenuto Cellini to Diego Rivera are full of incidents that prove this statement. The many outstanding successes in the radio field simply testify that their talented and alert artists are no exceptions to this rule. So if you fail to characterize your radio characters successfully, do not blame radio; blame yourself. In the preceding chapters, we have laid the foundations that are basic in all character creations, regardless of the particular medium, whether fiction, the stage play, the screen or radio. In this chapter, we shall stress the special feature in characterizing the story-actors that are peculiar to the field of radio.

The various taboos in short-story writing, about which you were warned in Chapter XVII, also apply to radio and the screen. Your drama character-heroes must not do or say anything that might be construed as offensive to the radio audience. Not only profanity, but also anything suggestive of a double meaning, is definitely taboo on the air.

Radio characterization is necessarily simple and broad in its outlines, for reasons we shall discuss as we proceed. *It makes fullest use of the art of suggestion*, leaving the listener to fill in details by the exercise of his own imagination. This involves no hardship for the reader, who welcomes the opportunity and enjoys it.

However, radio is no place for subtle, complicated characterization. Since radio characterization is necessarily simple, it naturally follows that it is easily learned and easily accomplished, once its basic principles, limitations, and special opportunities are clearly understood by the writer.

The main limitation and conditioning factor in radio characterization is that it appeals to the ear alone. At first glance, this may seem to be no more a limitation than that imposed by the printed word, which appeals to the eye alone, but in reality the limitation is much greater. The fiction writer has at his command not only dialogue, but narration, exposition, analysis, action, and description to use in characterizing his actors. He can go into the thoughts of his characters, tell the reader the gestures and movements they make, the changes in their facial expression. While the radio writer, with the exception of dialogue between his actors and, perhaps, very little help from the announcer and sound effects, can avail himself of none of these aids.

In the movie or stage play, the dramatist appeals as much to the eye as to the ear — perhaps more so. Throughout the play, the appearance, clothing, mannerisms, action, and background of each character, as well as what he says, are continuously before the audience. These means of making character-actors live are not available to the radio dramatist. He can *appeal* directly to only one of the five senses, the *sense of hearing*.

Radio writers are sometimes told to think of their audience as being blind. This advice might be of benefit were it not misleading. Hearing is, of course, the only channel through which you appeal to the imagination of your listener and mould it to a perfect mind-picture of the character portrayed. Remember, your listener is not blind. Your task as a writer would be easier if he were. He has seen with his eyes actual scenes similar to those that are being presented to his imagination through his sense of hearing over the radio. Just as the imaginative world is presented to the reader by the printed word and to the theatre-goer by the stage effects and action, so the radio listener is focusing his attention on the sounds emerging from his radio, which represents your only means of communication with him.

When we say, as above, that the radio listener is 'focusing his attention' on the program, we introduce, by contrast, one of the problems of the radio writer. In every home, there is a listener who, while trying to give his attention to your play, is looking about the living-room, hearing Junior ask to go to a movie, arguing with Junior's elder brother as to who shall have the car, is probably eating peanuts and reading the newspaper. Rare, indeed, is the fortunate person who can give his undivided attention to a radio drama without interruptions or distractions of any kind.

You realize, then, that your radio characters must fight for audience-attention as no other characters in no other medium have to fight for audience- or reader-interest. This is one of the reasons radio characters must be simple and not complex. Subtleties and fine gradations are lost on the radio listener, and you now understand why.

In radio, time, or rather the lack of time, is still another factor that limits characterization. Your listeners have to become interested in your characters in the first thirty seconds. There is no time, as there is in a stage or movie play or in a piece of fiction, to reveal your actors' characteristics bit by bit. Those characters must spring, like Pallas Athene, 'full-panoplied from the brow of Jove.' There are far more fifteen-minute dramatic programs on the air than there are thirty-minute dramatic programs. The full-hour dramatic program is on its way out. There are two reasons for this: The cost of radio time makes the hour show almost prohibitive. More important still, radio surveys show that the average listener begins to get restless at the end of a fifteen-minute program, and that it is almost impossible to hold his attention for more than thirty minutes with the same story and cast of characters. That is why most hour-shows are variety programs, with a swift change of situations, skits, gags, and offering perhaps one ten-minute drama. In view of all this, it is clear that your characterization must be done swiftly.

As well as the speed with which your radio characters must be characterized, a further limiting and conditioning factor in the *selection* of a character for a radio drama is the psychology of the average radio listener. He is not wrapped in the enchanted spell of the printed page, neither can he be influenced by the surroundings, the mood, and the crowd psychology of the theatre. He is relaxed, in his own home, an independent entity surrounded by distractions and the demands of, or opportunities for, other forms of entertainment. He may read a book or magazine, he may talk to his family, or to his friends who drop in, he may telephone on business or social matters, he may tune in on any one of a dozen programs, or he may go to a movie. *The listener's mood is one of challenge, rather than acceptance.* You have to prove that you can entertain him; he is, until you have captured his interest, extremely critical. If your characters bore him during the first two minutes he can — and probably will — tune them out with one turn of his wrist. Then, as far as he is concerned, those characters no longer exist.

I have emphasized all this so that you, the writer, may be fully aware of the special conditions that affect the presentation of your radio dramas. As in all writing, radio demands characters that are entirely convincing and completely natural. They are not separated from the listener by distance and by the barrier of footlights. They are not residents of a completely imaginary world as are the characters of a book or story. They are, in a sense, present in the listener's living-room, no farther away than he can reach. He can tune them out if they do not please him; if they do, he can enjoy their companionship in the intimacy and informal atmosphere of his home.

Does all this seem to make radio characterization a difficult feat? If so, your impression is incorrect and you have only to tune in on any one of dozens of dramatic programs, from the full-hour complete drama to the fifteen-minute complete drama or serial episode, or even the ten-minute sketch, to prove it. Good characterization is by no means uniform in these dramas, but enough excellent work is being done to convince any writer, unless he belongs to the 'arty' school, that *once the limitations and conditions of the medium are understood,* excellent characterization can be done on the air. In fact — and this is one of the surprising and pleasant discoveries of radio — characterization can hold, as no other means, the attention of listeners and, in the case of a serial or strip-show, establish large and loyal followings. Several of the most popular strip-shows on the air have no plot, and almost no dramatic action, but are made up of simple incidents happening to *everyday people,* with very little, and in some cases no, continuity or carry-over of listener-interest from episode to episode. This alone proves that characters themselves are of sufficient interest for the listeners to tune in day after day, week after week, and, in many cases, year after year, merely to hear them talk about the simple incidents of their lives. Though the original and, probably, still the most popular strip-show of this kind is 'Amos 'n Andy,' there are at present thirty-five similar programs on the national networks that hold their listeners almost altogether by the characters who appear in them.

What fundamental qualities are necessary for a character to fit him for radio presentation? First, as we have seen, *the character must be simple*, with *one dominant character-trait* and *one dominant emotion* and, provided you are writing a play complete in one performance, a *dominant purpose for that play*. Second, the character should *represent a type* that is familiar to a large majority of the possible listeners. This greatly reduces the necessity for detailed characterization, for, given the type, the listener will, in his own mind, characterize the actor accordingly. After that the dramatist need only individualize the character within the type.

For example, if you let your reader know in the first few seconds of dialogue that your main character is named Mrs. Moriarity and that she has nine children, you have established her type as an elderly Irish mother. This character-type is — unless definitely characterized otherwise — elderly, good-natured, unselfish, self-sacrificing, courageous, industrious, affectionate.

Perhaps you do it something like this:

POLICEMAN O'CONNOR

'Good mornin' to ye, Mrs. Moriarity! And how would ye be feelin' this mornin'?'

MRS. MORIARITY

'I'm feelin' fine, officer. And why not? With every one of me nine children home and workin' — and even himself with a nice, easy job of night-watchin' to do.'

Note this carefully: You have established your actor's name, approximate age, social status, position as wife and mother, and her characteristics of cheerfulness, unselfishness, self-sacrifice, courage, industry, and affection — that is, you have characterized her as to type — in forty words. But this is not all you have done. You have roused in the listener an emotion of liking, sympathy, and admiration for your character, and when *you have roused an emotion in the listener toward a character*, no matter what that emotion may be, *you have increased listener-interest* in that character. *The stronger the emotion, the stronger the interest*, of course. If you had, in the above lines, shown Mrs. Moriarity to be facing a serious problem of great emotional intensity you would have gained still stronger listener-interest in her.

Third, you should *individualize* the *character within the type*. There are countless ways of doing this. The character can be given a mannerism, or a peculiarity of speech. One of the best ways, however, is to assign to the character some special capacity that will later be used in the action of the drama.

How can you make Mrs. Moriarity more interesting to the listener and also individualize her within the type? Suppose you do it this way:

OFFICER O'CONNOR

'Good mornin' to ye, Mrs. Moriarity! And how would ye be feelin' this mornin'?'

MRS. MORIARITY

'I'm feelin' awful low in me mind, officer. Glory be, every one of me children is workin' and bringin' home their pay regular as clockwork, and I've got me health so I can do for 'em — but himself, officer, he gets weaker every day. I've always been a great hand for curin' people that was ailin', but with Tim — Tim just keeps slippin' away from me.'

Now you have given Mrs. Moriarity the special capacity of helping people to regain their health, perhaps as much by her cheerful personality and courage, as by her knowledge of nursing. You have also shown her faced by a crisis, the serious illness of her husband. The sum of the reader's emotion toward her has been increased by sympathy and pity, and curiosity as to how she will continue to meet this crisis. Doubt as to the outcome of the crisis — will she succeed in nursing Tim back to health, or will Tim die? — is another listener-interest hook that will help hold the listener until you can get further into your story.

The voice of an actor in a radio drama is of great importance in characterization, but selecting the voice for a part is the business of the director. All the *writer has to do is to characterize his radio actor so clearly that the director will know the type of voice suited to the part.*

Telling the occupation of the actor is one of the best means at your command for characterizing by type. If you let your listener know that your hero is a bricklayer, the listener instantly sees a middle-class workman, steady, dependable, intelligent but not intellectual. All that is left for you to do is individualize the bricklayer within the type. This you can do easily by one of several available means. The bricklayer may be individualized as industrious, and ambitious to become foreman on the construction job on which he is working. Or he may be mean, envious, and revengeful, engaged in an intrigue to frame the present foreman and get him fired. Or he may be in poor health, but continuing to work under great difficulties so that his daughter may finish school. He is still a bricklayer, but any one of the above characterizations will make him also an individual. A banker, a lawyer, a judge, a truck driver, a doctor, a musician, a nursemaid, a housewife: these start the reader's imagination in the direction the radio dramatist wants it to go. Thus the broad outlines are blocked in, leaving the finer work of individualization to be done by deft touches.

Social status is another help in characterizing by type. A man rich enough to own a yacht, the member of an exclusive club, the girl working her way through college, the farmer's son; each of these is characterized by his social status, as to type.

There are, of course, exceptions to this. For example, your character might have the occupation of dishwasher in a cheap restaurant, but his social status might be that of the highly educated son of the president of a railroad. Such a combination, while quite possible to handle in a radio drama, presents difficulties, since the combination of occupation and social status does not, in itself, clearly indicate the type to which the young man belongs, or if he belongs to any well-known and familiar type. He may be a black sheep, a drunkard, and a wastrel; or he may possess courage and initiative, and have left his home and wealth in order to escape intolerable tyranny. Where the type is not clearly indicated by either occupation or social status, the type as well as the individualization within that type may be communicated to the listener in one of the three ways that follow:

1. By dialogue between the major character and a minor character.
2. By dialogue between minor characters concerning the major character.
3. By the announcer.

Let us see how this can be worked out with the character described above:

1. *Characterization by dialogue between the major character and a minor character:*

Setting: Kitchen of a cheap restaurant. Richard is washing dishes.
Characters:
Major character — Richard Haldane, son of the president of a railroad.
Minor character — Pete Slosson, proprietor of the restaurant, Slosson's Eatery.

PETE

Say, fella, you ain't no dishwasher.
(*Rattle of dishes indicates that Richard is working fast.*)

RICHARD

Maybe not. But I'm trying to be, and a darned good one, too. Give me a chance, Mr. Slosson. I need the job.

PETE

Take it easy, son. I'm not goin' to fire you. You're the best dishwasher I've had in five years. You use your head along with your hands. That's how I know you don't belong in no job like this. And call me Pete, my boy. How come you're washin' dishes in Slosson's Eatery?

RICHARD

Look, Pete. You're a good scout. I'll give you the lowdown. Just because my father owns a railroad and sent me to Princeton doesn't mean I have to take orders from him about what I shall do and whom I shall marry, does it?

PETE

Ha! The old man pulled the old Simon Legree stuff on you, did he?

RICHARD

Yes. And I've got to eat, haven't I?

PETE

Sure!

RICHARD

And when a fellow has to pull himself up by the bootstraps, he better start pulling from the first place he can find, hadn't he?

PETE

You bet, son. Well, you already got in your first healthy yank on them bootstraps. How about takin' the job of buyer for the restaurant? I ain't so good at it and I figure a smart, educated fella like you that certainly ain't no mouse, could save me money — and at the same time make some for himself.

In this brief bit of dialogue we have characterized our main actor, Richard, as to type: the young man who runs away from wealth and security to preserve his independence of thought and action. He is individualized within the type by being shown to be determined, courageous, capable, and resourceful. We have also characterized a minor character, Pete Slosson, as to type — he is the almost illiterate owner of a cheap restaurant — and we have individualized him within the type as observant, kindly, and fair. In approximately two hundred words we have not only introduced and characterized two actors, but we have established the purpose of the main actor for the drama, to achieve financial independence in his own way and to marry the girl he loves, not one of his father's choosing. This is an example of the speed with which objectives, and especially the objective of characterization, must and can be achieved in the radio drama.

2. *Characterization by the comment of minor characters:*

Scene: Same as before.

Characters: Jan, the cook.

Luther, the waiter.

JAN

Hey, Luther! Look at that new dishwasher over there that the boss is talkin' to. Fine thing! An educated fella like him, wearin' swell clothes, washin' dishes in a joint like Slosson's Eatery. What's the idea?

LUTHER (*mysteriously*)

Oh, I guess he's got his reasons.

JAN (*sarcastically*)

And of course you know what they are!

LUTHER

Sure I know. At least, I got a pretty good idea.

JAN

How come you're so smart?

LUTHER

Because I read the papers, dummy. Yesterday there was a piece in the *Evening Blade* about him — with a picture. I recognized him in a minute. According to the newspaper, his old man owns the D. and T. Railroad. The old man give this here feller orders to marry some swell dame he'd picked out, but our friend that's rubbin' down dishes over there had another skirt in mind. So he give the old man a Bronx cheer and here he is, consortin' with you an' me.

JAN

Well, he won't be consortin' with us long. A fella that's got nerve enough to leave off bein' a rich man's son and take a job as dish souser in Slosson's Eatery is on his way up, or I'm a burned biscuit.

3. *Characterization by the announcer:*

This is the least desirable way of characterizing any radio actor, since it is done outside the drama itself. But this method is useful at times when it is difficult, if not impossible, to characterize the actor in the first few lines of dialogue, as is sometimes the case when the drama starts with fast, tense action. Let us see what an announcer can do for us in our problem of characterizing Richard Haldane before the radio play begins:

ANNOUNCER

Richard Haldane, a graduate of Princeton and son of Rodney Haldane, President of the D. & T. Railroad, had left his home in Riverside Drive a few days before our story opens. He left suddenly after a violent quarrel with his father, in which the older Haldane ordered Richard to marry Bettina Rossmore, daughter of a multi-millionaire business associate, and abandon what the old man called Richard's 'infatuation' for Lissa Snowden, Rodney's pretty, but penniless, secretary. Since Richard had only a dollar and seventy-nine cents in his pocket at the time, he took the first job he could get, that of dishwasher in the blowsy but prosperous restaurant called Slosson's Eatery. Richard, being as determined as his father, had no intention of remaining in the position of dishwasher very long, but it meant three meals a day and a place to sleep until he could decide what to do next. When our story opens Richard is having a little difficulty with Jan, the cook, and Luther, the waiter. Let's listen.

This is, as you see, designed to lead into an action scene, possibly a fight between Richard and Jan, during which little or no characterization or story-situation could be given the listener because of the fast tempo at which the scene would necessarily proceed.

Because characters in a radio drama must be simple, natural and convincing, the writer should never select for his radio drama characters with which he is not entirely familiar.

The time of day at which your play will be broadcast is another factor that enters into the selection of your characters for radio dramas. Careful surveys have determined that from nine in the morning to three in the afternoon, the majority of listeners are women, for the most part, alone. This audience likes women characters, at least in the leading rôles, who face problems that the listeners face or can easily imagine themselves as facing, and who are having a very, very hard time. Women, listening alone, like to cry and feel the deepest sympathy for the main character in all she is going through. Because this is true, if you are writing a drama to be broadcast between nine and three o'clock, select a main character who will lend herself to this kind of presentation.

From three until six, children make up a large part of the radio audience, and your choice of a character to lead in your radio drama must be guided by this fact. Brave, versatile, cheerful, and almost unbelievably intelligent children now share honors with cowboys, scouts, sailors, treasure hunters, and with district attorneys in the 'crime does not pay' type of drama.

From six-thirty until ten-thirty, family groups, in which men and women predominate, form the largest part of the radio audience, and this condition will of necessity influence your choice of characters. Your main character, especially, should be familiar to the majority of your listeners, be of interest to them and, in addition, should be skillfully individualized within the type. This is the most discriminating audience the radio dramatist has to please. These six-thirty to ten dramas should avoid deep sadness or pure tragedy. Not even the most lachrymose and emotional woman likes to cry over a play when other people are present, and a man hates a radio program that so much as forces him to blow his nose when the little woman and the kids, and maybe the neighbor from next door, are looking. The radio dramatist who hopes to succeed takes all these things into consideration when he selects the characters for his radio drama. For his characters determine his story.

After ten-thirty very few dramas are broadcast. From then on until midnight the majority of radio listeners want music, preferably dance music. And the day is over, as far as the radio dramatist is concerned.

Method of Study

1. What is the main limiting factor in radio characterization?
2. Why must radio characterization be simpler than that of any other medium?
3. Why must radio characterization be done more swiftly and with a greater economy of words than characterization in any other medium?
4. Create two or three characters whom you believe sufficiently interesting to hold listeners, for a twenty-six-weeks run, through a serial drama in which almost nothing happens. Write fifteen hundred words of dialogue between them.

5. Characterize the main actor in a complete fifteen-minute or thirty-minute drama, and establish the opening situation in not more than two hundred words and in the three following ways:

(1) Dialogue between the main character and a minor character.

(2) Dialogue between two minor characters.

(3) By the announcer.

CHAPTER XX

Characterization in the Stage Play and Moving Picture

HOW TO CHARACTERIZE FOR THE STAGE AND SCREEN

It is impossible in one brief chapter to discuss all the aspects of writing for the stage and screen. The subject is so broad and so much has been written concerning it that, for a detailed study of these media, the writer wishing to turn dramatist should consult a number of well-known authorities on the subject.

In this book we are analyzing the essentials of characterization and are considering it, not only basically as such, but in its relation to specific forms of presentation.

Before we begin our examination of characterization for the stage and screen, it will be well for the writer to review the chapters on static and dynamic characterization (Chapters III to X, inclusive), on motivation and contrast (Chapters XII to XIV, inclusive), and on emotion (Chapter XVIII). As in the preceding chapter on radio characterization, I shall again point out that each medium has its special ways of characterizing the actor. Likewise, each medium has its own specific requirements and limitations, both of which the wise writer will keep in mind when considering the form he shall choose. Regardless of the form of presentation or the medium, *all characterization has certain fundamentals in common*.

'Characters are themselves the play. It is their interrelation that works out the story presented,' to quote Arthur Edwin Krows in his 'Playwriting for Profit.' This is another way of phrasing what John

Galsworthy says, that 'Behind action lies the main trend of character.' That is, from this clash of character with character drama grows. This is as true of the short story or novel as it is of the stage play or the scenario. Never forget that *character must reveal itself*, whether the victim of circumstance, or whether that character shapes events to his own ends through his own force.

Character change comes slowly and with *difficulty*, owing to the fact that obstacles can be overcome only with difficulty. It is in this struggle that drama lies. Monologue, which is hardly ever used today and which formerly helped to show the progress of character change and states of mind, has now yielded almost entirely to facial expression, gestures and mannerisms, words and attitudes of other characters and their reactions to one another.

Of course, in that a full three-act play or a movie is equivalent to a novel, you will have more characters to delineate and more time to develop them, but you still will subordinate all others to the two star leads, who become the focal point of audience interest and sympathy. As always, the worth-while characters in a play are the morally good ones or, as Avery Hopwood said, 'Bad women have to be made attractive by giving them beautiful souls — for example, Camille.'

The moving picture and the stage play differ from the radio play in two important particulars that especially concern the writer. The screen and the stage appeal to the eye as well as to the ear, while, as we have seen, the radio play appeals to the ear alone. The screen and stage make far less demands upon the imagination of the audience than does radio. They differ from the book or story in that their presentation is visual, aural, and objective, rather than a mixture of the objective and the subjective appeals to the imagination.

The opportunities offered for characterization by the objective and visual nature of theatrical production, whether on the stage or screen, compensate for the loss of the subjective characterization possible to the writer when he discloses to the reader the thoughts of the actors, or analyzes those thoughts as he does in fiction writing. In dramatics, thought and psychological processes are evident only through speech and action. In other words, they must be shown objectively. Action as action is important as a means by which character can be shown as is dialogue, but the playwright should never neglect the other means at his command, such as appearance, clothing, setting, the general air and furnishings of the character's abode, and those many other means that were discussed in a previous chapter under the heading of 'Appearance Only' (Chapter IV).

CHARACTERIZATION FOR THE STAGE

The limitation of the stage play in characterization is that the audience can know nothing about the character except what it sees and hears during the action of the play. The number of scenes are, as compared to a screen play, very limited. The small number of scenes in a stage play is made necessary by two things: the time required to shift scenes; the cost of making suitable scenery and, in the case of the show going on tour, of transporting it.

This limitation is compensated by the actual presence of the actors, which has a subtle, but strong, psychological influence on the audience. Audiences are likely to react more strongly to actors in the flesh than to the shadows of actors on a screen. A person in the audience is more willing to believe in a character whom he sees before him in flesh and blood, than he is willing to believe in a character, regardless how convincing, whom he knows to be nothing more than a shadow and a sound-track.

Stage characterization has another advantage over the screen in the added time. Most stage shows run about two hours and a half, with intermissions or rest periods. Most screen productions run about an hour and a half with no intermissions or rest periods. Consequently, the writer for the legitimate theatre has more time at his disposal to delineate character, and his audience is not so mentally fatigued as is the case with the movie audience.

In the selecting of his characters, the dramatist is much more free than the writer for the radio or for the screen. The reason for this lies in the fact that the theatre audience is largely adult and is, in addition, a highly selective audience. The average theatre-goer does not attend a play unless he has read reviews of it, heard of it from friends, or in some way has learned what type of play it is, or likes the actor as an artist. Consequently, he knows before he goes the general type of play he is about to see. If he doesn't like that type, he seeks entertainment elsewhere. Hence, while the writer for the radio and the screen aims to please a large number of people, including as many types as possible, the writer for the stage has the same problem as the writer of a book or short story, in that he must slant his work toward a particular group. A group, moreover, that is exceptionally discriminating. Nevertheless, knowing he cannot please everyone, he selects a sufficiently large audience-group to make his writing the play worth while, and then selects characters whom he believes will interest that group.

In stage plays, life can be reproduced perhaps more nearly as it is, in spite of the obvious artificiality of the medium, than in any other form except that of the novel. Both mediums are selective; they appeal chiefly to adults who go to stage productions that they select, and buy books they *choose* to buy. These adults are prepared for and, at least, predisposed to accept your characters and what they do, far more than is the case with either the radio or the screen-play audience.

Because this is true, in a stage play you, as dramatist, may if you are skillful enough present psychological, mental, and physical abnormalities as characters so unusual and strange that very few of the audience, if any at all, have ever seen or known their like. Yet the only requisite for this acceptance is that your characters be convincing to your audience for the duration of the play; that is, while your spell of enchantment is still upon them. Of course, your best chance of success lies with portraying normal people in a highly dramatic period of their lives. With rare exceptions, this is the kind of stage play that attracts the largest audiences over the longest period of time and brings the greatest financial returns to the playwright. The rare success of the play that deliberately flaunts all the above requirements, makes it no less wise for the playwright, who wants to win fame and financial rewards, to remember that most of the people most of the time want to see stage plays about human beings more or less like themselves. Normal human beings facing the same old problems that most of us have to face, in one form or another, in our lives.

CHARACTERIZATION FOR THE SCREEN

Screen characterization, in spite of the wide differences occasioned by the addition of the visual element, has much in common with characterization for radio in that for the picture to be a money-maker, it is slanted toward the same average audience. For that reason, the characters chosen will, of necessity, be fairly simple, and their types familiar to the audience or made familiar by the device of giving them one or two well-understood character traits and emotions. While there is more time actually available for characterization to the writer for the screen than for the radio, the demands of the producers are that this time must be largely given to *advancing* the story and to crowding the play with highly dramatic and emotional scenes.

The pace of the moving picture is every bit as fast as that of the radio play, and much more is demanded of it in the way of richer characterizations, more plot complications and, as a rule, a larger cast of which everyone of any importance has to be more or less fully characterized. This offers no unsurmountable difficulties to the trained dramatist, since he can appeal to the sense of sight, as well as the sense of hearing. His audience can *see* the character of his actors in their faces, their manners, their gestures, their clothing, their background.

The screen writer is very little, if any, more free in his choice of characters than is the radio-play writer; that is, if he wants his picture to have a wide audience appeal. As yet, the screen is not the medium for presenting the completely rounded character of the psychological character-conflict story. While many movie stories have themes, as yet many stories of mental conflict of a psychological and philosophical nature have not been filmed, probably because such subject matter, with the emphasis upon character development rather than upon action, has a limited audience appeal. However, *The Informer*, *The Scoundrel*, *Winterset*, and *Wuthering Heights* have been more or less box-office successes. It is to be hoped that we shall have an ever-increasing number of such pictures.

As with all writing, sympathetic characterization is the most important factor in the film story. The audience is interested in the chief actor and what *happens* to him and in what *action* he is involved. Through him the audience experiences vicariously a wide range of emotions and a varied life. Through their imaginations, for the duration of the picture, they are the hero, they would act from the same motive he acts; he is their model, the suggestion for their ideas.

Characterization for the screen must be very definite, with not more than two dominant major characters usually opposing each other and, as a result, arousing in the audience contrasting emotions. What was said in Chapter IV about the importance of names and reader-reactions to them, also applies to theatre audiences.

However, the screen has one serious disadvantage in presenting convincing characters, from the audience point of view as compared either to the stage or to radio; that is, the double-feature performance. But since he has no power to ban it, the screen writer has no means of overcoming this handicap; hence, he need not concern himself with it. Yet what of this fact, from the point of view of audience emotional reaction, when the *same character* is in both features, in either a major or a minor rôle!

As is often the case in the first feature, an actor may be cast in a likable rôle, let us say that of a generous bachelor uncle of several impecunious nieces and nephews. Of course, the audience has seen the actor time and again before in other rôles, but months have passed and they accept, for approximately two hours, the illusion that is presented to them with the actor as a generous bachelor uncle. The picture ends with the nice bachelor surrounded by his affectionate foster family. Comes feature two. The first scene is flashed on the screen and the audience sees the man who, only five minutes before, was a self-respecting, wealthy, kindly member of society, has become Bull Crauch, a sodden drunk and father of six dirty, unpleasant-looking children. This requires considerable emotional readjustment on the part of the audience, sometimes more than a majority of them are able to make, no matter how great the skill of the screen writer and the interpretive skill of the actor may be.

The artist in any medium should make the fullest use of the opportunities of his medium, and this is true of the artist who writes for the screen as it is of the artist who expresses himself through the medium of paint, or clay, or marble. The unique opportunity that the screen offers for characterization is the *swiftness and ease with which it can change scenes*. True, radio can change scenes without expense and without waiting for scene shifters and the lowering and raising of a curtain, as is demanded on the stage, but the radio is forced to set the new scene either through description, however brief, by the announcer, or by dialogue between the actors themselves. True, radio writers are becoming more and more clever at shifting scenes clearly and with the minimum of words, but the limitations of their medium will never allow them to entirely dispense with the use of words and the consequent spending of time in which to say them in scene-shifting.

On the contrary, the screen, in dozens of scenes and a handful of seconds, permits the spectator to see character growth or change that in reality took many years to accomplish. This is done by swift series of scenes, many or all of them merely flashes on the screen, showing significant moments in the life of the character being portrayed. This method is called a lap-dissolve or a wipe sequence. The names are derived from the fact that the scenes either overlap slightly and dissolve into each other, or they seem to be wiped off the screen. *This device allows the screen writer to characterize his actors visually and aurally, with a speed and effectiveness available in no other medium.*

In addition to the lap-dissolve device, which is so extremely useful in characterization, the screen writer can show his actor as reacting characteristically in dozens of situations, places, and circumstances, or to one situation, place, or circumstance. This is impossible in a story, book, radio play, or stage play. The only limitation in this regard that faces the scenario writer is the budget for making the picture. Since directors are convinced that the frequent change of scene is highly conducive to holding audience-interest, the added cost of filming a hundred or even more short scenes need not worry the writer. For example, you might have a young man in your screen play who shrinks from any display of physical force, and who some actors in your cast think is a coward. You take your reader back to a scene in his childhood when as a small, sensitive boy his father overpowered him and gave him a brutal beating because of some small disobedience. This is followed by a lap-dissolve sequence showing the boy witnessing a brutal fight between a big man and a little one in which the small one was badly injured and he, the boy, set upon by a group of small ruffians and beaten into unconsciousness. There might be other scenes of a similar nature. In each one the boy is a little older, until the lap-dissolve brings him to the present of your play, his character-trait of hatred and fear of physical violence firmly entrenched as mental and emotional habits. All this may be accomplished in a little less or a little more than a minute's time.

And yet, there are limitations of characterization on the screen: Your characters must appeal to many types of people and degrees of mentality. They must be readily understood and universally acceptable. The screen audience is only one degree more selective than the radio audience. Practically everybody goes to the movies, and probably less than fifty per cent deliberately choose the movie to which they shall go. Even that choice is often limited by what is showing that afternoon or evening, the decision to go to a movie, any movie, often preceding the choice as to what movie it shall be. Therefore, complex characters, characters having abnormal mental attributes, qualities, states, or psychological curiosities, these are not good material for screen plays. That there are exceptions to this in the more lurid mystery and horror plays is quite true. But these are exceptions and, compared with the number of wholesome plays about normal people that are filmed, such types are only a small minority.

Both the screen and stage play have one tremendous advantage over the radio play in the immediacy of the character-appeal to the audience.

There is the power of the crowd psychology, a crowd being much more susceptible to emotional suggestion than any individual in it if that individual were alone. There is the focusing of attention on a single point, the stage in one case, the screen in the other; by the darkness of the theatre itself and the focusing of bright light on the action going forward. There is the absence of interruptions, of distractions. All this allows the writer to paint his characters with far greater detail. He can use a camel's-hair brush instead of a whitewash brush. Consequently be can achieve much more subtle effects.

The wise artist looks for the limitations and the advantages of his medium. He wastes no time bemoaning its limitations. Frankly accepting them, he turns them to his own use wherever possible and seeks new and better methods of compensating for them. This can best be done by a careful study of the advantages of any medium, and the opportunities it offers for artistic expression. A determined effort to make the fullest and most intelligent use both of the limitations and advantages of a medium has many times resulted in a masterpiece of achievement. The best-known example of this that comes to mind is the painting of the story of the Creation by Michelangelo on the broken surfaces of the ceiling of the Sistine Chapel. Perhaps no great work of art was ever produced under such limitations and disadvantages. Yet if Michelangelo voiced a single complaint, it has not come down to us. He accepted the limitations and used them toward his own ends, producing one of the greatest masterpieces of painting the world has ever seen.

So, use the limitations of these different media insofar as they affect characterization as a means to finer, more artistic work, not as unsurmountable obstacles in your path to the successful creation of *characters that live.*

Method of Study

1. What is the chief limitation in the movie, in reference to characterization?
2. What is the chief limitation of the stage play in reference to characterization?
3. What is the chief advantage of each of the above?
4. Characterize a likable character and a villain-character as fully as possible in one page of dialogue written for stage presentation.
5. Characterize a likable character in one scene and a lap-dissolve sequence suitable for screen presentation.

CHAPTER XXI

Characterization in the Novel

HOW TO SHOW CHARACTER-CHANGES

It has been said by people qualified to judge that the novel is the highest form of art. This does not mean that every novel is an artistic production of any kind or to any degree. It means that the true artist, working through the novel form, may reach greater heights of artistic expression than with any other medium since, in the novel, life may be approximated more closely and in more of its aspects than in, for example, a short story, a poem, a picture, a statue, or a symphony. Whether or not this be true, it will be generally agreed that, for the portrayal of character, the novel offers a wider field than any other of the arts, or than any other literary form. Poetry, even in the epic, concerns itself with character to a less degree. The play, whether presented on the stage or screen, is limited in two respects. In the first place, it must *condense* into a certain number of scenes to meet audience-endurance; and second, its objective presentation allows no opportunity for *subtle* analysis of character-reactions as expressed in thought or action. The limitations of the radio are too obvious to require capitulation here. The short story, because of its brevity, can present only a partial picture of any character, and can almost never fully show either character-growth or character-deterioration. The characterization in a short story, in the sense that it can show so little change, is static, and all action is kept consistent with the character as it is first delineated.

In the novel, however, the major characters, at least, should show either growth or deterioration, if the writer is to take advantage of the wider field offered him by this medium. The wide scope of a novel affords the time, and the wide variety of impacts from without, that are necessary to character-change. There will be changes of environment, changes in situation, and in emotional reaction.

Novels in which character-change does not take place do not fulfill the highest functions of this literary form, though they may be entertaining and make the writers a great deal of money. They are not novels at all in the real sense of the word, but long stories that, provided they are interesting, fulfill a real need. No criticism of them is intended; they are merely being classified.

In this chapter we are considering characterization in the novel. It is at once evident that characterization in the novel takes advantage of all the ways and methods of characterization used in other literary forms, except the use of the voice as in radio. This is, of course, barred to the novelist. But the novel form has three advantages that the other forms lack:

1. The large number and wide variety of scenes, situations, and interchanges that are possible.
2. The great number and length of descriptive passages that the reader will accept, provided they are entertainingly written.
3. The possibility, even advisability, of much more analysis and interpretative comment on the characters.
4. The development of a theme or philosophy or 'message' that the reader will accept as part of the story.

All these tend to create fuller and more subtle shadings of characterization. The advantages listed under number 1 enable the writer to show character-change, whether growth or deterioration, under the impact of many physical, mental, and emotional stimuli. The advantages listed under number 2 permit the writer to show a character reacting to a number of different and perhaps highly contrasted environments and settings. The advantages under number 3 permit the writer to clarify the significance of what is, presumably, the purpose of the novel; namely, the character-change of the main actor and the influences that brought it about. Number 4 gives the opportunity to 'point a moral' subtly, it is to be hoped, and as an integral part of the novel material.

Since the characterization of the people in your novel is necessarily so much more complete than would be the case in any of the other literary forms, it follows that your *understanding* of your characters must also be more complete. As always, *this understanding must precede any successful attempt to communicate these characters to the reader by means of words.* Neither is understanding all that is required. *You must also feel strongly toward them and about them.* Understanding has to do with the mind. Feeling has to do with the emotions. And if you are going to rouse any emotion in your readers toward your characters, it is necessary that you understand them, be intensely interested in them, and feel emotionally toward them. In other words, your characters must seem just as real to you, as you hope to make them seem to the reader. They cannot seem real to you until you know their past as well as their present environment, their heredity, education, preferences in clothing, food, hobbies, pet hates, and dozens of other things. You will then know what they will wear on all occasions, what they like to do, their philosophy of life, and how they will *react* to any and all situations and circumstances. More than this, you must understand the movement of ᵗheir minds.

The source, the very fountainhead of all knowledge of character and, therefore, of characterization, is in the writer himself. As no stream can rise higher than its source, no writer can create characters that he himself does not understand, because in him is something of that created character. No man who has not within himself some of the qualities of sainthood can create the character of a saint. No man who has not in himself some of the qualities of a villain can create a convincing villain. It is not enough to look at the people about you and try to understand them, though that, too, is important. But you must look within yourself for the final touch of reality that will make the characters, in your novel, live for the reader.

Novels are, in the very nature of things, to a greater or less degree biographical. With the young novelist, I believe this to be almost entirely true. You may change the incidents, the settings, the names past all recognition, but your life, your experiences, your emotions, and your philosophy will live again in the characters of your novels. This you cannot help — even if you would. Indeed, you should not attempt to do so, since your life, experiences, emotion, and philosophy all will contribute richly to your work and help you to achieve a temporary, if anonymous, immortality.

Now let us make a closer and more specific examination of the greater advantages for characterization offered by the novel form than by those of other literary media.

1. *The large number and variety of scenes, situations, and interchanges*
   In the novel, you may, if you wish, begin with your main character or

characters as children, thus showing their heredity, that is, their parents and the environmental influences of their formative years. You may devote few or many scenes to any phase of your story, as seems best, with interchanges between widely contrasted characters, and their emotional and character-forming results. You may then take your characters on through adolescence and into adult life, showing them living under the different environment of a farm, a small town, and a city, or vice versa. Or you may keep the same general environment throughout, securing a variety of situations and actions by the *reactions of contrasted characters to each other and to varying situations and complications.*

2. *Number and length of descriptive and analytical or interpretative passages*

Character is often, if not always, influenced by environment. Therefore, descriptions of environment, whether it be a room, a village, a city, or a lonely mountain-peak, are often very significant indications of character-traits, both in themselves and as they combine to make a character. This calls for a certain amount of interpretative comment, or interpolations by the writer, in order that the significance of the descriptions in relation to the character may be clear to the reader.

3. *More analyses and interpretative comment concerning the characters themselves*

In other literary forms, analyses of characters and interpretative comment regarding them, either by other characters or by the writer, should be done very briefly if at all. In the novel both these ways of characterizing may be used freely, provided, of course, they are written in an arresting manner. This permits the writer to give a well-rounded impression of his characters and their conflicting or contrasting character-traits as they appear to other characters and as the reader himself sees them. The advantages of this to the novel are of the utmost importance.

In short stories and even to a great extent in plays, the major characters must act at all times in a manner consistent with their dominant character-trait, but the *wider scope of the novel allows the writer to show his characters as motivated now by one desire and now by another.* Consistence is achieved by having the character act in harmony with his *general trend of character-growth or character-deterioration,* as the case might be. If character-growth, his admirable actions would tend to increase in frequency and his wrong actions to decrease in frequency; while if his general character-changes were toward deterioration, the condition would be reversed.

Novels can be classified under two broad headings: novels that depend mainly on characterization for their interest, and novels that depend mainly on plot. In neither can characterization be neglected, or even slighted. The finest novels of our time depend neither on one nor the other; rather, to a marked degree on both. A sound plot is necessary to show characters in action, and character must be in action to sustain the attentive interest of the reader. 'Living' characters are needed to carry a plot forward, for a plot acted out by puppets is a sure way of putting the reader to sleep. Of the two, plot and character, the characters should come first, as in Chapter XVI we have seen that characters create their own plots.

In the psychological novel, action is less necessary to reveal character, because psychological states can be depicted by the author or interpreted by other characters instead of their being visualized in action. This particular type of novel has a definite appeal to the special reader whose interest lies, because of his understanding, in the reasons or causes that underlie the inhibited action of the character. Hence such a reader is not concerned by the fact that 'nothing happens' in the psychological character-conflict story. His interest is in the mental states of that character.

Take time to create the characters for your novel. Let them *grow and develop in your mind*, as you get to know them. The first hour, or day or week, that you know a man you do not get to know his real character. You have to see that man under varying conditions and over a period of time before his character becomes 'round' to you. The same is true of your characters that you expect to put in a novel. Live with them. Think about them. Visualize them in different environments and in different situations. See how they would react under this stimulus and that stimulus. Imagine these scenes as if they were scenes in all their details. After you have done this for a few weeks or months, you will have no difficulty in making your characters seem real to your readers, because they will *seem real to you*. Then be sure that the central or chief problem of the hero is a vital one to him. A real character with a real problem are the ingredients out of which is built a real story.

Then, when the time comes to write your novel, take advantage of every technical device you know for characterizing your brain-people, and *deliberately plan* to use to the fullest the special advantages for characterization offered by the novel form, the one in which you have chosen to work.

Method of Study

1. Why is the novel said to be the highest art form that has yet been developed?
2. What are the advantages of the novel form for characterization?
3. Is characterization in novels simpler or more complicated than in other literary forms?
4. Write a brief description of an environment with interpretive comments on the way a character was influenced by the environment described.
5. Write an analysis of a character in order to interpret him to a reader.

CHAPTER XXII

Characterization in Juvenile Writing

HOW TO CHARACTERIZE CHILDREN

How to characterize children is not one problem, but two problems; and while these problems are related, they do not overlap, though a few general principles apply to both. The first problem is that of characterizing children for adults; the second is that of characterizing children for other children. In juvenile characterization, more completely perhaps than in any other field of writing, *your choice of a definite method is determined by the audience or group for which you are writing.* We shall return to this subject later when we come to observe the specific differences between characterizing children for adults, and characterizing children for children.

Let us examine the fundamental and generally accepted laws that govern juvenile characterization both for the adult and juvenile audience. *The first requisite for convincing juvenile characterization for either audience is that you know children.* You must know them so completely and so thoroughly that you will experience no difficulty in depicting your story-characters as thinking, speaking, and acting as real children of their age, background, and character-traits might reasonably be expected to think, act, and speak. Don't attempt to write a story about a five-year-old boy, unless you know or have known a five-year-old boy who at least approximates the character in your story. Don't try to write a story about an adolescent girl unless you know just such an adolescent girl, and know her well. It is preferable that you know several. A composer can write variations on a theme only when he is completely familiar with that theme. You may be successful in putting the girl you know into a story, but if you want to *vary* the theme in *other* stories you should know several adolescent girls, each differing from the other in basic character-traits.

Children neither think, speak, nor talk like adults, except in rare cases. These rare cases do not often make good fictional material because of the extreme difficulty of making these children plausible and convincing to the reader.

No child-character, of whatever age and created for whatever audience, should be characterized as wholly bad. The bad things the plot of the story requires him to do are shown to be the result of environment, wrong or mistaken action of one or both parents, or of other persons in authority. There is no such thing in fiction as the thoroughly bad child. Reader-liking, or at least reader-sympathy, must be kept for the child-character. In stories where naughty children appear, their naughtiness is excused explicitly or tacitly, for the reason that they *are* children; or because their naughtiness is only temporary, induced by lack of understanding, or knowledge of the facts; or they are impelled to do what they do by the act or influence of an adult. This is because most people believe, or find it more pleasant to read stories that stress the belief, that good environment and wise guidance are all that are needed for the development of the model child and, in time, the model citizen. This conception, whether true or false, must be accepted as a fact by the writer who uses juvenile characters in his stories.

Still another important point in juvenile characterization is the matter of word selection, or vocabulary. Children, no less than adults, are characterized and made to seem real by the *words* they use and by the arrangement of those words. Here again it is imperative that you know the living prototypes of your juvenile fictional characters. If you do not, how can you be sure that the children of your brain talk as similar children in real life talk? Of course, wide latitude in vocabulary usage is possible and permissible. However, any marked deviation from the generally accepted mode of speech would demand explanation and become, in turn, an element of characterization. For example, an only child, without playmates, who has been brought up among intellectual, even scholarly, adults and, never having been allowed to go to school, has received his education from a private tutor, would not speak as a normal child, brought up in the normal American way. In a case of this kind, the child's unusual vocabulary would be an aid to truthful characterization, but the reason for his using it would have to be made clear. This, also, would have to be used with care, in order that it might show the mentality and thinking processes of a child, expressing themselves through an adult vocabulary, or the vocabulary of a child much older mentally than his actual age.

While there is nothing that will take the place of first-hand familiarity with the vocabulary actually used by the age-group to which your characters belong, writers can obtain valuable help with individual words through certain books arranged by educators for the teaching in schools of vocabularies to various age-groups. These lists, which are compiled of words in general use by children, are helpful guideposts against such vocabulary blunders as the following, put into the mouth of a seven year-old boy:

> 'Father, what you say is incomprehensible to me and your constant interruptions destroy my pleasure in the game of checkers I am playing with my friend James, who has recently moved into the neighborhood.'

No, this is not impossible or exaggerated. In student manuscripts, I have read hundreds of such speeches, put forcibly into the mouths of child-characters. Of course, I have read many more where the fault was not so glaring, yet still sufficient to destroy all illusion of reality in the character being portrayed. *Words used, word arrangement, and the way words are spoken, cannot be given too much careful thought in the characterization of children, if you want your story-children to 'come alive' and not to be mere stilted caricatures of the real thing.* Never forget the importance of dialogue in characterization.

Very few writers make the mistake of characterizing children for an adult story in a way suitable only to a child audience. It is a common error, however, for them to characterize children in a story obviously slanted toward child readers in a way that would appeal only to the adult reader. This mistake is possible only when the writer forgets the group for which he is writing, and writes for his own pleasure, not for his reader's entertainment. In such a case, the writer allows his own feeling and his own viewpoint to predominate. *In no field of writing is it safe to forget for a moment the group for which you are writing.* This mistake is especially unfortunate in its results when it is made in stories written for juveniles. The reason is that children do not and cannot have more than a vague notion of the adult viewpoint, while one adult group may sense to some extent, and be partially able to comprehend, the viewpoint of another adult group. Neither can children understand words outside their vocabulary, nor can they follow introspection, except of the simplest kind. This is true in varying degrees from the youngest group for which writing is done, up to and including the adolescent group.

I wish to mention here that it will make your writing easier if you will remember that in stories written for juveniles, adults, if they appear at all, should be given decidedly minor rôles and be treated as background characters. There is considerably wider latitude, in this respect, in the use of children in stories for adults. Sometimes all the characters in a story for adults are children; sometimes the major characters are children and adults enact minor rôles, and sometimes children and adults are almost equally balanced in importance, with their separate stories woven together into a unified plot. The reason for this difference is that children, while dependent upon adults, are deeply interested only in their own affairs. Their interest in adult affairs and problems rarely goes beyond the point where those affairs and problems affect their own lives in immediate ways that they can understand. But, on their part, most adult readers are deeply interested in and sympathetic toward children and their problems.

CHARACTERIZING CHILDREN FOR ADULT READERS

Let us now turn our attention to the problem of how to characterize children in stories for adults. But before we begin to characterize, however, we must select a character. To do this, let us make a list of the emotions an adult is most likely to feel toward a child. These must, of course, be fictionally acceptable. The following incomplete list is presented merely for illustration:

1. Tender amusement.
2. A desire to protect.
3. A trust that is justified.
4. Regret, even sorrow, because of a lack of understanding and sympathy on the part of the adult character.

We see the reason when we remember that adults read stories of children to reminisce about their own childhood. If you question this, re-read Booth Tarkington's 'Seventeen' or 'Alice Adams' or Mark Twain's 'Huckleberry Finn.' On the other hand, when adults read stories written for children, it is usually for the enjoyment of the whimsy, the exquisite presentation, the symbolism, the philosophy, or the satire. In other words, the adult reads stories written for children for other reasons than the mere story; he reads for the entertainment value that comes from his adult point of view or the implications inherent in the story; whereas a child reads just to be entertained or to enlarge his field of experience. If you have not re-read in recent years Kingsley's 'Water Babies,' Andersen's 'Fairy Tales,' Carroll's 'Alice in Wonderland,' and 'Through the Looking-Glass,' do so; then analyze the reason for your enjoyment and you will know how true this is.

These emotions not only suggest characters, but they suggest plots as well: Tender amusement suggests adolescent characters with their infinite capacity for suffering and their earnestness in matters that seem so unimportant to the adult mind. A desire to protect suggests an unhappy child who is the victim of circumstances. A trust that is justified suggests a modern adolescent faced with the problems of his age, whose fine character brings him safely through temptations and dangers. Regret and sorrow suggest the juvenile character repressed or misunderstood to the point of tragedy by an adult who does not realize his responsibility in the matter until too late.

In characterizing a child for the adult reader, emphasis may be placed on the psychological states and mental conflicts of a complicated nature. Of these, of course, the child is only dimly conscious. It is clear that he cannot understand or analyze them. For example, a little girl of eight may react violently toward her stepmother who is both understanding and affectionate. This child has no idea that the underlying reason is her resentment at having someone take the place of her own much-loved mother, as well as usurping her own unique place in her father's formerly undivided attentions. Such a child would be fundamentally sensitive, affectionate, responsive to love, and, no doubt, thoroughly admirable, once she is understood. Her psychological and mental states would be objectified in action, and the reader would get to know her through characterization based on analysis. Once the child is characterized and her *motives* shown, she may act in a very disagreeable manner without forfeiting reader-sympathy.

Or your juvenile character may be a shy, timid little boy, who feels that he is unloved and unwanted when the new baby comes, because all attention, even that of his mother, is centered on the new arrival. Show him acting in shy timid ways, shrinking from attention, seeking to efface himself, contemplating running away from home. The result will surely stir reader-sympathy.

While no hard and fast rules can be laid down, it is usually better when characterizing juvenile characters for adults to accomplish your purpose as objectively as possible; that is, not to go into the character's mind any more than is absolutely necessary. There are two reasons for this. One is to avoid sentimentality, or the 'Oh, you poor darling!' type of writing, and yet, at the same time, to appeal to the imagination of the reader by showing what the child does, rather than what he thinks. The other reason is, it takes an exceptional adult to know what a child thinks, let alone express his thoughts and make them sound convincing. The truth of the matter is, no adult knows how or what a child thinks, unless that child is an adolescent, and even then the matter is somewhat in doubt. Perhaps some adults can remember the mental attitudes, states, and thoughts of their childhood, but usually any thinking back is hazy and unreliable. Yet adults do know what children *do*, and can get from their actions a fairly accurate picture of their emotions. That is why it is better, in the main, when writing stories about juveniles for adults, to depend largely on actions to express mental states and emotions.

It is well to remind the writer that the younger the child, the less he thinks, in the true sense of the word. His thoughts about any except the simplest experiences are formless and incoherent. Small children live almost completely through feeling and action. Therefore, their thoughts are of very little use, even if writers knew what they were, in characterizing the child actor for the adult reader; for, as I said above, the characterization must take into account mental and psychological states of which the child himself is only dimly, if at all, conscious. The situation is somewhat different in characterizing children for children, as we shall see when we come to discuss that phase of juvenile characterization.

The points to keep in mind, then, when characterizing children for adult readers, are:

1. Know the child.
2. Be sure that his vocabulary and actions are natural and convincing.
3. Use, as much as your material permits, the objective and analytical methods of presentation.

CHARACTERIZING CHILDREN FOR JUVENILE READERS

When choosing a juvenile character that will interest juvenile readers, our task is much simpler than when choosing a juvenile character to interest an adult reader. A likable, lively child of approximately his own age, or preferably a little older, who does interesting things, is practically sure to hold the attention of the juvenile reader. In order to please the editors and the parents, give the main juvenile character a good purpose for the story, and this purpose should be a natural outgrowth of his good character. When writing for girls, you may give the main rôle either to a girl or a boy, but when writing for boys, girls are only allowed in background rôles, if at all. It is best to study the publication to which you intend to submit your story to find out its particular bias in this respect.

In writing juvenile fiction, it is well that you bear in mind that, although the pill is sugar-coated, the purpose of the story is to teach the child reader a lesson wherein right is always rewarded and wrong is always punished. The villains in stories for children are usually situations, forces of nature, conflicts within the child-character himself, or misunderstandings between the children-characters themselves or between them and adults. There are exceptions, of course, but generally speaking, the villain in a story for children is not a person, either juvenile or adult, but some force or trait.

For juvenile readers the characterization must be simple, and such that the reader, whatever his age-group may be, can readily understand. Children often have very complex characters, but such character complications are understandable and interesting only to the adult reader.

For example, let us characterize a little girl of about eight years for juvenile readers, and then for adult readers, and use the same character-traits and the same scene. The characterization for the juvenile readers will necessarily have to be simple and direct:

> Ettie took two sugar cookies from the blue jar on the kitchen shelf and tucked them into her red-and-white braided straw lunch basket. Just as she was fastening the basket shut she remembered something.
>
> 'Mother,' she said, 'may I take two more cookies?'
>
> 'What for, dear?' her mother asked.
>
> 'I want to give them to Susie. She's a new girl at school. Yesterday was her first day, and she hasn't any special friend. If I give her the cookies maybe she'll know I'd like to be her special friend.'
>
> 'Of course you may take the cookies,' said Ettie's mother.
>
> 'Oh, thank you!' Ettie cried, as she dashed out the door.

Ettie is a simple character that other eight-year-olds can understand. She wants to be kind to the strange new girl at school and she is grateful to her mother for furnishing her the means by which she hopes to accomplish her purpose. The child reader is interested because he understands Ettie's purpose and wants to know whether she and Susan become friends or not.

Now, how would we characterize Ettie in a story for adults?

'Hurry, Ettie, or you'll be late to school,' said Mrs. Lander, Ettie's stepmother, as she piled the breakfast dishes in the sink.

'Yes, Mother,' Ettie said, as she took two sugar cookies from the blue jar on the kitchen shelf and tucked them into her red-and-white braided straw lunch basket. Just as she was fastening the basket shut, she thought of something she'd planned the afternoon before on her way home from school.

'Mother,' Ettie said, 'may I take two more cookies?'

'Why, what for, dear?' her mother asked. 'You can't possibly eat so many.'

'I want to give them to a new little girl who only started to our school yesterday. Her name is Susie, and I like her an awful lot.'

'But darling, she brings her own lunch, doesn't she?'

'Yes, Mother, but ——' Ettie stood wiggling the lid of her lunch basket up and down, as though struggling with an idea that was too big for her.

'Go on, sweet.'

'Susie is a stranger,' Ettie frowned intently as she tried to explain. 'She looked like she didn't like being a stranger, but she didn't know how to stop being one. It's — it's a hurting feeling, mummy.'

Suddenly Mrs. Lander knelt down by Ettie and put her arms around the little girl. 'Why, honey, how do you know?'

'Because,' Ettie almost whispered, 'when I started to school here — that was before you married Daddy and came to be my mother — I felt just like Susie looked yesterday. I thought,' she went on, her voice getting stronger, 'that if I gave her two of your good sugar cookies she'd know I don't feel like a stranger to her and then maybe she wouldn't feel like a stranger to me any more.'

Mrs. Lander made a little choking sound, then got up suddenly and busied herself with the dishes, her back to Ettie. It was a moment before she spoke, then she said: 'Take the cookies, darling, and run along. You might ask Susie to come home with you after school if you want to. I'll make you chocolate ——'

'Oh, Mother, you're the friendliest person!' Ettie cried as she slammed her lunch basket shut and raced out the door.

This second characterization shows Ettie as a much more complex person, feeling much more complicated emotions than the characterization for juvenile readers. It centers the attention of the reader on

Ettie, as a person, rather than on her Purpose, and her stepmother is also characterized much more fully. Both scenes are objectively presented; that is, the story is told through what Ettie did and what she said.

Simplicity and naturalness are the two most important requisites in characterizing children, whether the characterization be done for children or for adults. It all goes back to the fundamental principle that to communicate to your reader the true character of an actor in your story, you must know that character thoroughly and from the inside, not superficially, and from the outside only. You must understand him subjectively as well as objectively, even though you should present him entirely from the objective viewpoint. *For actions and words are nothing but emotions and mental states objectified.* Actions can be made convincing and emotionally moving only when the light of characteristic emotions and mental states shines through, illuminating them and making them significant.

Method of Study

1. What are the two main problems, or phases, of juvenile characterization?
2. What is the position or rôle of adults in stories written for children?
3. What are the fundamental requisites of the major story-character in a story written for children?
4. Write a character-analysis of Ettie and of her stepmother, setting down the character-traits and emotions of each as shown by the characterization of Ettie for juvenile readers. For adult readers.
5. Write an original characterization of:
   (*a*) a child for juvenile readers.
   (*b*) the same child for adult readers.

CHAPTER XXIII

It's Easy—After You Learn How

'But in Art excuses count for nothing;
good intentions are of no avail.'

MARCEL PROUST

THE familiar remark, 'It's easy — after you learn how,' when applied to characterization, is not merely a smart, flippant saying; it embodies a profound truth. Really good characterization cannot be written until it has become easy, for the same fundamental reason that one does not play good golf until one has developed a faculty in playing good golf.

Characterization in fiction is an art, just as surely as portrait-painting is an art, or that sculpture is an art. No matter how talented a person may be, he cannot attain proficiency in any art until he has mastered the technique and the special skills demanded by his medium.

Gaining proficiency in any art is not entirely a matter of acquiring a set of mental conceptions or memorizing a list of technical rules, though these play an important part. *The more important phase of acquiring skill is that which has to do with the growth and development of the artist* himself. Three things are necessary to facilitate this growth and development: definite *knowledge* of specific procedures that are likely to produce the best results; *experimentation,* to determine the line of development best suited to the talents of the artist; and *practice* in applying what is learned. The sooner the writer realizes that a *knowledge* of the craftsmanship, of the *how* to do, frees him to concentrate on the artistic presentation of his material, the sooner will he become the successful writer.

Whatever his field may be, the feeling of the artist toward his material is of such tremendous importance that I do not believe any worth-while piece of work can be created if this feeling is absent. Certainly countless thousands of stories, books, and plays have failed to reach publication because their authors did not *feel* keenly about their material. A large percentage of stories, books, and plays that do reach publication or production would have been vastly better and more successful if their authors had been more emotionally involved in the lives and fates of their characters. When you feel strongly about some-one in real life, you do not have to stop and think how to communicate the character of that person to someone else. If you hate a man, you do not fumblingly search for words to tell your listener what an unmiti-gated rascal that man is. If you admire someone greatly, you find it quite easy to present that person to others as you see him. You know what words to say and how to say them and, where feeling is strong, you do it without conscious thought.

Of course, writing has a great advantage over extemporaneous speech in that a story, book, or play can be *planned* before the words are writ-ten, and they can be checked for effectiveness after they are written. But *ease and facility in the actual creative effort of writing do not come until practice enables the mind to select and arrange the material and the words below the level of conscious thought to a greater or less degree.*

This being true, you can see the importance, even the necessity, for experimentation and practice *before* the writer sits down with the con-sidered purpose of writing a story for *The Saturday Evening Post, The Atlantic Monthly, Harper's Magazine, Esquire,* or whatever publication may be his goal. Writers do not often sell their first story to a top mag-azine, or to any magazine at all, though such things do happen. When this does occur, the result is often highly disastrous to the writer, be-cause he then thinks he is a professional and has nothing more to learn. Sometimes years go by before he discovers his mistake, years of striving, of discouragement, and of failure, until he realizes that his first sale was an accident in almost the same way that it would be an accident if he hit the bull's-eye the first time he shot a rifle in target practice. Continued success in any activity, whether art, profession, trade, or business, must rest on a solid foundation of specific knowledge and acquired skills, plus a certain amount of talent. Perhaps it seems strange that I place talent last in my list of requirements for success, but I have seen too many people with a small amount of talent achieve remarkable success by hard, intelligent, and directed work, not to believe firmly that specific ability or talent, while necessary, does not play the important part in artistic achievement that it is popularly supposed to do. Certainly, even

great talent is no guarantee of success, because many people who possess
talent almost to the point of genius achieve no success whatsoever until
they *direct* and control their talent by hard work, practice, and intelligent discipline. I like to remember the advice of Zola: 'Work! This says
it all. The worst misfortune that can befall a beginner is to arrive too
soon. Behind every solid reputation are twenty years of effort and toil.'

The first step toward learning how to characterize your fictional
actors is to find a method of work that appeals to you as practical and as
being devised along commonsense lines. The next step is to follow this
method, varying it as little as possible and only when you are convinced
that such variation is necessary to make it more nearly meet your individual needs. Discipline yourself to regular hours of work, and to controlled thinking. Do not be afraid to experiment. Your mistakes may
be more valuable to you in the beginning than your successes. Much of
the learning of any art is concerned with the discovery for one's self of
what not to do. Don't rush the words down on paper. Instead, learn to
think creatively, to *plan* your characters as you must plan your plot.

There is only one way to gain facility in doing anything, and to gain
facility in characterization is no exception to this rule. That way is by
practice. *Not until you are freed from the necessity of giving the greater part
of your attention to the mechanics of an art can you really use that art as a
channel for your creative power.* So practice writing characterization.

Fortunately, the raw materials for characterization are all around
you. Unlike the painter and the sculptor, you do not have to pay a
model to pose for you. Every person you know, every person to whom
you are introduced, even every person you meet by chance on the street,
is a potential model for the practice of your art. And you do not even
have to ask his permission.

Before you begin to use one of these countless models that are available to you, analyze yourself and discover what emotion, if any, you
feel toward that person. If you do not feel any emotion, pass that person
by as not a good model for you, because, since *you* feel no emotion, you
will be unable to rouse any emotion toward that person in your reader
and without emotion of some kind there can be no interest.

Perhaps you see an old woman sitting on a busy downtown corner
playing a battered violin for the coins passersby may toss into her tin
cup. What is the emotion she rouses in you? Not the emotion you think
you ought to feel, but the one you really do feel. Perhaps, believing her
poverty to be real and seeing in her face the evidences of a toil-filled and

unselfish life, you are moved by a profound pity. In that case, *let the reader see her as you see her*, and so rouse in him the emotion that is yours.

But perhaps the old woman's face looks hard and her eyes bold and scheming. Now what emotion do you feel toward her? Perhaps your emotion is compounded of contempt and a pity that she has lived so long and learned so little of how to achieve real happiness. Whatever your emotion may be, let it help you to communicate the character of this old woman, as you see it, to your reader.

The emotion you feel toward these models of yours need not necessarily be somber, or especially significant. Perhaps it is one of mild amusement, or curiosity. Practice putting these people down on paper so the reader will feel amused, or curious. Remember, it is the character of these models, as you saw it, that made you feel amused or curious. So it is in presenting them characteristically that you will amuse your reader or make him curious.

Characters are your raw material. Thumbnail characterizations of the people you know, meet, and see are comparable to the sketches the artist makes in large numbers all his active life and particularly when he is planning a new piece of work. The characterization you make of the man who sits opposite you on the bus may be the germ of a plot for either a short story, a play, or a book. *Characters are plots.* So, while you are gaining facility in characterization, you are building up a stock of potential plots that will be worth a great deal to you as an active professional writer. Never throw one of these away, but file it under the proper heading where you can find it again when in need of such a character for either a major or a minor rôle.

While you are practicing characterization, strive always for exactly the right word to express your exact meaning, the original and charming phrase or figure of speech that will make your work pleasing and give it the element of surprise. Train your mind to search for and find the one best way of communicating the character of your model to the reader, the one way most interesting, the one most pictorial and emotional way. Never be content with mediocrity or triteness in word or phrase. Neither allow yourself to go to the other extreme and make it obvious to the reader that you are striving for an effect. You may work hard to characterize your model, but never let the reader suspect you have worked hard. Everything you write should appear spontaneous and as if you thought of it for the first time just as you wrote it down. An appearance of simplicity and ease must be an integral part of even your most subtle and complicated characterizations. As soon as artifice appears, art disappears. The reader's attention should never be distracted from the effect by the mechanics used to achieve the effect. Suppose we went to a moving picture and were shown, along with the progress of the story, even a few of the mechanical *means* that are necessary to the build-up of the illusion. The effect of that moving picture would certainly be ruined for us. Always strive for the art that conceals art.

That is one reason it is important to show character through action or dynamic description as much as possible, and as little as possible through analysis and exposition. The reader must be given the illusion that he arrives at his conclusions about a fictional character independently of the writer. The writer, if he has done his work well, has presented the action and description in such a way that the reader could not possibly arrive at any other conclusion than the one predetermined by the writer's plan before he began to write.

The trend in present-day characterization is away from the long analysis or exposition setting forth the character-traits of the fictional person and toward characterization that is an integral part of the necessary action of the story as the plot unfolds. That is, the reader of today *depends more upon what the story-people do and the way they do it* to find out what people they are. Furthermore, today's trend in fiction is more and more toward character stories; for instance, note the numbers that now appear in such popular magazines as *The Saturday Evening Post* and *Redbook*. Formerly, character stories appeared almost exclusively in such quality magazines as *The Atlantic Monthly* and *Harper's Magazine*.

When learning the art of characterization, or developing it, much practical help may be obtained by reading the work of the best modern writers. Of course, mere reading as reading will do you little, if any, good. It is only *analytical* reading that counts. You should read critically, alert to every instance of characterization in the material before you. When you have finished a short story, play, or book, ask yourself which characters you liked and which you disliked. This is where nearly everyone stops in his thinking about fictional characters, but this is the point where the writer *begins to think*. Ask yourself: 'Why do I dislike that character, and why do I like this character? Exactly *how* and *by what means* did the writer cause me to *feel* as I do about each of these characters? *How* and *at what points* was my emotion toward each character intensified?' Write down your answers to all these questions so that you will be forced to read with attentive care and to think clearly and definitely. Fuzzy thinking will do you no good whatsoever; in fact, it will do you harm, in that it will encourage a wrong way of thinking and cause you to miss the whole point of this mental exercise.

Analyzing a dozen books and a dozen stories exhaustively by this method will help you to solve your own problems of characterization more surely than you, at the moment, believe possible by any one method. *It will be hard work. It will take time.* But if you are not willing to work hard and to spend time and to direct your efforts toward learning the technique of your art, the chances are you will never succeed in the practice of that art. If you do not know by *what means* you were *made* to be involved emotionally and imaginatively in the stories you read, how can you expect to *know how* to substitute an active for a passive enjoyment in *your* reader?

After you have done the work suggested above, you will have set up mental habits of observation and analysis that will pay increasing dividends, provided you make these mental habits permanent by continued practice. A good plan is never to sit down to read anything, not excepting the daily paper, without a pencil and paper at hand to record unusual, effective, pictorial, and emotionally appealing examples of characterization. Then rewrite these, seeing if you can improve them in any way. Such a procedure can be even more fun, and far more productive of results, than working crossword puzzles.

The will to learn, plus a definite objective, is as important in mastering the art of characterization as it is in the mastery of anything else, whether it be learning to play the saxophone, to build a bridge, or to paint a masterpiece. If you really determine to learn characterization with the purpose of writing first-rate fiction, you are already well on the path to success. If you have no such determination, you are about as likely to succeed in your writing as a boat without power or rudder is likely to make port.

Inasmuch as we have within ourselves the will to direct our own energies intelligently toward the fulfillment of a dream, have we within ourselves the power to bring about the results of certain failure or positive achievement.

Method of Study

1. Why is it important that the writer feel definite emotions toward his characters?

2. What is the value of experimentation and practice in learning how to characterize?

3. Next to practice in writing characterization, what is the best method of learning to write interesting and convincing characterization?

4. Characterize someone you know well in not more than one hundred words, by what he says and the way he says it.

5. Characterize someone you know very slightly in not more than one hundred words, using dynamic description and at least one figure of speech.

Appendix

THE four stories that follow were selected as models primarily because of the outstandingly fine characterization they contain. But qualities other than that of fine characterization also entered into their being chosen. They vary widely in structure, viewpoint, and effect, and the many technical problems involved in each story have been solved with the sure touch that comes only when writing talent of a high order has been combined with specific knowledge and skill attained by much practice. While it is no doubt true that the perfect story is yet to be written, each of the models that follows is highly admirable, and the earnest student of writing will find in them much that is worthy of his most careful attention, analysis, and appraisal.

While characterization will be stressed in the analyses of the models given here, other important technical points that are, strictly speaking, outside the subject under discussion will be touched upon. It is distinctly advantageous to separate writing technique into its component parts for *purposes of study*, but in actual practice all important phases of the technique of fiction writing are inextricably woven together into a unity of fabric and design. Therefore, any study of characterization must, if it is to be of practical use to the writer, take into consideration, even though briefly, such matters as structure, viewpoint, setting, and effect.

In these stories the number of words devoted to characterizing each actor, and the number of specific means used to characterize him, are in direct ratio to the importance of the character in relation to the story-action and the story-problem. For example, the main character in each story is characterized many more times and in many more ways than the character next in importance to him, and so on, down to the background characters, who are not really characterized at all, sometimes not even named. This is true of all stories that reach a professional standard, and the result attained is one of proportion and balance. Characterization serves as a spotlight, concentrating reader-attention, reader-emotion, and reader-interest on that character. The portioning out of this spotlight of characterization should be carefully observed by the writer when analyzing published stories, and he should take care to handle it with judgment and skill in his own creative work.

Notice carefully that in each of these stories the characters, as well as the action of the story, are influenced very largely by the setting, and are the logical outgrowth of that setting. This will be discussed more fully in the analysis of each story as a whole. Descriptive passages, passages that indicate the lapse of time and action and thoughts, which are merely natural to the character but that do not emphasize the specific character-traits that are stressed in the story, are left unmarked in order to concentrate attention on the passages where characterization is definitely accomplished.

In these stories, as in all professional writing, two or more ways of characterization are often combined in one sentence, or in one paragraph. This combining of ways will be clearly indicated. For convenience of study, the numbers in the stories and in the analyses are arranged consecutively in order that the culminative effect of characterization, the importance of which cannot be overestimated, will not be lost to the writer whose aim is to get the greatest amount of practical help from his study, that he may with increased ease and facility write stories that editors will gladly buy.

You will derive greater benefit from your study of these models if you will read them for the first time, not as a writer, but as a reader, content to be emotionally moved and entertained. Lull your critical and analytical faculties into as nearly a somnolent state as possible. Attempting to analyze how the effect of a story is secured is almost a waste of time until you know *what that effect is.* You cannot know what the full effect is until you have read the last line of the story. Once the story is read through in its entirety and you see it whole, then you may profitably proceed to a critical analysis of the technical devices used by the writer to produce a successful story.

Sunday Afternoon

BY FANNIE HURST

(Reprinted by permission of the author and *Woman's Home Companion*)

1. *Once or twice during the hot Sundays of July or August, Papa was almost sure to say to me on the Saturday before: 'How about Cherokee Highlands for you and me tomorrow, Lora? Ask your mother.'*
2. *I liked the Sundays Papa got Cherokee Highlands into his head. Mama would always say the same sort of things: 'Go if you want, but I wouldn't go out to that black-fly nest and get stuck up with chiggers if you gave me the Cherokee River with a fence around it. Besides, those rapids are dangerous. See that you don't go near them. Be sure you catch the nine o'clock trolley back, at the latest.'*
3. *I could tell when Papa was going to get that Cherokee Highlands look on his face. After he had been talking to old Mr. Brown who boarded at the Lelands' he'd get it. Mr. Brown had once been assistant pilot on the same Mississippi boat with Mark Twain, and Mama used to say it really was a privilege to hear him reminisce about 'Sam Clemens.' Mama really wasn't interested in anything historical like that but she knew she ought to be. Mama never read. She only liked to talk about personal things, such as people she knew, and the cost of things, and how husbands treated their wives, and the other way around. Mama's face kind of fell in when people got to talking about books or McKinley or Free Silver or anything that wasn't about something or somebody she knew.*

But just the same, Mama said once when Mr. Brown got to describing Mark Twain when he was Sam Clemens the pilot:

4. *'You know, Mr. Brown, speaking of steamboat pilots, I think Mr. Kirk would have made a fine sea captain. His Scotch grandfather was one, you know. There is something bottled up and kind of caught-on-the-land about my husband. You always know your husband by what he says in his sleep. Mr. Kirk's favorite nightmare has sea words like "ship-ahoy" and "fore-and-aft" in it.'*
5. *Well anyway, it was usually after Papa had had a long talk or a walk with old Mr. Brown, or had been looking at his little ship in a bottle that had belonged to his grandfather, or had been re-reading 'Lord Jim,' that he was pretty sure to come out with: 'How about a little Cherokee Highlands, Lora?'*
6. *'For a boy raised just outside Kansas City, Kansas,' Mama used to remark, 'where all the water you ever saw must have been in the rain-barrel, and*

then not much, you certainly act as if you were born with your grandfather's taste of salt water in your mouth.'

Something I once overheard Mrs. Townsend say to Mrs. Holton about Papa, even though it wasn't entirely about him, certainly made me think.

Mrs. Townsend and Mrs. Holton were sitting down in the reception hall one Saturday noon after lunch, and on my way from the bathroom to our room I leaned over the banister, really just to see if Mama was with them, when I caught the name of a nephew of Mrs. Townsend's, Ted Hallip, who was awfully handsome and sometimes came to visit her, and I guess I just listened. Mrs. Townsend had a letter in her hand. It seems she had just read that this nephew had quit Missouri University where he was studying to be a doctor, in order to get married and take a job in his father-in-law's mill somewhere in Ohio. 'Ted comes from a family of doctors,' Mrs. Townsend went on to say as she put the letter back in its envelope. 'Just you wait and see! Along about the time his children are growing up and the mill has worn him down, Ted is going to be eating out his heart because his fingers were made to perform operations instead of fumble with textiles in a mill. I hate a trapped look in human eyes. We've got an example of it right in this house,' went on Mrs. Townsend, lowering her voice so that I had to bend over the banister.

7. '*I never look at Fred Kirk that I don't say to myself, he's frustrated. It's in his face.'*

8. '*You would be too,' said Mrs. Holton, 'if you were married to a talking machine.'*

    'Shh-h-h, walls have ears,

9. '*Mrs. Kirk isn't so bad. The trouble with Mr. Kirk is that he married without getting that something or other out of his system beforehand, and then along came the baby and, just like my nephew here, bing, the trap!'*

10. *Mrs. Townsend, with all her faults that got so on Mama's nerves, was right! Papa hadn't ever said much to me, but every time he looked at his ship in a bottle, or talked to Mr. Brown about navigating, he got that look in his eye of a person who had his body in one place and his mind, or rather his spirit or something, in another. He got it when he said, 'Well, Lora, how about Cherokee Highlands?' He just loved water, even if it was only a river like the Cherokee.*

On the Sunday I am going to tell you about, I was glad Papa wanted to spend it at Cherokee Highlands, because it was just beautiful weather, blue June.

Cherokee Highlands was a big grove on the edge of the quiet part of the River Cherokee. Where you got off the street-car was a long pavilion where they sold soda pop and beer and wienies. At the foot of some wooden stairs, right in the trees, was the boathouse where you rented skiffs and canoes and fishing tackle.

11. *Papa right away breathed in deep when we reached the vicinity where we stretched out on the grass for an hour or two before starting out in our skiff to*

have our lunch under a tree on the other side of the river. He always read the
Sunday paper while I strolled and picked dog-violets for Mama and looked for
four-leafs. It was long after two when we finally started out in the skiff.

First we rowed straight across the river to our tree where we sat in our
skiff under a weeping willow and opened the shoebox of lunch.

I'll never forget that afternoon rowing slowly on the shady side of the
river!

12. *Papa said such wonderful things to me, things I knew he wouldn't say if*
Mama were along. Mama being lovely but — well, the way she is.

Looking back, it now seems the most peaceful afternoon in the world to
me because of the contrast of what was to come later.

I can see it now. The river like glass. The dragonflies skimming over it.
The weeping willow we were under trailing in the water. Papa leaning
back on the boat-cushions and talking with his hat over his face.

13. *'There's nothing like peace, Lora. It clears the air like a thunderstorm.'*
14. *I thought it was a funny thing to compare peace to a thunderstorm, but I*
knew what Papa meant.
15. *'If people cultivated more harmonies within themselves, there would not be*
so much outside conflict.'

'You mean wars and things, Papa?'

16. *'Not only wars. Just the hand-to-hand disharmonies in everyday business.*
The Lord meant harmony, or he could not have created such harmonies as sun-
rise and rivers and trees.'

'I guess God made lack of harmony, Papa, so we can enjoy peace all the
more when it comes.'

'That's right, Lora,' he said, 'work and ye shall reap.'

That wasn't from the Bible, but Papa said it as if it were.

'You've worked, Papa. Hard, too. You must reap.'

17. *He sighed. Beneath his hat I could see his mouth twist. It hurt me somehow,*
to see Papa lying there in that skiff with all the wrong clothes on. Business
man's suit, vest, heavy watchchain and nicely blackened shoes.
18. *'I've no complaint to make, Lora. God has been good to me and mine.*
We've our health.'

'Well, Papa, having health is what you have in order to help you enjoy
having other things too.'

He laughed. 'I suppose if I had it to do all over again ——'

'Oh Papa, what would you do if you had it to do all over again? You
would have me, if you had to do it all over again, wouldn't you, Papa?'

19. *'Without you, I wouldn't want to do it all over again.'*
20. *Oh, Papa, what a lovely thing to say!*
21. *It was funny the way we both remembered Mama at the same moment.*
'Without you and Mama,' Papa added to what he had been saying.

'Know thyself, Daughter, is a grand saying. But many of us wait too long,
and meanwhile life is almost lived up. Then it's too late, so we have to content
ourselves with living in the present and dreaming the dream.'

22. *'But it's nice to have a dream to dream, Papa. Some people haven't.'* I

meant Mama. You couldn't hold against her that she didn't have a dream. But she didn't.

'One of my best dreams is for you, Lora.'

'Oh Papa, I'll try to make it come true.'

The lovely day turned bluer and bluer, and after a while Papa began to row softly, always away from the direction of the rapids, and I began to sing soft, school songs such as 'Sweet and Low,' and 'Fays and Elves.'

23.   *Just as we were nosing back in the direction of the little pier where we had rented our skiff, a big dark fellow in old pants and an undershirt so open that it showed the black hair all over his chest, jumped into a little red canoe and pushed off with a very fast paddle that must have made Papa's two heavy oars feel pretty cheap.*

'Hi, brother,' he called when he saw Papa, giving him a salute with his paddle, 'been riding the rapids in a bathtub? Come along for some real goin'. I'm shootin' to the moon!'

I wish you could have seen Papa!

24.   *Where you would have thought he would not even have answered this rough fellow, his head shot out of his neck and he said, of all things for Papa to say: 'No kidding, Bo?'*

'Sure. Hop in.'

I declare, I think Papa just forgot I existed, because he raised his foot to step over into the canoe before he even remembered to look down at me.

25.   *His face, when he did remember, just seemed to fall to pieces.*

26.   *Suddenly, more than anything I could think of, I wanted Papa to go with Bo and shoot the rapids, no matter what! I was going to have Papa free to shoot to the moon!*

'Why, Papa,' I said taunting, 'you aren't afraid, are you? Even kids shoot the Cherokee Rapids.'

27.   *'Your mother ——'*

'Mama's not here.'

28   *Papa clicked then, just as if you had closed a purse. 'Wait until I get my girl moored, Bo. I'll go shooting with you.'*

You should have seen Papa maneuver our skiff alongside the pier.

'I'll keep your coat and things, Papa, and wait for you here while I read the Sunday papers.'

I wanted to add: 'Don't fail to be back in good time for the nine o'clock trolley.' But I didn't. After all, Papa didn't go off shooting to the moon every day. Before I knew it, Bo's canoe was sliding out in midstream.

It was only a little after four o'clock.

I liked it down near the little wooden pier where I could wait for Papa when he came back and where I could spread myself on the grass and read and just sort of drowse. I could have felt all relaxed, except for the arrival of the black flies. It was a long fight between keeping them off and keeping awake, and when they got worse and worse, so sleepy that I scarcely knew what I was doing, I moved up the hill way, way back under some trees, where there wasn't a soul around, and covered my ankles with Papa's coat and my shoulders with Papa's vest and my face with Papa's hat, and decided to doze a little while before it got time to go downhill again to meet Papa.

The strangest thing woke me up! It was an electric light burning! But before I opened my eyes to see it, I saw it in my dream. It was over on the trolley platform and as I gathered myself together enough to remember where I was, I realized it was darkish and much cooler.

It was late! I must have overslept! Papa must have come back from shooting to the moon and not found me where I said I would be. Papa! Yoo-hoo! I began to run down the hill, calling. Papa — he must be looking for me everywhere!

Not a car or a soul in sight, either at the trolley platform or any place around. I called and then I ran down to the soda-pop place and the lady and the man who ran it and lived in the back, were putting up the wooden shutters.

'Has a man in shirtsleeves been looking for me?'

29.   *They were Poles or something. The woman didn't answer at all, because I don't think she understood and he just grunted a 'No.'*

- *'Is the nine o'clock trolley next?'*

'Ten minutes to nine,' he said, thinking I had asked him the time.

30.   *Good heavens! Oh, good heavens. Mama would be insane with worry if we missed the nine o'clock. Papa. Where was Papa? I began to run down to the boathouse again.* This time a young fellow was there.

'Do you know a man named Bo?' I asked, trying not to let him see how terribly scared I was.

31.   *'Nope.'*

'Are all the boats in?'

'Nope, they keep coming. What's the matter, sister? Lonesome?'

'I've lost my father. He went out in a canoe with a man named Bo. You wouldn't know Bo's canoe?'

'Bo?'

Suddenly I realized that Bo's name wasn't Bo just because Papa had called him that.

'I'm not sure what his name is, but he is tall and rangy, with an open shirt and hair on his chest.' The fellow stopped dipping water out of his canoe and looked up at me with a wink. 'I'm not so bad meself,' he said and jerked open the V of his shirt and I began to run up the hill again. I wanted Papa.

The Polish people, now that they had closed up the front, were sitting in back of the soda-pop stand.

'My father,' I kept repeating. 'I can't find my father.' And the more I kept repeating the more the man kept pointing with his pipe down the hill where I had come from. I started there again and then changed my mind and ran back to the trolley platform. This time there was a woman sitting there.

'Have you seen a smallish man in shirtsleeves, looking for someone?'

She shook her head and rose, as the trolley, an immense headlight whitening the track, appeared around the curve.

'You're the only person I've seen since I'm waiting.'

32.   The car came. *A nice-looking man* was the only one who got off.

33.   *I felt so helpless. As if I ought to take this car back to town and see if Papa had gone home; as if I ought to go to Mama who would be worried sick if neither of us came on this car.* I couldn't be sure which way to turn.

I ran after the man who had got off the car.

'I've lost my father,' I said. 'Do you know how I can go about finding him? He went canoeing. I don't know whether he's back or not.'

I kept running in quick little steps alongside the man, explaining.

34.   *It was wonderful, the difference in people. With this man, things began to happen right away. He owned the Goldenrod Hotel, which wasn't yet open for the season, and was living there with the caretakers. First thing he did was to check off with that horrid fellow down at the boathouse and see how many boats were not yet accounted for. But with the boathouse locked, there was no way of telling whether they were canoes or skiffs. It was nothing unusual, it appeared, for boats which had carried parties to Mound Park to return after midnight.*

'*Either your old man went home, or is taking his time at Mound Park. Got a telephone in your house?*'

35.   *That brought West Pine Street before me suddenly. Mama! No matter how you looked at it, even if Papa had got home, he had got there without me. Mama must be almost crazy by now.*

We hurried up to the hotel which was even higher up on the hill than where I took my nap. It was big and empty, but there was a pay telephone in the office and I called up Mrs. Ettens, who lived across the street from us, and who was paid ten cents every time one of the boarders got an incoming call on her telephone and she had to send across the street.

It took so long to get Mama over to Mrs. Ettens that the man who owned the hotel brought me a chair. Finally, even before Mama's voice came over the wire,

36.   *I could hear the commotion of her entering Mrs. Ettens' and the crying noises she made, and in a flash I knew Papa wasn't home.*

'*Something terrible has happened to them. My child. My husband. Oh my God — hello — hello — hello ——*'

'*Mama, it's me. Lora. If Papa isn't there, it's all right. He's out here somewhere — canoeing.*'

I just had to tell her that much.

Mama began to scream:

'*My husband! He drowned. Lora, where are you? Mama's coming. Tell me where to come. Oh my God! Here, Mrs. Ettens — I can't hold the receiver — I'm weak — you find out where I'm to go — no, let me. Lora, where are you?*'

'*I'm at Cherokee Highlands, Mama, and everything is all right, only ——*'

'*Where is your father, Lora? Lora, where is your father? He's dead. I know he's dead.*'

'*No, no, Mama! He only went boating and I waited on the bank and he's somewhere out here, trying to find out where I am waiting for him. We missed each other. That's all, Mama. Don't worry, Mama. I'll bring him home.*'

I tried not to cry, but it was getting dark and I began to know that bad accidents happened all the time on those rapids with inexperienced canoeists. I began to know that if Papa was looking for me on the grounds he would have found me.

'*Oh my God — my husband. Lora, stay where you are. I'm coming. My husband — they can't find my husband — I'll be there.*'

I dropped the receiver and the hotel man had to hang it back on the hook for me.

'*My mother is coming. Oh, sir, we must find my father before* ——'

'Now look here, let's give this thing a little time. We'll telephone and see if anybody at the Mound Park Hotel can tell us anything. Meanwhile we'll take a bite. My caretaker's wife has got it ready.'

'Oh, sir, my mother will be out here in about fifty minutes. She mustn't find him gone. Couldn't we go through the woods, calling?'

'Hold your horses and let's try Mound Park, first.' They didn't even answer their telephone at Mound Park, and so we got lanterns and started through the woods, calling.

'Yoo-hoo,' I kept shouting between my hands. 'Papa. Papa. It's Lor-a.' But our voices just came back. Finally the man said:

'Sister, this is a waste of time. Either your old man has had a tip-over and is spending the night somewhere in the woods, or is on his way back here. We've got to give him a little more time before we send out an alarm. He'll probably be along any minute now. We'll go back and have a bite. He'll show up.'

I didn't like to insist any more. I knew we ought to wait longer before turning in an alarm. Lots and lots of people come back from canoeing hours late.

Oh God, I got to saying over and over again to myself, don't let anything happen to Papa.

Watching the hotel man and the lady and man caretakers who ate at the same table with us gave me the queerest feeling. Here was Papa, lost; Mama on a trolley nearly crazy with worry; and these three people eating just as if it were the same unconcerned world I had known that morning.

'Isn't it almost time for me to go to the trolley and meet my mother?'

'Not for another twenty-five minutes. After dark those trolleys don't keep any more schedule than a titmouse.'

37. *The caretaker seemed to have his mind on me. He was a heavy-set man about fifty, with a beard that must have been a week old and tattooing on his arms.*

'I've hauled too many out of those rapids to trust 'em,' he said suddenly *out of a clear sky, and his wife, a puny woman in a washed-out blue dress* cried: *'Oh, Pete, where's your manners!'*

My heart was right up in my mouth.

'Oh, Mr. Pete,' I cried and jumped up from the table, 'take me down those rapids! Please. Please. Please. Please get a boat and take me.'

'I don't know as I need to take you, but I'll get my boat and go alone.'

'Please — please — I can't stand it if you don't take me.'

38. *'All right. I'd do as much for a kitten that had lost its cat.* Get me my boots, Mother, and my hooks.'

I didn't know what hooks meant then. If I had, I think I would have fainted.

'You're not a-goin' to take that child, Pete?'

'She wants to go. What say, Boss? 'Twon't hurt to scan a bit.'

'It's going to rain,' she said.

'Windjammers,' he replied.

Then Mrs. Pete brought me a sort of jacket which I know now is called a windjammer, and Pete and I went out into the woods which were filled with lightning-bugs.

Pete's canoe was much older than the one Papa and Bo had started out in,

39. *but you could tell from the minute he dipped paddle that Pete and his canoe had rhythm.*

'Yoo-hoo, Papa,' I began at once as we pulled off. 'Yoo-hoo, Papa!'

The voice came back at me from black woods that were all lighted with little lightning-bug lamps that gave no light. How dark. How mysterious.

'Pa — pa — Fath — er — it's Lo — ra — Pa-pa!'

It must have gone on that way for a half-hour. Suddenly I knew we were hearing the rapids' far-off roar. I was much too numb to be afraid. I just sat and prayed and called and shivered in my windjammer.

We could see the rapids like something grinning white in the dark, and Pete now began to look from one side to another, paddling faster and faster. It suddenly felt as if we were going downhill, and then, more by the feeling of something tugging from underneath than anything else, I knew, as we started to swirl, that we were in the rapids.

40. *For some freak reason I still wasn't sorry I had let Papa come down here. Papa, wherever he might be, had at least felt that first plunge into something that wasn't all little and harnessed and white-collared. But to hear me talk, you'd never believe what a knot of misery I was, sitting there in that boat holding on for dear life.*

There wasn't any use trying to call now, although I did keep at it. I couldn't even hear myself above the roar of the water and the spray came all over me and then the water itself and several times we spun, and all I could see through the foam and confusion was Pete's teeth.

Suddenly he began to call and you bet you could hear his voice above the roar. 'Hullo. Hullo.'

What I had thought was all spray turned out to be rain and I could see and feel slanting needles of it pouring right onto my face.

'Hullo. Hul — lo.'

'Papa. Yoo-hoo — Papa — it's Lora — Papa ——'

There wasn't any wind and not much thunder and lightning,

41. *but I thought of Mama, who was afraid of lightning.* We kept spinning and turning, Pete — between shouts — looking, looking, from right to left. From left to right.

Suddenly, like a cat that sees in the dark, Pete took his paddle and reached over the side of the boat until we teetered and made a stab at something as far away as the end of his paddle. It lightened just then, and I saw the paddle hit the bottom-side-up of a red canoe that was bobbing along the fast waters, upside down!

It was red all right, red as blood, and like a flash, Pete, reaching over, giving us an awful tip, had it fastened, right side up, to the end of our canoe.

Oh my God. Oh Mama — poor Mama — Papa!

Never once did Pete look at me after that. He just paddled, turning around after he had found the canoe, and looking harder than ever from left to right and shouting louder than ever: 'Hul — oo. Hul — ooo.'

I stopped calling. I hadn't anything to call with. Horror had my voice. Horror of that thing bobbing along behind us. Empty!

'Hu — loo — hu — loo.'

To my dying day I'll never forget what Pete did then. All of a sudden, without a word, and so deftly that the boat never even shuddered, he stepped out of it, giving me the most terrible feeling of being left alone! The water was only about up to his thighs, but when I saw what he was doing, I closed my eyes.

The water went off deeper just ahead and formed a little falls. Pete had the pair of grappling hooks he had brought along, and he was feeding their rope into the water and fishing for something down below the falls. I knew! He was fishing for Papa and Bo! He must have seen something that caused him to jump out of the boat that way. What he finally brought up on one of the hooks was a big bunch of old weeds. That seemed to satisfy him, because he got back into the canoe without a word, and presently we were at it again, spinning and hullo-ing. Spinning and hullo-ing.

By now everything was water and rain and blackness and pain in a horrible sort of swirl, but suddenly, to Pete's hullo, there came a faint sound that wasn't water or swirl. We both heard it at the same instant and suddenly we both saw the same thing at the same time. Deep off in a sort of bay, behind trees, was a small bonfire, a feeble little affair trying to make itself seen.

We finally maneuvered into the bay and stumbled through those woods. I don't think I would have recognized Papa if I hadn't been looking for him. In the glow from the pitiful fire they had been trying to keep alive, his face was all streaked, and he had no shirt at all. He certainly didn't look like Papa. I know! He looked like a painting called The Agony I had seen at the Exposition. He didn't get up, but kept whispering and looking down into his lap. Then I saw! Bo covered with blood, was lying in Papa's lap, his head hanging backward and his mouth open as if he were dead.

Papa couldn't talk. He just whispered. I didn't do anything. I just stood. I just stood and I don't believe at first he even saw me or knew me if he did. He never talked about it afterward, so I was never to know. He had horror in his lap.

42. *I'll never forget Pete. I still think he is one of the most wonderful men! He leaned Bo up against a tree and poured liquor down him from a bottle in his hip-pocket. He laid Papa down. He built up the pitiful little fire with some dry wood he found heavens knows where, and boiled some water in an old tin can. He took off his windjammer and mine to wrap them in. He stripped off Papa's wet pants and hung them beside the fire and then sort of dug his knees into Bo's back and began to massage him for all he was worth.*

After a while Papa could talk a little and laid his head in my lap and cried and kept asking for Mama. Bo opened his eyes and felt the back of his head and said, 'Hell.'

43. *Pete washed Bo's face and Papa's, and I put Papa's sock back on, we couldn't find the other one. I tried to help Bo too, but he said, 'Hell, no,' and put on his own socks and kept feeling the back of his head which Pete had tied around with a handkerchief and saying, 'Hell.'*

'A coupla stitches will fix that. Better than a coupla spades of dirt on your face,' said Pete.

'You said it!'

I couldn't take my eyes off Papa all the time we were getting ready to start back. The rain had stopped and the lightning-bugs were out again, and after Bo sort of got his senses together, the sum total of the story came out in snatches.

Papa was a hero!

44. *Bo made no bones about it. Papa saved his life. Papa, more annoyed than I had ever seen him with another man, kept saying: 'Cut that out, fellow. The canoe upset. We spilled. You happened to hit your head on the rock that turned us over and I dragged you here. There is the thing in a nutshell, no fancy business.'*

'The hell, that's the thing in a nutshell. You saved my life. Hell, you did!'

'My daughter is present, sir,' said Papa in his Mrs. Leland's boarding-house manner and Pete added: 'Cut it, Bo.'

I give you my word, worried as I was, I could have giggled.

45. *Poor Papa, now that he was pulling himself together, I don't think anything much was really on his mind except Mama, sitting back there waiting for us, although I must say he kept touching me as if he couldn't keep his hands off the reality of having me there. Poor Papa, being a hero didn't fit him.*

Getting out of the rapids didn't take long on the way back. The four of us got into Pete's canoe, the little one bobbing along behind. I just sat with my hand on Papa's, pretending I didn't feel it trembling. 'Don't forget to give Pete some money,' I whispered once. Papa nodded.

The night was almost clear now, with a watery-looking moon drifting along behind clouds. It made everything cream-colored and silky. In the quiet waters the stillness was just beautiful.

Then came the light on the front porch of the hotel and

46. *Mama's loud crying voice:*

'*My husband. The best man that ever lived. God, give me back my good considerate husband. I have so much to make up to him for. I'll be the kind and gentle wife I never was. I need him. His child needs him. Oh God, give me my husband — best, kindest and most considerate of husbands. Best man a woman ever had. What have I done to deserve this.*'

46a. '*My husband! No woman ever had a better. His child needs him. I need him. Best, kindest, most considerate ——*'

You could hear another woman's voice, Mrs. Pete's, no doubt, trying to quiet her.

And then we rounded the curve and in the creamy moonlight Mama saw us all at a clip, and stopped in the act of wringing her hands to get hysterical at the top of her voice, so that Mrs. Pete, standing beside her, had to grab and hold her back from jumping toward our boat.

'*Fred! Lora! Oh my darlings — oh my God — oh my husband — come, come, come!*'

47. *Papa's hand in mine began to sweat. I knew why. He was suffering the way I was. The way we were always suffering for Mama. We were both so sorry for her, so embarrassed for her, and for ourselves, and so grateful and so — unnerved ——*

48. *Papa stumbled out of that canoe as if he were going to fall in his tracks and took Mama in his arms and held her and then held both of us together and shook hands with Bo and whispered to Pete that a check would be in his mail.*

Mama thanked Mrs. Pete and then, as the three of us stood kind of exhausted and looking at one another, Mama began to cry softly and Papa laid his hand on her arm and said: 'Now, Clara, don't give way. It's all over. I know what you've been through.'

49. *That was all Mama needed to remind her what she had been through. More tears came now, the quick mad kind. In floods.*

'*All over, is it! You know what I've been through, do you? Nobody knows what I've been through, because the most inconsiderate man on earth thinks of nobody but himself. Any other man would say to himself, "I've one day a week at home, I'll spend it with my wife." But no! My husband has to go gallivanting! All over, is it? Wait until we get home and I'll tell you how all over it is. All over, is it? Well, Fred Kirk, if any one should ask you, I've just begun!*'

Characterization-Analysis of 'Sunday Afternoon'

Main character: Mr. Kirk

Minor characters: Mrs. Kirk, Lora

Background characters: Mrs. Townsend, Mrs. Holton, Bo, Mr. Pete and his wife, the man who got off the car, the young man at the boathouse, and the couple who kept the 'soda-pop place.'

Structure

This is an off-pattern, unplotted story, as distinguished from the pattern, or plotted, story in which the main character has a purpose for the story, or is faced by the necessity for making a decision. Although without plot in the strict sense of the word, it has a *clearly defined plan* and one that is often used with excellent effect. The plan is that of building a strong emotion in the reader toward the main character.

Setting

The setting is a small town and river resort in the Middle-West; time, about forty-five years ago.

Viewpoint

The story is told from the viewpoint of a minor character, Lora, in the first person.

Effect

The effect is a build-up of profound sympathy and admiration for Mr. Kirk.

BRIEF SUMMARY OF STORY

Mr. Kirk, whose dream is a life with a background of water and ships, is married to a woman who is dictatorial, nagging, possessive, and his inferior mentally and spiritually. The responsibility of his wife and daughter effectually bars him from any realization of his dream. The action of the story shows that he possesses the innate courage and daring required to lead the life of which he dreams. At the end of the story, he returns, after his brief adventure, to the chains of responsibility that, his character being what it is, he will never break.

COMMENT

This story is definitely slanted toward women readers, in spite of the fact that the main character is a man and the 'villain' character a woman. Most of its scenes are highly charged with emotion expressed through the words of a young girl, Lora. Observation shows that while Lora is the daughter of Mr.

and Mrs. Kirk, she has in reality been assigned the 'mother' rôle; that is, she understands, sympathizes, loves, and tries to protect and shield both Mr. Kirk and Mrs. Kirk. This helps to give the story its fundamental appeal to women readers.

It is a fine example of the way in which an 'unhappy' ending can be made acceptable to the reader. The reader is made to feel, subconsciously, by means of characterization, that the ending is inevitable. Mr. Kirk being what he is, will never break away from his responsibilities, and Mrs. Kirk, being what she is, will never be any more understanding or kind. The reader does not want Mr. Kirk to assert his independence, knowing that if he did, he would be even more unhappy because he would feel that he had been disloyal to his family. Therefore, the ending is the best possible ending, under the circumstances, and the *least unhappy* for the main character, Mr. Kirk.

CHARACTER-ANALYSES

Main character, Mr. Kirk

He loves anything connected with boats and water. Is loyal, affectionate, peace-loving, philosophical, a dreamer.

Minor character, Mrs. Kirk

Superficial, talkative, selfish, dominating, lacking in understanding.

Minor character, Lora.

Understanding, gentle, affectionate, sympathetic. A perfect choice as a minor character narrator. In no other way could this material have been presented so effectively as through the eyes of this sensitive girl who loved both her father and her mother. Because Lora herself is understanding, the reader does not hate Mrs. Kirk, but feels pity for her, too, though in a less degree than for Mr. Kirk.

Note that these character-traits are not presented to the reader once, but many times, and in many ways.

Of the background characters, Mrs. Townsend and Mrs. Holton are not even individualized. They play no part in the unfoldment of the story itself, and their sole function is to characterize Mr. and Mrs. Kirk by their comment, after which they are not heard of again. The other background characters, of which there are an unusually large number, are deftly individualized and become convincing and real.

'*Sunday Afternoon*' is an admirable example of a character and psychological story presented by means of dramatic action.

CHARACTERIZATION-ANALYSIS

1. The three main characters are introduced, their relationship established, and some setting indicated. Characterizes Mr. Kirk by his speech.
2. Lora's habit of thought. Mrs. Kirk is characterized by her speech.

3. Characterization of Mr. and Mrs. Kirk by exposition of the minor character narrator.
4. Characterization of Mr. Kirk by words of Mrs. Kirk.
5. Characterization by exposition of the minor character narrator.
6. Characterization of Mr. Kirk by words of Mrs. Kirk.
7, 8, 9. Characterization by minor character comment.
10. Characterization by minor character narrator exposition.
11. Both Mr. Kirk and Lora characterized by action.
12. All three major characters are effectively characterized here in one sentence: Mr. Kirk as philosophical and thoughtful; Lora as understanding, affectionate, and loyal; Mrs. Kirk as 'the way she is,' that way having already been clearly established.
13. Mr. Kirk characterized by his speech.
14. Showing Lora's character-trait of understanding.
15, 16. Characterizing Mr. Kirk by his own speech.
17. Action, facial expression, clothing, characterize Mr. Kirk.
18. Patience, loyalty, steadfastness, shown by Mr. Kirk's words.
19. Emotion felt characterizes Lora.
20. Affection, appreciation, sensitivity, shown by Lora's words.
21. Shows both feeling loyalty to Mrs. Kirk. Characterizes Mr. Kirk by means of his speech.
22. Characterizes Lora by her speech. Characterizes Mrs. Kirk by Lora's thoughts.
23. Characterizing Bo by action, static description, clothing, speech.
24. Mr. Kirk characterized by action and speech.
25. Facial expression.
26. Characterizing Lora by thoughts, and speech.
27. Characterization of Mr. Kirk by speech, showing his thought.
28. Mr. Kirk characterized by action and words.
29. Background characters individualized by their nationality and by speech.
30. Characterizing Lora by her actions and thoughts, and Mrs. Kirk by Lora's thoughts.
31. Individualizing a background character by speech, action, and physical appearance.
32. Individualizing a background character by appearance.
33. Lora characterized by her thoughts and feelings, Mrs. Kirk characterized by Lora's thoughts.
34. Individualizing a background character by exposition, telling the reader that he owns the Goldenrod Hotel, by the man's action and speech.
35. Characterizing Lora by her concern for her mother shown by her thoughts. Characterizing Mrs. Kirk by Lora's thoughts.
36. This is a long passage in which Lora and Mrs. Kirk are both characterized by action, by what they say and how they say it, and Lora is characterized by her thoughts.
37, 38, 39. Background characters individualized by static description clothing, speech and way of speaking, and action.

40. Lora characterized by her thoughts, emotions.
41. Characterizing both Lora and Mrs. Kirk by Lora's thoughts.
42. Individualizing a background character by action.
43. Pete, Lora, Bo, in characteristic action. Pete and Bo characterized by speech.
44. Mr. Kirk characterized by minor character comment, by his own speech, by his observable emotion and manner. Bo further individualized by his speech.
45. Mr. Kirk characterized by Lora's thoughts, and by his actions.
46, 46a. Characterizing Mrs. Kirk by her voice and words, and actions.
47. This direct statement by Lora characterizes Mr. Kirk, Mrs. Kirk, and Lora.
48. Characterizing Mr. Kirk by action and speech.
49. Characterizing Mrs. Kirk by action and words.

Singlehanded

BY HUGH MacNAIR KAHLER

(Reprinted by permission of the author and *The Saturday Evening Post*)

1. *When old George Rucker was ready to haul his winter's cut of saw logs down to the mill, it didn't occur to him to drive over to Canastego and complain to the highway commissioner about the mudholes in the Hogback Road. The spring floods had washed up a bed of first-rate gravel in a handy place in the creek. Rucker hooked his team to his dump wagon and filled the holes himself.*

2. *He didn't see anything foolish about this. His forebears had stayed alive in this harsh hill country by learning to do most things for themselves, and Rucker had inherited, along with that self-dependence, their idea that there was wisdom in it, and virtue.*

    It was a raw day, and overcast. By the time he was dumping l•s last load, dusk had fallen, and the car which came toward him down the hill needed its head lights. They shot a long beam downward, a beam that swung drunkenly to the lurch and jolt of the wheels.

3. *Rucker wagged his head. One of these days Ollie would come down Hogback a little too fast. Rucker knew, though, that it wouldn't do any good to tell Ollie so. Ollie was like the rest of the young fellows — always in a hurry.*

4. *He was in a hurry this time. The car stopped just short of Rucker's team, its brakes squealing, and Ollie's voice, cheerfully impatient, came through the dazzle of the lamp.*

    'Hi, old-timer. Elected you pathmaster again, have they?'

    George Rucker grinned. He knew Ollie would expect him to. Ollie and the rest of them had the notion that there was something comical about saying things they didn't mean.

    'Pathmaster don't have to haul saw logs down Hogback,' Rucker said. 'Won't break none of his bones if a load tips over in a mudhole.'

5. *He heard Ollie's chuckle. Ollie always seemed to find something funny in what you said, no matter how sensible it was.*

    'Well, make it snappy, will you, so I can get by? I'm in a hurry.'

6. *'What for?' Rucker tugged at a plank of the wagon bed and a gush of gravel splashed down into the puddle. 'Train won't be in for half an hour yet, even if it's on time. Don't seem hardly worth while to risk your neck just so's to wait an extry ten-fifteen minutes down to the deepo.'*

7. *There was a short pause, and when Ollie spoke, his voice had sobered a little.*

'What makes you so sure that's where I'm going?'

Rucker shrugged his shoulders.

8. *'Been coming over this way every other Friday for quite a spell,'* he said. *'I can see your lights when you go across the flats. No place excepting the deepo for you to go to, over yonder. Notice you always go back, too, right after the train's gone through.'*

Ollie's chuckle had a touch of annoyance in it.

9. *'Forgot what a hand you are to notice things,'* he said. *'Expect you've got a notion, haven't you, what I'm up to?'*

'Wouldn't wonder but what I had,' Rucker said. 'Pay off the hands over to the dam every other Sat'day, don't you? Seems's if you might be coming over this way after the money to do it with.'

He twisted another plank. Ollie laughed, a little shortly.

10. *'Don't need to ask you if you've mentioned it to anybody,'* he said.

'Guess you'd ought to know me by now,' Rucker said dryly.

'That's right.' Ollie stopped. 'Why, of course! I ought to've thought of you first off. Come over here, will you?'

Rucker walked over to the side of the car. Ollie reached under the dash and brought out a small package, wrapped in stout paper and tied with thick string. There were two big splashes of red sealing wax on it.

'This is a dummy,' Ollie said. 'It looks just like the real one that's coming up on the train. Even if you tore it open it might fool you. It's full of bundles of blank paper, but there's a real bill on the outside of each of 'em. I carry it in a kind of wire basket I fixed up back of the dash. Soon as I start away from the station, though, I put the real package in the basket and carry this one on the seat. Even if somebody was watching me pretty close they'd never see me making the switch, and if they held me up I figure there'd be a first-rate chance of their just grabbing the dummy and making a quick getaway with it. Even if they took the car they wouldn't be apt to find the money in it and we'd have a chance, anyhow, of getting it back.'

11. *'Smart,'* Rucker said admiringly. *'Took brains to figure out that idee, Ollie.'*

'I don't think it's so dumb, myself,' Ollie admitted. 'The only thing wrong with it is that I didn't feel like telling anybody over at the dam about it. Not even the boss.'

12. *'Dead right,'* Rucker said warmly. *'One mouth can stay shut a sight longer'n two.'*

'Yeah.' Ollie laughed. 'Only if I happened to get knocked off in a hold-up my mouth would stay shut quite a while. That's where you come in, Uncle George. If any robber bumps me off you can tell Jim Dawson where to look for his cash. Scheme's airtight, now you know about it.'

13. *George Rucker nodded. It was one time, he could see, when there was some sense in splitting up a secret.* Ollie seemed to feel easier in his mind now. He leaned back and lighted a cigarette. The flare of the match and the smell of smoke prodded George Rucker's memory.

'About out of tobacco, Ollie. Might fetch me up a couple of sacks when you come back, if it ain't too much trouble.'

Ollie promised. Rucker dumped the rest of his load and pulled out of the way. The car went past him, its tires crunching in the gravel, the spark of Ollie's cigarette making a bright scar in the darkness as he waved his hand. Rucker watched the lights go dancing down the hill.

14. *He saw them flatten and steady when they struck the smooth paved road across the valley, and that made him feel easier in his mind. Hogback was a mean road for a car, and that fresh gravel wouldn't make it any safer. He guessed it was kind of dumb, the way he kept worrying about Ollie, but he couldn't seem to quit doing it.*

Ollie could certainly take care of himself. He was foreman over yonder at the new dam, with three-four hundred men under him. He earned as much in a year as George Rucker's place was worth. It was right down ridiculous to keep feeling as if he was still nothing but a little boy, fresh from the city, who didn't even know the difference between a bull and a cow. Rucker guessed that when you'd had the raising of a boy you never really got over the notion that you had to look out for him, even after he'd proved that he was a long sight brainier than you.

As he put up his team and did his chores Rucker stopped every now and then to look down across the valley. The train was pretty late. He had eaten his lonesome supper before he saw its lights creeping along at the foot of the other hill. A little later he saw the moving splash of brightness which told him that Ollie had started back. He went out on the porch to wait, so that Ollie could give him his tobacco without having to stop. He saw the beam from the headlights tilt upward. It held fairly steady for a little while and then, suddenly, it shot sidewise and winked out.

15. *Even then, Rucker didn't exactly hurry. He took time to put on his cap and mackinaw and to light his lantern, and he didn't try to run down the hill. He walked pretty fast, though.* It didn't take him more than ten minutes to find Ollie's car, wedged in between two hickory saplings at the side of the road. Ollie was in it, huddled over the steering wheel. It didn't take Rucker very long to make sure that he was dead. The lantern didn't give much light, though, and it took him a little while longer to find the bullet hole behind Ollie's ear.

The dummy package wasn't anywhere in sight, but there were two muslin sacks of tobacco on the seat. Rucker stood still, hefting them, one in each hand, for quite a while. Then he put them in his pocket and reached in under the dash.

There was a package in there. He brought it out. It looked just like the dummy one that Ollie had shown him, but when he worried it open at one corner, he found that it was full of money. The scheme had worked. Rucker wished that Ollie could know that.

16. *It had been smart of Ollie to tell him about it too. If he hadn't done that the scheme wouldn't have done any good. Nobody would have thought of hunting for the money; everybody would have taken it for granted that the robbers had it.*

17. *There were a lot of other things to think about, but Rucker was used to thinking about one thing at a time, slowly. He couldn't seem to get his mind away from the package in his hand, from the idea that he was the only man who knew about it.*
   Somehow that knowledge seemed to matter, to matter more than anything else. After a while Rucker began to see that it did matter, and to see why.

   He had been rigging up a new skidway from which to load his saw logs. It was just across the road, with a long parade of logs ranked beyond it, waiting for a cant hook to roll them out on the skids and onto a wagon. Stepping gingerly on shale outcrops, so as not to leave footprints, Rucker went across the road and hid the package of money between two of the logs.

18. *Then he went down the hill, holding the lantern low and taking care not to step on any of the footprints in the mud. There were only two sets of them, one pointing uphill and the other, wider spaced and deeper, pointing down, all made by the same smallish shoe.*
   Rucker nodded almost approvingly. According to what he'd heard, up-to-date robbers and murderers mostly worked in gangs, but this one seemed to be kind of old-fashioned. At any rate, it looked as if he held to George Rucker's back-number notion that if you had a one-man job to do, it was a pretty good scheme to pitch in and tend to it yourself, singlehanded.

   The footprints led Rucker down to the place where the robber's car had been hidden in the scrub, just a few yards above the foot of the hill. Tire tracks ran down to the paved turnpike and turned eastward, but Rucker couldn't follow them very far along the concrete.

   He kept on to Joe Magruder's place and got Joe out of bed to telephone the state police.

19. *He didn't tell Joe that he'd found the money. He didn't tell the two brisk young state policemen, either, nor the sheriff, nor the long-nosed, gabby young fellow who worked on the Canastego paper, nor Jim Dawson, when he came over from the dam, nor any of the other people who kept him busy, the next few days, answering their questions.*

20. *It would have been harder to keep his knowledge to himself if he'd had to lie to do it. He wasn't much of a hand at lying. But there was no need for any lies:* the state police went over Ollie's car, inch by inch, looking for fingerprints, but they didn't find the wires behind the dash, or, if they did, they didn't guess why they were there. They took it for granted, like everybody else, that the murderer had the money. All George Rucker had to do was to hold his tongue. He was used to doing that.

   At first there wasn't much chance for him to work at anything except answering questions, but after four days, people began to let up on him, and there was time, between callers, to go ahead with that skidway. He was working on it when he saw Ed Lithgow's battered little truck turn off the highway and start up the hill.

   He climbed down and went out to wait at the edge of the road. He was worried. Sooner or later, somebody was coming up that hill to try and find out what had happened to that money. He was afraid that maybe Ed Lithgow might be the one to do it.

21. *He'd kept thinking about Ed pretty steadily, these four days. He'd tried not to, but he couldn't help it. He couldn't help remembering the way Ed had looked and sounded, last month, when he'd come up to borrow a little money, or the way he'd kind of grabbed at the bills when Rucker gave them to him.* He couldn't help remembering that Ed's place was on the road across the flats, where he was bound to see Ollie going by, every other Friday, and bound to guess — even old George Rucker had guessed it, hadn't he? — what Ollie must be up to.

Ed had been a young hellion of a boy, too, always up to his neck in mischief till he got big enough to run off. Nobody knew where he'd spent the five or six years he stayed away, but George Rucker guessed that he'd found plenty of mischief there.

22. *He'd come home looking like a sheep-killing dog, afraid to look you in the eye. He'd got over that, though, after a while. He buckled down and worked like a nailer on his father's farm, and after the old man died, he kept on working harder than ever. It wasn't much of a place, but he made it pay him a living and a mite over. He'd made people like him and respect him, a decent, sober, steady-going youngster. Last summer, when the word went around that Milly Warren was going to marry him, even George Rucker, who set a sight of store by Milly, had been glad to hear it.*

It made him feel a little easier in his mind to see that Milly had ridden up with Ed. He guessed that if Ed had been coming up to try and find out about that money, he wouldn't have brought her along. When they were near enough for him to see their faces, though, he could see that they had something on their minds, something pretty serious,

23. *and he began to worry again.*

24. *He waited for them to do the talking. It was a minute, maybe, before Milly spoke. She had the kind of a voice Rucker liked best, low-pitched and quiet, and she kept her words separate. After the talk Rucker had been hearing for these four days, listening to her was almost the same as resting.*

'Ed knows something I thought we ought to come and tell you, Mr. Rucker.'

Something of the sheep-killing look had come back to Ed Lithgow's face. He kept his eyes away from Rucker's.

25. *'I know who killed Ollie,' he said. His hand tightened slowly on the steering wheel. It was a big hand, warped and knotted with work. Somehow the look of it suddenly made George Rucker feel ashamed of having wondered whether it might have done a murder.*

'It was a man named Brusso,' Lithgow said. 'I got to know him in —— ' He stopped. 'In the state's prison down to Stillburn. That's where I was, the last part of the time I was away. Busted in a speak-easy one night, hunting for a drink, and they got me. Gave me two years. Brusso was in the same cell with me. He was in for life. Murder. Got sentenced to the 'lectric chair, but the governor commuted him.

26. *Used to lay in his bunk and brag about how many he'd killed, same's a man might brag about catching fish. He'd done it for wages, even, same as if it was a trade. Wasn't worried a mite, neither, about being sent up for life. Wanted to bet me he'd get out ahead of me. Did too. Two months ahead of me.'*
He stopped.

27. *Rucker kept still.* He'd been finding out that questions didn't make it any easier for a man to talk.

'When I got out, I come straight home. Hadn't told 'em my right name nor where I hailed from, and I figured there wasn't much chance of their finding me up here, so I didn't report back to the parole officer. Knew that if I did, somebody would be bound to find out.'

Rucker nodded. After a moment, Lithgow went on:

'I made out all right till a couple of months back. Then one night I was over to the deepo after some freight, and the train came in while I was on the platform. Brusso was on it. He seen me and got off.'

Again the big hand tightened on the steering wheel.

'He was real glad to see me. The murder business ain't been any too good lately, seems as though. Guess the way I acted give Brusso the idee 't he could get money out of me for not squealing on me. He's been getting it, anyhow. All I could lay my hands on. That's why I had to come over and borrow off of you, Mr. Rucker. He'd got all I had by then and he was back for more. He'd got so he didn't even bother to say what he was after.

28. *'Just grinned at me and kind of rubbed his fingers against his thumb, like this.'*
The gesture didn't carry much meaning to George Rucker's eye, but he guessed that maybe a murderer's hand would do it better.

'Don't know when or how he caught on about Ollie,' Lithgow said, 'but I know he done it. He was up here Friday. I seen him driving up the turnpike past Magruder's. He was trying to get past a truck that kept in the middle of the road, so he didn't see me, I guess, but I seen him close enough to be dead sure it was him. Went off the concrete, getting by the truck, and pretty near turned over. Saturday morning, when I heard about Ollie, I come up here and looked at the tire tracks where he hid up his car. I went back along the turnpike and found the same tracks in the soft shoulder, right where I seen Brusso go off the road.'

29. *Rucker took plenty of time. There were a lot of things to think about, but first and mostly he thought about Ed and Milly, and what it would mean to them when this story got around the valley. He knew how fast and far it would travel if even the sheriff knew it, or the state police. They were pretty smart, most ways, but it seemed as if they hadn't ever caught on to the knack of keeping their mouths shut. Anything you told them you could read, next day, in the Canastego paper. It was a queer thing, the way folks hankered to see their names in print, even smart folks who didn't need to have a newspaper tell them how brainy they were, and big and important.*

Rucker had served on juries. He remembered how lawyers talked and acted, and how hard they worked to make things look different from the way they were. He remembered about the funny rules that lawyers and judges had made up, rules that kept a witness from telling more than a little of what he knew. He remembered about the crowd in the courtroom, clapping hands and yelling when a prisoner got off, no matter what he'd done or how well it had been proved.

Ollie wasn't the first man Brusso had killed, either. He'd killed a sight of others. And the one time when the police had made out to catch him and the court had made out to convict him and the judge had sentenced him to the chair, the governor had kept him alive and the parole board had turned him loose.

Rucker thought about Ed's story, too, and the way it would sound in court, what little of it the lawyers and the judge would let him tell. Rucker made up his mind.

30.   *'Real glad you ain't told nobody but me, Ed,' he said. 'I ain't much of a hand to talk. It won't go no further.'*

He saw Lithgow's head jerk upward, saw hope come suddenly into his hopeless face. Milly spoke, her voice quietly triumphant:

'I knew you'd look at it that way, Mr. Rucker. That's why I wouldn't let Ed go tell the sheriff without coming up here and telling you first. If it would help to catch Brusso and kill him, I'd want Ed to tell, but it won't. He hasn't got a mite of proof, the way lawyers look at things. Those marks in the mud don't prove that Brusso was in that car. There's only Ed's word for that, and' — she stopped, a little catch in her voice — 'and he'd have to own up about being in prison. Any smart lawyer could make the jury believe Ed was just making up the story so as to get even with Brusso for squeezing money out of him. Brusso would be bound to get off and——'

'And Ed wouldn't get off,' Rucker said. 'Nor you, neither. No, sir. This stays right where 'tis, between us three.'

31.   *'Seems as though it wasn't right,' Lithgow said doggedly. 'Leaving Brusso to go ahead and kill somebody else. Somebody like Ollie, maybe.'*

'Telling ain't going to stop him from doing that,' Rucker said. 'You'd be back in jail and he'd be on the outside, figuring up some way to get even with you for telling on him. Guess he might do it too. Apt to find out about you and Milly, anyhow, and, by what I hear, his kind ain't too puhtickler to kill womenfolks.'

32.   *Lithgow's shoulders jerked and his mouth went tight. There wasn't much doubt, Rucker guessed, about its staying shut.*

33.   *'Done enough talking, ain't we?' he said. 'Guess you got plenty else to do, weather like this.' His glance moved to the skidway and came back. He managed to twist his mouth into something like a grin. 'I have, anyhow.'*

Lithgow started his engine and turned the truck. It went down the hill almost gaily, Rucker thought. He went back to his work at the skidway — hard work, but simple. It didn't keep him from thinking. He did quite a lot of thinking before he hit on the notion he was hunting for.

34.   *After that he kept on thinking, slowly and patiently, about the notion. He*

had plenty of time. It was three nights afterward that he heard quiet foot steps on the porch. He didn't move or speak. He sat up a little straighter, though. There was no knock. The door opened; a man came in and kicked it shut behind him. He pointed a flat pistol at George Rucker's stomach.

In the yellow light of the glass lamp the gun looked kind of wicked and dangerous, like

35. *the fattish, grinning face above it. George Rucker wasn't much scared, though. He was pretty sure that Brusso wouldn't shoot. Not right away, anyhow. There wouldn't be any sense to doing that, and you could tell from Brusso's face that he was smart.*

36. *Rucker waited for him to do the talking, but Brusso didn't bother to talk. He just held out his left hand and rubbed his fingers against his thumb.*

It was real easy to understand that gesture, Rucker thought, when it was done by somebody that knew how, somebody who had the right kind of hand for it. Brusso's hand was just about right — fat and soft and kind of whitish, like the belly side of a snake or a toad, a hand that didn't know much about work or sun or snow.

37. *'Gimme, grampaw.' Brusso kept on grinning, and his voice was kind of merry too. 'No use stalling. I know you found that sugar. Come through and live awhile.'*

Rucker didn't speak. Brusso's grin flattened.

'Wanna be coaxed, huh? Okay. Stretch out on the floor, face down. Come on, or you might get a slug in the leg.'

The muzzle of the gun moved a little. Rucker got down on the floor.

'Put your hands back of you. That's right.'

The gun pressed against the back of Rucker's neck. A strap went around his wrists, bit into them. Another was slipped over his feet and pulled tight.

38. *That was smart, he thought, fetching straps along, instead of a rope. You could buckle a strap one-handed.*

39. *Brusso's foot rolled him over. Brusso was lighting a cigarette. He took it out of his mouth and blew gently at the glowing tip. Then he held it close to Rucker's cheek.*

'Want to feel that in your eye awhile before you tell me where you got that money hid?'

'It's down to my skidway,' Rucker said. 'Side of the road, right where you — right where the car was. You'll see some poles piled on the ground, right between the skids. All you got to do is move 'em and look under a big flat stone. The money's in a tin can under the stone.'

'It better be,' Brusso said. He stood up. 'If you're stalling me, it's gonna be just too bad about that eye of yours when I come back, grampaw.'

'It's there,' Rucker said. 'Know it wouldn't be no use lying to you.'

'You said it.' Brusso snickered. He blew out the lamp. The door opened and shut.

40. *George Rucker lay still for a little while before he began inching himself over toward the table. Under it, a butcher-knife blade was wedged firmly between the floor boards, edge upward. It was pretty sharp. Rucker only had to saw the strap against it once before his wrists were free. He unbuckled the strap around his legs and stood up. He didn't light the lamp. He didn't need it to find his way to the chimney cupboard where he kept his shotgun.*

He took down the lantern from the peg beside the door as he went out, but he didn't light it, either. He went out to the road and waited there, waited till he heard a noise a long way below him.

He started down the hill then. At the skidway he lit the lantern, not because he needed light to tell him what had happened to Brusso when his fat, toad-belly hand moved those poles, but because he wanted to make sure that nobody else guessed how it had come to happen. He didn't think there was much danger that those young state policemen would guess, nor the long-nosed boy from the newspaper, but the sheriff might. The sheriff was a kind of a back number himself, and he'd been raised in the hills. It might not look to him as if Brusso had just happened to push the prop out from under that skid and let a few tons of saw logs drop on him. The sheriff might notice the notches on those broken poles and remember what a Figure 4 trap looked like.

It took a little time and some hard work to prize up and replace three of the saw logs, but George Rucker had always been a good hand with a cant hook and there wasn't any need to hurry. When he had finished, he was easy in his mind about the way things would look to anybody else. With those notched poles out of sight, with that flat stone shifted far enough to show the money package in the wet earth under it, almost within reach of the outstretched toad-belly hand, even the sheriff would be bound to figure that Brusso must have got scared when, just after killing Ollie, he saw George Rucker's lantern coming down the hill toward him, must have decided to hide the money and come back for it afterwards, sooner than run any risk of being caught with it on him.

When Rucker started down the hill toward Joe Magruder's telephone, he could see a dot of light far out on the flats. It was kind of good to think that there wasn't any reason, now, why that lamp shouldn't be burning there a long, long time for Ed Lithgow and Milly. That newspaper boy's long nose wasn't going to poke itself into their story, spoiling two lives just to give strangers something to gab about for a day or two. It hadn't hurt Joe Dawson any to wait a little while for his payroll money. And Brusso was back yonder, under those saw logs. Lawyers and judges and juries and governors, nor the good-hearted, soft-headed people who believed in babying up murderers, weren't going to turn him loose again this time, to go back to his trade of killing men like Ollie.

George Rucker wasn't much of a hand to set store by himself, but he couldn't help feeling as if he'd handled things kind of well. More than ever, it seemed to him as if there might be a sight of sense in the old-fashioned notion that when there was a job of work that you wanted done to suit you, it was a first-rate scheme to pitch in and tend to it yourself, singlehanded.

Characterization Analysis of 'Singlehanded'

Main character: George Rucker.

Minor characters: Brusso, Ollie, Ed Lithgow, Millie Warren.

Background characters: Jim Dawson, Joe Magruder, the sheriff, the newspaper reporter, two state policemen.

Structure

This is a pattern story, plotted as a story of purpose accomplishment by means of Special Capacity. George Rucker's purpose for the story is to kill Brusso, the villain, and do it singlehanded. He accomplishes his purpose by means of his character-traits and his special knowledge as a lumberman.

Setting

The setting is a rural one in which lumbering and agriculture are carried on. Time, the present.

Viewpoint

The story is told from the viewpoint of the main character, George Rucker, third person.

Emotional Effect on Reader

Satisfaction that justice has been done. Brusso is defeated, Ed and Millie are going to be happy and safe, Jim Dawson gets his money back, Ollie is avenged; and, of course, admiration is built for George Rucker, who brought about the happy conclusion.

BRIEF SUMMARY

George Rucker is faced with the problem of catching Brusso, a thief, blackmailer, and several-times murderer; thereby protecting Ed Lithgow, Millie Warren, and society from a ruthless criminal, and saving the payroll money for Dawson. He moves toward the solution of his problem by the exercise of his dominant character-traits. He plans to catch Brusso and bring about his death singlehanded, in such a way that no one except himself will know how it was done. Using his knowledge as a lumberman, he sets a figure-four trap with his logs, placing the payroll money near by. Then he sends Brusso to get the money. Brusso springs the trap and so is himself the direct instrument of bringing about his own death. The story ends, of course, in success for George Rucker.

COMMENT

This story is slanted toward masculine readers, though most of the large group of women who read *The Saturday Evening Post* would also read it with equally deep interest. It is highly dramatic and emotional in content, but written with great restraint. This restraint is achieved by two means. The major and minor characters, with the possible exception of Millie, are naturally restrained in action, speech, and thought. Much of the presentation is objective; that is, the reader is told what is done, what happens, what is said. The reader is left free to exercise his imaginative faculty regarding the strong emotions that motivate the actors in what they do. This increases the power and vitality of the story. 'Singlehanded' is an especially good model of the rare story in which the main character commits a crime and goes undetected and therefore unpunished. The technique used is correct in every detail. George Rucker kills Brusso for unselfish reasons; he himself gains nothing from Brusso's death, except a sense of satisfaction in an unpleasant but necessary job well done. By killing Brusso he protects two likable characters, Ed Lithgow and Millie Warren, assuring them happiness and release from fear. He causes Jim Dawson to recover the payroll money. He protects society from Brusso's further depredations. In no other way could all these ends have been accomplished. Therefore, the reader feels that George Rucker was completely justified in what he did and the story ends with complete reader-satisfaction. An especially deft touch in bringing about this reader-satisfaction is that of having Brusso himself spring the trap as he reached for the money that was not rightfully his.

CHARACTER-ANALYSES

Main character: George Rucker

Dominant character-trait for the story: a strong desire to do whatever needs doing 'singlehanded.' Other character-traits: observant; thoughtful; patient; willing to wait, plan, and work things out slowly; deliberate in thought, speech, and action; extremely reticent; feels responsibility keenly; a good lumberman; concerned about other people.

Minor character: Brusso

Brusso is, of course, the villain, and since the main character is going to kill him he must be a very black villain indeed. Mr. Kahler has done a thorough job here. Brusso is a several-times murderer, a thief, a blackmailer, cruel and clever, in his way; altogether, a thoroughgoing enemy of society in general, and of two helpless and likable characters, Ed Lithgow and Millie Warren, in particular.

Minor character: Ed Lithgow

Weak, but well-intentioned, industrious, ambitious to rehabilitate himself and make a home for Millie.

Minor character: Millie Warren

Strong, determined, and likable.

Minor character: Ollie

Impatient, cheerful, and clever. The reader likes Ollie, but since he is to be killed early in the story the reader's feeling toward him and interest in him is purposely kept mild, so the reader will not feel too sharp a regret at his death and so be distracted from the main forward movement of the story, which concerns the struggle between George Rucker and Brusso.

Background characters:

These background characters never come on the stage at all, but are simply mentioned. They influence George Rucker's actions to some extent and serve to make the situation clear to the reader.

CHARACTERIZATION-ANALYSIS

1. In this paragraph George Rucker is characterized by setting, approximate age, occupation, habit of thought, and action.
2. Characterization by exposition.
3. Rucker characterized by his own thoughts. Ollie characterized by Rucker's thoughts.
4. Ollie characterized by action, tone of voice, speech.
5. Ollie characterized by his chuckle and by what he says.
6. Rucker characterized by his words.
7. Ollie characterized by his tone of voice. A serious side to his nature shown.
8. Rucker characterized as observant by his words.
9. Rucker characterized as observant by Ollie's words.
10. Rucker characterized as reticent by Ollie's speech and by Rucker's answer.
11. Ollie characterized as smart by Rucker's speech and by Ollie's speech.
12. Rucker characterized by his speech, and the way in which he said the words.
13. Rucker characterized by his thought as a reticent man.
14. This long passage in Rucker's thoughts presented indirectly characterizes him as considerate, generous, warm-hearted, and protective toward young people. This plays an important part in the story-development.
15. Rucker is shown by his actions as deliberate, thoughtful, taking time to do everything necessary to be done without haste or excitement.
16. Rucker's thoughts characterize Ollie as 'smart.'
17. Rucker is characterized by exposition. The writer tells the reader that he thinks slowly, of one thing at a time.
18. Rucker is characterized by action and thought as observant and thoughtful, and his dominant character-trait, a settled belief that it is best to do things singlehanded, is emphasized.
19. Rucker is characterized by exposition; the writer telling the reader what Rucker *did not* do.
20. Further characterization of Rucker by exposition, telling the reader that Rucker is honest, and whenever possible truthful. He dislikes lying.

21. Characterizing Rucker by his kindly, fearful thoughts about Ed Lithgow. Characterizing Ed Lithgow through Rucker's thoughts about Ed, as he remembered Ed's appearance, actions, and his way of speaking.

22. Ed Lithgow is characterized by a descriptive figure of speech, 'looking like a sheep-killing dog,' in the thoughts of George Rucker, given indirectly. Then, Ed is further characterized in the same way as an industrious, hard-working fellow.

23. Characterized by exposition, telling the reader his state of mind.

24. Rucker characterized by action. Millie characterized by tone of voice and way of speaking.

25. Ed Lithgow characterized by what he says, and by the static description of his hand. Rucker characterized by his thoughts as he looks at Ed's hand.

26. Brusso characterized by Ed's speech.

27. Characterizing Rucker by his action, or rather, his refraining from action.

28. Brusso characterized by description of facial expression and a gesture.

29. Rucker characterized by his action, his mode of thought, and the thoughts themselves, which concern Ed and Milly, not himself. Rucker thinks carefully here, summing up the whole situation. Then he makes up his mind.

30. Rucker characterized by his speech.

31. Characterizing Ed by his own speech. He is intrinsically honest and wants to do what is right, even at great sacrifice to himself.

32. Ed characterized by action, or muscular movement, at this threat to Millie.

33. Rucker characterized by his speech.

34. Characterizing Rucker by his mode of thought.

35. Brusso characterized by description of his face.

36. Rucker characterized by his action, Brusso by his. Brusso by description of his hand.

37. Rucker characterized by his speech and facial expression.

38. Brusso characterized by Rucker's thoughts.

39. Brusso characterized by his actions and by his speech.

40. From here to the end of the story Rucker acts and thinks consistently in character. He does not hurry. He makes sure that his plan has worked as he expected it to do. And he looks ahead calmly, seeing what the outcome will be, and this is made clear to the reader through his thoughts.

A Day in Town

BY ERNEST HAYCOX

1. *They reached Two Dance around ten that morning and turned into the big lot between the courthouse and the Cattle King Hotel. Most of the homesteaders camped here when they came to town, for after a slow ride across the sage flats, underneath so hot and so yellow a sun, the shade of the huge locust trees was a comfort. Joe Blount unhitched and watered the horses and tied them to a pole. He was a long and loose and deliberate man who had worked with his hands too many years to waste motion, and if he dallied more than usual over his chores now it was because he dreaded the thing ahead of him.*

2. *His wife sat on the wagon's seat, holding the baby. She had a pin in her mouth and she was talking around it to young Tom: 'Stay away from the horses on the street and don't you go near the railroad tracks. Keep hold of May's hand. She's too little to be alone, you remember. Be sure to come back by noon.'*

    Young Tom was seven and getting pretty thin from growth. The trip to town had him excited. He kept nodding his sun-bleached head, he kept tugging at little May's hand, and then both of them ran headlong for the street and turned the corner of the Cattle King, shrilly whooping as they disappeared.

3. *Blount looked up at his wife. She was a composed woman and not one to bother people with talk* and sometimes it was hard for a man to know what was in her mind. But he knew what was there now, for all their problems were less than this one and they had gone over it pretty thoroughly the last two-three months.

4. *He moved his fingers up to the pocket of his shirt and dropped them immediately away, searching the smoky horizon with his glance. He didn't expect to see anything over there, but it was better than meeting her eyes at this moment. He said in his patiently low voice: 'Think we could make it less than three hundred?'*

    The baby moved its arms, its warm-wet fingers aimlessly brushing Hester Blount's cheeks. She said: 'I don't see how. We kept figuring — and it never gets smaller. You know best, Joe.'

    'No,' he murmured, 'it never gets smaller. Well, three hundred. That's what I'll ask for.' And yet, with the chore before him, he kept his place by the dropped wagon tongue. He put his hands in his pockets and drew a long breath and looked at the powdered earth below him with a sustained gravity, and was like this when

5. *Hester Blount spoke again. He noticed that she was pretty gentle with her words:* 'Why, now, Joe, you go on. It isn't like you were shiftless and hadn't tried. He knows you're a hard worker and he knows your word's good. You just go ahead.'

6. 'Guess we've both tried,' *he agreed.* 'And I guess he knows how it's been. We ain't alone.' *He went out toward the street, reminding himself of this. They weren't alone. All the people along Christmas Creek were burned out, so it wasn't as if he had failed because he didn't know how to farm. The thought comforted him a good deal; it restored a little of his pride.* Crossing the street toward Dunmire's stable, he met Chess Roberts, with whom he had once punched cattle on the Hat outfit, and he stopped in great relief and palavered with Chess for a good ten minutes until, looking back, he saw his wife still seated on the wagon. That sight vaguely troubled him and he drawled to Chess, 'Well, I'll see you later,' and turned quite slowly toward the bank.

There was nothing in the bank's old-fashioned room to take a man's attention. Yet when he came into its hot, shaded silence Joe Blount removed his hat and felt ill at ease as he walked toward Lane McKercher. There was a pine desk here and on the wall a railroad map showing the counties of the Territory in colors. Over at the other side of the room stood the cage where McKercher's son waited on the trade.

7. *McKercher was big and bony and gray and his eyes could cut. They were that penetrating, as everybody agreed.* 'Been a long time since you came to town. Sit down and have a talk,' *and his glance saw more about Joe Blount than the homesteader himself could ever tell.* 'How's Christmas Creek?'

8. *Blount settled in the chair. He said,* 'Why, just fine,' *and laid his hands over the hat in his lap. Weather had darkened him and work had thinned him and gravity remained like a stain on his cheeks. He was, McKercher recalled, about thirty years old, had once worked as a puncher on Hat and had married a girl from a small ranch over in the Yellows. Thirty wasn't so old, yet the country was having its way with Joe Blount. When he dropped his head the skin around his neck formed a loose crease and his mouth had that half-severe expression which comes from too much trouble. This was what McKercher saw. This and the blue army shirt, washed and mended until it was as thin as cotton, and the man's long hard hands lying so loose before him.*

McKercher said, 'A little dry over your way?'

9. 'Oh,' *said Blount,* 'a little. Yeah, a little bit dry.'

The banker sat back and waited, and the silence ran on a long while. Blount moved around in the chair and lifted his hand and reversed the hat on his lap. His eyes touched McKercher and passed quickly on to the ceiling. He stirred again, not comfortable. One hand reached up to the pocket of his shirt, dropping quickly back.

'Something on your mind, Joe?'

'Why,' said Blount, 'Hester and I have figured it out pretty close. It would take about three hundred dollars until next crop. Don't see how it could be less. There'd be seed and salt for stock and grub to put in and I guess some clothes for the kids. Seems like a lot but we can't seem to figure it any smaller.'

'A loan?' said McKercher.

'Why, yes,' said Blount, relieved that the explaining was over.

'Now let's see. You've got another year to go before you get title to your place. So that's no security. How was your wheat?'

'Burnt out. No rain over there in April.'

'How much stock?'

10. '*Well, not much. Just two cows. I sold off last fall. The graze was pretty skinny.' He looked at McKercher and said in the briefest way, 'I got nothing to cover this loan. But I'm a pretty good worker.'*

11. *McKercher turned his eyes toward the desk. There wasn't much to be seen behind the cropped gray whiskers of his face. According to the country this was why he wore them — so that a man could never tell what he figured. But his shoulders rose and dropped and he spoke regretfully: 'There's no show for you on that ranch, Joe. Dry farming — it won't do. All you fellows are burned out. This country never was meant for it. It's cattle land and that's about all.'*

He let it go like that, and waited for the homesteader to come back with a better argument. Only, there was no argument.

12. *Joe Blount's lips changed a little and his hands flattened on the peak of his hat. He said in a slow, mild voice, 'Well, I can see it your way all right,' and got up. His hand strayed up to the shirt pocket again, and fell away —* and McKercher, looking straight into the man's eyes, saw an expression there hard to define. The banker shook his head. Direct refusal was on his tongue and it wasn't like him to postpone it, which he did. 'I'll think it over. Come back about two o'clock.'

'Sure,' said Blount, and turned across the room, his long frame swinging loosely, his knees springing as he walked, saving energy.

13. *After he had gone out of the place McKercher remembered the way the homesteader's hand had gone toward the shirt pocket. It was a gesture that remained in the banker's mind.*

Blount stopped outside the bank. Hester, at this moment, was passing down toward the dry-goods store with the baby in her arms. He waited until she had gone into the store and then walked on toward the lower end of town, not wanting her to see him just then. He knew McKercher would turn him down at two o'clock. He had heard it pretty plainly in the banker's tone, and he was thinking of all the things he had meant to explain to McKercher.

14. *He was telling McKercher that one or two bad years shouldn't count against a man. That the land on Christmas Creek would grow the best winter wheat in the world. That you had to take the dry with the wet. But he knew he'd never say any of this. The talk wasn't in him, and never had been.* Young Tom and

little May were across the street, standing in front of Swing's restaurant, seeing something that gripped their interest. Joe Blount looked at them from beneath the lowered brim of his hat; they were skinny with age and they needed some clothes. He went on by, coming against Chess Roberts near the saloon.

Chess said: 'Well, we'll have a drink on this.'

15. *The smell of the saloon drifted out to Joe Blount, its odor of spilled whisky and tobacco smoke starting the saliva in his jaws, freshening a hunger. But Hester and the kids were on his mind and something told him it was unseemly, the way things were. He said: 'Not right now, Chess. I got some chores to tend. What you doing?'*

'You ain't heard? I'm riding for Hat again.'

Blount said: 'Kind of quiet over my way. Any jobs for a man on Hat?'

'Not now,' said Chess. 'We been layin' off summer help. A little bit tough this year, Joe. You havin' trouble on Christmas Creek?'

16. *'Me? Not a bit, Chess. We get along. It's just that I like to keep workin'.'*

After Chess had gone, Joe Blount laid the point of his shoulder against the saloon wall and watched his two children walk hand in hand past the windows of the general store. Young Tom pointed and swung his sister around; and both of them had their faces against a window, staring in. Blount pulled his eyes away.

17. *It took the kids to do things that scraped a man's pride pretty hard, that made him feel his failure. Under the saloon's board awning lay shade, but sweat cracked through his forehead and he thought quickly of what he could do. Maybe Dunmire could use a man to break horses. Maybe he could get on hauling wood for the feed store. This was Saturday and the big ranch owners would be coming down the Two Dance grade pretty soon. Maybe there was a hole on one of those outfits. It was an hour until noon, and at noon he had to go back to Hester. He turned toward the feed store.*

Hester Blount stood at the dry-goods counter of Vetten's store. Vetten came over, but she said, 'I'm just trying to think.' She laid the baby on the counter and watched it lift its feet straight in the air and aimlessly try to catch them with its hands;

18. *and she was thinking that the family needed a good many things. Underwear all around, and stockings and overalls. Little May had to have some material for a dress, and some ribbon. You couldn't let a girl grow up without a few pretty things, even out on Christmas Creek. It wasn't good for the girl. Copper-toed shoes for young Tom, and a pair for his father; and lighter buttoned ones for May. None of these would be less than two dollars and a half, and it was a crime the way it mounted up. And plenty of flannel for the baby.*

She had not thought of herself until she saw the dark gray bolt of silk lying at the end of the counter, and when she saw it something happened to her heart. It wasn't good to be so poor that the sight of a piece of silk made you feel this way. She turned from it, ashamed of her thoughts — as though she had been guilty of extravagance. Maybe if she were young again and still pretty, and wanting to catch a man's eyes, it might not be so silly to think of clothes. But she was no longer young or pretty and she had her man. She could take out her love of nice things on little May, who was going to be a very attractive girl. As soon as Joe was sure of the three hundred dollars she'd come back here and get what they all had to have — and somehow squeeze out the few pennies for the dress material and the hair ribbon.

19. *She stood here thinking of these things, and so many others — a tall and rather comely woman in her early thirties, dark-faced and carrying an even, sweet-lipped gravity while her eyes sought the dry-goods shelves and her hand unconsciously patted the baby's round middle.*

20. *A woman came bustling into the store and said in a loud, accented voice: 'Why, Hester Blount, of all the people I never did expect to see!'*

Hester said, 'Now, isn't this a surprise!' and the two took each other's hands and fell into a quick half embrace. Ten years ago they had been girls together over in the Two Dance, Hester and this Lila Evenson who had married a town man.

21. *Lila was turning into a heavy woman and, like many heavy women, she loved white and wore it now, though it made her look big as a house. Above the tight collar of the dress, her skin was a flushed red and a second chin faintly trembled when she talked.* Hester Blount stood motionless, listening to that outpour of words, feeling the quick search of Lila's eyes. Lila, she knew, would be taking everything in — her worn dress, her heavy shoes, and the lines of her face.

'And another baby!' said Lila and bent over it and made a long gurgling sound. 'What a lucky woman! That's three? But ain't it a problem, out there on Christmas Creek? Even in town here I worry so much over my one darling.'

'No,' said Hester, 'we don't worry. How is your husband?'

'So well,' said Lila. 'You know, he's bought the drugstore from old Kerrin, who is getting old. He has done so well. We are lucky, as we keep telling ourselves. And that reminds me. You must come up to dinner. You really must come this minute.'

They had been brought up on adjoining ranches and had ridden to the same school and to the same dances. But that was so long ago, and so much had changed them.

22. *And Lila was always a girl to throw her fortunes in other people's faces.*

23. *Hester said, gently, regretfully: 'Now, isn't it too bad! We brought a big lunch in the wagon, thinking it would be easier. Joe has so many chores to do here.'*

'I have often wondered about you, away out there,' said Lila. 'Have you been well? It's been such a hard year for everybody. So many homesteaders going broke.'

24. *'We are well,' said Hester slowly, a small, hard pride in her tone. 'Everything's been fine.'*

'Now, that's nice,' murmured Lila, her smile remaining fixed; but her eyes, Hester observed, were sharp and busy — and reading too much. Lila said, 'Next time you must come and see us,' and bobbed her head and went out of the store, her clothes rustling in this quiet. Hester's lips went sharp-shut and quick color burned on her cheeks. She took up the baby and turned into the street again and saw that Tom hadn't come yet to the wagon. The children were out of sight and there was nothing to do but wait. Hearing the far-off halloo of a train's whistle, she walked on under the board galleries to the depot.

Heat swirled around her and light flashed up from polished spots on the iron rails. Around her lay the full monotony of the desert, so familiar, so wide — and sometimes so hard to bear. Backed against the yellow depot wall, she watched the train rush forward, a high plume of white steam rising to the sky as it whistled to warn them. And then it rushed by, engine and cars, in a great smash of sound that stirred the baby in her arms. She saw men standing on the platforms. Women's faces showed in the car windows, serene and idly curious and not a part of Hester's world at all; and afterward the train was gone, leaving behind the heated smell of steel and smoke. When the quiet came back it was lonelier than before. She turned back to the wagon.

It was then almost twelve. The children came up, hot and weary and full of excitement. Young Tom said: 'The school is right in town. They don't have to walk at all. It's right next to the houses. Why don't they have to walk three miles like us?' And May said: 'I saw a china doll with real clothes and painted eyelashes. Can I have a china doll?'

Hester changed the baby on the wagon seat.

25. She said: 'Walking is good for people, Tom. Why should you expect a doll now, May? Christmas is the time. Maybe Christmas we'll remember.'

'Well, I'm hungry.'

'Wait till your father comes,' said Hester.

When he turned in from the street, later, she knew something was wrong. He was always a deliberate man, not much given to smiling. But he walked with his shoulders down and when he came up he said only: 'I suppose we ought to eat.' He didn't look directly at her. He had his own strong pride and she knew this wasn't like him — to stand by the wagon's wheel, so oddly watching his children. She reached under the seat for the box of sandwiches and the cups and the jug of cold coffee. She said: 'What did he say, Joe?'

'Why, nothing yet. He said come back at two. He wanted to think about it.'

She murmured, 'It won't hurt us to wait,' and laid out the sandwiches. They sat on the shaded ground and ate, the children with a quick, starved impatience, with an excited and aimless talk. Joe Blount looked at them carefully. 'What was it you saw in the restaurant, sonny?'

'It smelled nice,' said young May. 'The smell came out the door.'

26. Joe Blount cleared his throat. 'Don't stop like that in front of the restaurant again.'

'Can we go now? Can we go down by the depot?'

'You hold May's hand,' said Blount, and watched them leave. He sat cross-legged before his wife, his big hands idle, his expression unstirred. The sandwich, which was salted bacon grease spread on Hester's potato bread, lay before him. 'Ain't done enough this morning to be hungry,' he said.

'I know.'

27. *They were never much at talking.* And now there wasn't much to say. She knew that he had been turned down. She knew that at two o'clock he would go and come back empty-handed. Until then she wouldn't speak of it, and neither would he. And she was thinking with a woman's realism of what lay before them. They had nothing except this team and wagon and two cows standing unfed in the barn lot. Going back to Christmas Creek now would be going back only to pack up and leave. For they had delayed asking for this loan until the last sack of flour in the storehouse had been emptied.

He said: 'I been thinking. Not much to do on the ranch this fall. I ought to get a little outside work.'

'Maybe you should.'

'Fact is, I've tried a few places. Kind of quiet. But I can look around some more.'

She said, 'I'll wait here.'

28. *He got up, a rangy, spare man who found it hard to be idle.* He looked at her carefully and his voice didn't reveal anything: 'If I were you I don't believe I'd order anything at the stores until I come back.'

She watched the way he looked out into the smoky horizon, the way he held his shoulders. When he turned away, not meeting her eyes, her lips made a sweet line across her dark face, a softly maternal expression showing. She said, 'Joe,' and waited until he turned. 'Joe, we'll always get along.'

He went away again, around the corner of the Cattle King. She shifted her position on the wagon's seat, her hand gently patting the baby, who was a little cross from the heat. One by one she went over the list of necessary things in her mind, and one by one erased them. It was hard to think of little May without a ribbon bow in her hair, without a good dress. Boys could wear old clothes, as long as they were warm; but a girl, a pretty girl, needed the touch of niceness. It was hard to be poor.

Coming out of the bank at noon, Lane McKercher looked into the corral space and saw the Blounts eating their lunch under the locust tree. He turned down Arapahoe Street, walking through the comforting shade of the poplars to the big square house at the end of the lane. At dinner hour his boy took care of the bank, and so he ate his meal with the housekeeper in a dining-room whose shades had been tightly drawn — the heavy midday meal of a man who had developed his hunger and his physique from early days on the range. Afterward he walked to the living-room couch and lay down with a paper over his face for the customary nap.

A single fly made a racket in the deep quiet, but it was not this that kept him from sleeping.

29. *In some obscure manner the shape of Joe Blount came before him — the long, patient, and work-stiffened shape of a man whose eyes had been so blue and so calm in face of refusal.* Well, there had been something behind those eyes for a moment, and then it had passed away, eluding McKercher's sharp glance.

They were mostly all patient ones and seldom speaking — these men that came off the deep desert. A hard life had made them that way, as McKercher knew, who had shared that life himself. Blount was no different than the others and many times McKercher had refused these others, without afterthoughts. It was some other thing that kept his mind on Blount. Not knowing why, he lay quietly on the couch, trying to find the reason.

The country, he told himself, was cattle country, and those who tried to dry-farm it were bound to fail. He had seen them fail, year after year. They took their wagons and their families out toward Christmas Creek, loaded high with plunder; and presently they came back with their wagons baked and their eyebrows bleached and nothing left. With their wives sitting in the wagons, old from work, with their children long and thin from lack of food. They had always failed and always would. Blount was a good man, but so were most of the rest. Why should he be thinking of Blount?

He rose at one o'clock, feeling the heat and feeling his age; and washed his hands and face with good cold water. Lighting a cigar, he strolled back down Arapahoe and walked across the square toward the Cattle King. Mrs. Blount sat on the wagon's seat, holding a baby. The older youngsters, he noticed, were in the cool runway of Dunmire's stable. He went into the saloon, though not to drink.

'Nick,' he said, 'Joe Blount been in for a drink yet?'

The saloonkeeper looked up from an empty poker table. 'No,' he said.

McKercher went out, crossing to Billy Saxton's feed store. Deep in the big shed Billy Saxton weighed hay bales on his heavy scales. He stopped and sopped the sweat off his forehead, and smiled. 'Bankin',' he stated, 'is easier.'

'Maybe it is,' said Lane McKercher. 'You know Joe Blount well?'

'Why, he's all right. Used to ride for Hat. Old man Dale liked him. He was in here a while back.'

'To buy feed?'

'No, he wanted to haul wood for me.'

McKercher went back up the street toward the bank. Jim Benbow was coming down the road from the Two Dance hills, kicking a long streamer of dust behind. Sun struck the windows on the north side of town, setting up a brilliant explosion of light. Joe Blount came out of the stable and turned over toward the Cattle King, waiting for Benbow.

In the bank, McKercher said to his son, 'All right, you go eat,' and sat down at his pine desk. Benbow put his head through the front door, calling: 'I'll need five thousand this week, Mac — until the stock-check comes in.'

'All right.'

He sat quite still at the desk, stern with himself because he could not recall why he kept thinking of Joe Blount.

30. *Men were everything to Lane McKercher, who watched them pass along this street year in and year out, who studied them with his sharp eyes and made his judgments concerning them. If there was something in a man, it had to come out.* And what was it in Joe Blount he couldn't name? The echoes of the big clock on the wall rattled around the droning silence of the bank like the echo of feet striking the floor; it was then a quarter of two, and he knew he had to refuse Blount a second time. He could not understand why he had not made the first turndown final.

Blount met Jim Benbow on the corner of the Cattle King, directly after Hat's owner had left the bank. He shook Benbow's hand, warmed and pleased by the tall cattleman's smile of recognition. Benbow said: 'Been a long time since I saw you. How's Christmas Creek, Joe?'

'Fine — just fine. You're lookin' good. You don't get old.'

'Well, let's go have a little smile on that.'

'Why, thanks, no. I was wonderin'. It's pretty quiet on my place right now. Not much to do till spring. You need a man?'

Benbow shook his head. 'Not a thing doing, Joe. Sorry.'

'Of course — of course,' murmured Blount. 'I didn't figure there would be.'

He stood against the Cattle King's low porch rail after Benbow had gone down the street, his glance lifted and fixed on the smoky light of the desert beyond town. Shade lay around him but sweat began to creep below his hatbrim. He was closely and quickly thinking of places that might be open for a man, and knew there were none in town and none on the range. This was the slack season of the year. The children were over in front of the grocery store, stopped by its door, hand in hand, and their round, dark cheeks lifted and still. Blount swung his shoulders around, cutting them out of his sight.

Suddenly Ben Drury came out of the courthouse and passed Blount, removing his cigar and speaking, and replacing the cigar again. Its smell was like acid biting at Blount's jaw corners, and suddenly he faced the bank with the odd and terrible despair of a man who has reached the end of hope, and a strange thought came to him, which was that the doors of that bank were wide open and money lay on the counter inside for the taking.

31. *He stood very still, his head down, and after a while he thought: 'An unseemly thing for a man to hold in his head.'* It was two o'clock then and he turned over the square, going toward the bank with his legs springing as he walked and all his muscles loose. In the quietness of the room his boots dragged up odd sound. He stood by Lane McKercher's desk, waiting without any show of expression; he knew what McKercher would say.

McKercher said, slowly and with an odd trace of irritation: 'Joe, you're wasting your time on Christmas Creek. And you'd waste the loan.'

Blount said, mildly and courteously: 'I can understand your view. Don't blame you for not loanin' without security.' He looked over Mc-Kercher's head, his glance going through the window to the far strip of horizon. 'Kind of difficult to give up a thing,' he mused. 'I figured to get away from ridin' for other folks and ride for myself. Well, that was why we went to Christmas Creek. Maybe a place the kids could have later. Man wants his children to have somethin' better than he had.'

'Not on Christmas Creek,' said McKercher. He watched Joe Blount with a closer and sharper interest, bothered by a feeling he could not name. Bothered by it and turned impatient by it.

'Maybe, maybe not,' said Blount. 'Bad luck don't last forever.' Then he said, 'Well, I shouldn't be talkin'. I thank you for your time.' He put on his hat,

32. *and his big hand moved up across his shirt to the pocket there — and dropped away.* He turned toward the door.

'Hold on,' said Lane. 'Hold on a minute.' He waited till Blount came back to the desk. He opened the desk's drawer and pulled out a can of cigars, holding them up. 'Smoke?'

33. *There was a long delay and it was strange to see the way Joe Blount looked at the cigars, with his lips closely together. He said, his voice dragging on the words, 'I guess not, but thanks.'*

34. *Lane McKercher looked down at the desk, his expression breaking out of its maintained strictness. The things in a man had to come out, and he knew now why Joe Blount had stayed so long in his mind. It made him look up. 'I have been considering this. It won't ever be a matter of luck on Christmas Creek. It's a matter of water. When I passed the feed store today I noticed a second-hand windmill in the back. It will do. You get hold of Plummer Bowdry and find out his price for driving you a well. I never stake a man unless I stake him right. We will figure the three hundred and whatever it takes to put up a tank and windmill. When you buy your supplies today, just say you've got credit here.'*

'Why, now —' began Joe Blount in his slow, soft voice, 'I ——'

But Lane McKercher said to his son, just coming back from lunch, 'I want you to bring your ledger over here.' He kept on talking and Joe Blount, feeling himself pushed out, turned and left the bank.

McKercher's son came over. 'Made that loan after all. Why?'

35. *McKercher said only, 'He's a good man, Bob.' But he knew the real reason. A man that smoked always carried his tobacco in his shirt pocket. Blount had kept reaching, out of habit, for something that wasn't there. Well, a man like Blount loved this one small comfort and never went without it unless actually destitute. But Blount wouldn't admit it, and had been too proud to take a free cigar. Men were everything — and the qualities in them came out sooner or later, as with Blount. A windmill and water was a good risk with a fellow like that.*

36. *Hester watched him cross the square and come toward her, walking slowly, with his shoulders squared. She patted the baby's back and gently rocked it, and wondered at the change. When he came up he said, casually, 'I'll hitch and drive around to the store, so we can load the stuff you buy.'*

She watched him carefully, so curious to know how it had happened. But she only said: 'We'll get along.'

He was smiling then, he who seldom smiled. 'I guess you need a few things for yourself. We can spare something for that.'

'Only a dress and some ribbon, for May. A girl needs something nice.'

She paused, and afterward added, because she knew how real his need was, 'Joe, you buy yourself some tobacco.'

He let out a long, long breath. 'I believe I will,' he said. They stood this way, both gently smiling. They needed no talk to explain anything to each other. They had been through so much these last few years. Hardship and trouble had drawn them so close together that words were unnecessary. So they were silent, remembering so much, and still smiling. Presently he turned to hitch up.

Characterization-Analysis of 'A Day in Town'

Main character: Joe Blount.

Minor characters: Lane McKercher, Hester Blount.

Background characters: The children: Tom, May, and the baby. Chess Roberts, Vetten, the storekeeper, Lila Evanston, Nick the saloonkeeper, Billy Saxton, Jim Benbow, Ben Drury, Plummer Bowdry.

Structure

This is a true character story, in which a man accomplishes his purpose, not by struggle in accordance with a plan for accomplishing that purpose, but due to his innate character traits.

Setting

The setting is a small cow-town in the West. The characters have been moulded and influenced by the setting.

Viewpoint

The story is told from the omniscient viewpoint. Most writers consider this the most difficult viewpoint to use, but it is a favorite with Ernest Haycox, who has mastered its intricacies, and uses it fearlessly, with a rich, satisfying effect. In this story the reader is taken into the consciousness of the main character and each of the minor characters. Also the writer himself, in his capacity of omniscience, gives information and explanation. Yet there is no aimless and unnecessary shifting of viewpoint. Each shift is made clearly and for a definite reason.

Effect

Reader-satisfaction that courage, honesty, and self-respect bring to Joe and Hester Blount the three hundred dollars they need so desperately, and the windmill and well that will enable them to succeed in making a home for themselves and for their children on Christmas Creek.

BRIEF SUMMARY

Joe Blount and his wife, Hester, have come to Two Dance to ask for a loan of three hundred dollars. They have no security to offer, and if they do not get the loan they will have to abandon their homestead on Christmas Creek. The story-action is concerned with showing the courage, self-respect, and self-control of Joe and his wife. Nothing that they can consciously do or say will get them the loan. But Joe's dominant character-traits, as shown through conscious and unconscious action, convince the banker that Joe is good for the loan of three hundred dollars, and the well and windmill besides.

COMMENT

This is a story slanted toward both men and women, though the masculine interest is the stronger of the two. There are many devices used to heighten the suspense and increase the importance of what depends upon the outcome. It is Mr. Haycox' remarkable skill in building these and in his moving characterization that enables him to hold reader-interest with so slight a thread of action. 'A Day in Town' is told with the admirable restraint and attention to significant detail that characterize all of Mr. Haycox' work.

CHARACTER-ANALYSES

Main character: Joe Blount

Dominant character-traits for the story: self-respect and pride in his own integrity and ability to provide for his family. Other traits: courage, self-denial, self-control, industry, tenacity.

Minor character: Lane McKercher

Dominant character-trait: a desire to be fair in his judgment of others. Other character-traits: observant, firm, kindly, willingness to back his own judgment.

Minor character: Hester Blount

Dominant character-trait: unselfishness. Other character-traits: courage, loyalty, self-respect, industry, devotion to her husband and children.

Background characters

The background characters in this story, of which there are a large number, are flat, scarcely individualized at all. With the exception of the children, and

Lila, they are not even characterized. Yet they are named. The reason is clear. Two Dance is a small town. Everyone knows everyone else. Therefore it is natural that the background characters should be named. Their function is to furnish atmosphere and give opportunity for the characterization of the main and minor characters by dialogue.

CHARACTERIZATION-ANALYSIS

1. Characterization by setting and occupation. They are homesteaders in what is really cattle country. Joe Blount is characterized by his action, his appearance, and information given by the writer from the omniscient viewpoint.
2. Hester is characterized by action and by speech.
3. Hester is characterized by exposition. The reader is told she is composed, restrained, controlled.
4. Joe is characterized by action, an instinctive, almost unconscious gesture. Also by his tone of voice and by his words.
5. Characterizing Hester by the way she speaks, and her choice of words. Characterizing Joe by Hester's comment.
6. Characterizing Joe by his speech, by his thoughts, and by exposition; that is, the writer telling us that Joe's thoughts restored his pride.
7. Characterizing McKercher by facial contours and expression of his eyes. Also by speech.
8. Characterizing Joe by Joe's appearance, as seen by McKercher, manner, facial expression, clothing, and what McKercher knows about his past life.
9. Joe subtly characterized by speech and action; the significant gesture is repeated. Pride and restraint shown.
10. Characterizing Joe by his simple, straightforward speech, stating his case, making no plea.
11. Characterizing McKercher by lack of facial expression, gesture of his shoulders, way of speaking, words used.
12. Characterizing Joe by facial expression, action, the significant gesture again, and his speech.
13. Characterizing Joe by McKercher's thoughts.
14. Characterizing Joe by his thoughts, his estimate of himself.
15. Characterizing Joe by action.
16. Characterizing Joe by his speech.
17. Joe characterized by his attitude of mind and by his thoughts.
18. Hester characterized by her thoughts as she plans for May and longs for pretty things for herself, but gives them up.
19. Hester characterized by appearance, age, facial expression, and action.
20. Lila characterized by manner, tone of voice, manner of speaking, and words used. Her sharp contrast to Hester intensifies the character of each of the women.
21. Characterization of Lila by the lineaments of her body, clothing, appear-

ance, manner. Again the women are sharply contrasted, both here and in the paragraph that follows.

22. The writer characterizes Lila for the reader by summing up past conduct.
23. Hester characterized by her manner and speech.
24. Same as above.
25. Hester characterized by her patient speech.
26. Joe characterized by his speech.
27. Characterizing both Joe and Hester by exposition.
28. Characterizing Joe by description and exposition.
29. Characterizing Joe through description of his bodily lineaments and the expression of his eyes, through the thoughts of McKercher.
30. Characterizing McKercher by exposition.
31. Characterizing Joe by his thoughts.
32. Joe characterized by this significant gesture.
33. Joe characterized by facial expression, way of speaking, and by his speech.
34. Characterizes McKercher by facial expression and words. The actual characterization by words is done in the sentence, 'I never stake a man unless I stake him right.'
35. Characterizing Joe by McKercher's speech and thought.
36. Throughout this last paragraph Joe and Hester act and speak in the manner that is characteristic of each. They are as restrained and self-controlled in victory as in defeat.

No Flourishes

BY LUCRETIA PENNY

(Title changed afterward to 'Limbs is a Flourish Word' and published under
that title)

(The following is the *first version*, as submitted to me by the author. After
many revisions, this story was published in *The Saturday Evening Post*. Read
it carefully, note the weaknesses in plot construction, characterization, and
emotion; note that there is little interest in 'Sister's' problem, no action, and
that the story opens with a long narrative passage, without reader-interest,
and unfolds with much irrelevant detail. However, the student will recognize
in this draft the *material* out of which a strong, interesting story was *built*.)

First Draft

That Mr. Syl Faulkner was truly great I never doubted. His life was an
open book, plainly readable. As a matter of fact, because of Mr. Syl and his
memory that he claimed had never been worth a bawbee, our neighborhood
was a community of open-book lives.

Mr. Syl began his public diary many years before I was born. The first
entry written on the pine wall of his big front room was: 'Pa died at 9:12 A.M.
tolerably easy. His memory was the best thing he had.' The next day Mr.
Syl asked the pallbearers to write their names on the wall but after that he
never allowed anyone else to write there. 'Half of 'em sloped their letters,'
he said, 'and the rest made flourishes; I sure hate flourishes.'

His own round and modestly plain handwriting had been acquired at a
penmanship school Professor Hunt held up Scummy Creek one winter. For
accuracy in this class Mr. Syl won a book on etiquette which he treasured but
never consulted. 'I took to penmanship because it don't require a memory,'
he'd say; 'my memory is from Ma's side and not worth a bawbee; either I set
a thing down while it's fresh or I don't keep it straight.'

Mr. Syl's father had been a neighborhood authority on all matters of dates
and ages and similar detail over which persons of fallible memory dispute.
Feeling keenly his own lack of such a gift and wanting to do what he could
toward taking his father's place in the community, Mr. Syl hit upon the plan
of making use of his skill in penmanship by keeping a wall diary and making
it available to the neighborhood for reference.

Some said that he felt a wife would interfere with his lifework. At any rate he remained single and after his father's death lived alone. Every evening when he had wound the Seth Thomas clock he took a pencil out of the clock case, sharpened it painstakingly, and wrote on the wall the date and whatever of interest the day had brought to his attention.

Perhaps he would write nothing more than 'Sure a bleak bad day' or 'Fine growing weather.' He might make such a note as 'Had Old Am shod all round' or 'Left off woolens' or 'Daisies is sure as heck taking my bottom lot.' He might record an expenditure, 'Curry comb 50 cents,' or a bit of useful information, 'Plaintain seed stewed in milk for cholera morbus.' Sometimes he put down a line of song he wished to remember: 'Dan Patch that horse of mine done quit running and gone to flying.'

His record was by no means limited to personal and local matters. One read there: 'Gen'l U. S. Grant elected president; there sure ain't no law against hoping for the best though' and 'Bad cyclone in Texas; a mean wind can sure play the mischief.'

With neighborhood news Mr. Syl took meticulous pains. (He never had any luck with erasers, he said.) News brought him by persons of questionable accuracy never went on the wall until verified. He'd explain: 'I got to be strictly one hundred per cent accurate like Pa was or there ain't no point to all this.'

Once he was sure of his facts he went ahead fearlessly and if he chose to add an unflattering comment to a news item he added it in clear round letters with a freshly sharpened pencil and whoever didn't like it could 'Sure go read off somebody else's wall.' 'It's my own house, ain't it?' Mr. Syl would ask mildly.

Gus Stowers once took exceptions to a pine-planking editorial comment that followed the announcement of his foreclosure of the mortgage on a widowed in-law's home. He sent Mr. Syl word that if the plank wasn't sawed out by Saturday night he'd be down to see about it and all hell and high water couldn't stop him. Mr. Syl replied that the height of the water was in the hands of Providence but hell could sure be had for the asking. Mr. Stowers was in bed with a toothache by Saturday and nothing further came of the incident. (Mr. Syl, even in his old age, was so strong that farmers boasting of a good work mule used to say 'he's strong as Syl Faulkner but easier drove.')

I always thought that married men envied Mr. Syl and I know that all the neighborhood's children did. The women spoke of him condescendingly and when a visitor came from a distance the first wonder presented to her would be an account of this diary-keeping strong man who had won a prize for penmanship but didn't have any better sense than to eat his own cooking. If a lucky boy who had had a meal with Mr. Syl — the highest honor to which a child could aspire — spoke up to declare that the hot biscuits had been big and fine and heaped with honey, the women of the household sniffed: 'May have tasted all right to *you!*'

No child ever objected to being sent on an errand to Mr. Syl's and I envied the boys of the family this privilege more than I envied them their sling shots and suspenders. 'Run find out what year it was the spring flood washed away the swinging bridge and Doc Jasper's no-top buggy and brought the hog-scalding trough from who-knows-where right to Shad's barn lot' was a welcome command at any time and 'Let me go see' was every child's ready response when adults began to speculate on how long it had been since Cousin Captain ran for sheriff or what tobacco sold for in '91. Sometimes a letter would come from a relative who had moved away and wanted us to find out what year York's barn burned or the Bailey bridge was put in, so that, by these, other dates — of personal importance — might be established.

I was nine when I went with my father to consult The Wall for the date of the last epidemic of hog cholera, and all of my heart's hope was fixed on Mr. Syl that day. He alone could take from me the curse of being a person of no importance. For months I had nursed this secret plan, shaping and reshaping it by day, distorting it in my dreams at night. By it, if at all, I should establish my greatness in the sight of an outspoken group of children of whom I was youngest, homeliest, the one least likely to win at mumble peg, the only one afraid of lightning.

I hadn't really expected my father to consent when I asked to go with him, but he was in a good humor — it was the morning after the day he won three checker games from Dr. Jasper — and he said he supposed I might go if I'd get my hair out of my eyes and not talk everybody's head off.

We found Mr. Syl sitting on his front steps in the February sunshine smoothing a hickory axe handle with a triangle of broken glass. His hair and whiskers were a wiry white frame about a youthful face and his sharp old eyes gave back the faded blue of his overall jacket. The mulberry tree threw its bleak shadow over his stiff, straight figure and the scraped hickory fell before the broken glass to powder the toes of his shoes.

Just standing there watching him made me feel important, as if the glass slipper he could give me was already upon my feet. Here was a man who wrote without fear upon the walls of his house, a man who without asking permission had huddled his furniture to the middle of his room to make way for something of greater consequence, a man who settled the arguments of adults, a man stronger than mules and able to set a copy better than that in the copybooks — and for all of his power and greatness there was kindness in his face. In my opinion anyone who would hesitate to change places with Mr. Syl didn't have the sense the Lord promised geese.

'You ought to have a thinner piece of glass for that,' my father said.

Mr. Syl ran his forefinger over the length of hickory he had just polished. 'Bud,' he said tolerantly, 'is there anything on God's good earth you won't give advice on?'

My father started talking about the checker games. It was the first time he'd won more than one a day from Doctor Jasper since the year the hog cholera was so bad, but he didn't mention that, he just said as if he were changing the subject, he'd like to know what year the cholera came last. I edged impatiently, and I hoped, inconspicuously, toward the door.

Mr. Syl said, 'West, wall, left of the mantel, Bud.'

My father said, 'Don't worry, I'll find it.'

'About head high to your young one, maybe two-three inches higher

Throw on wood if the fire's low. I'll be in soon's I've slickened this handle a little more.'

I didn't ask for directions, for fear my father would complain that I was talking too much, but I brushed back my hair and went inside and began to search for my birth date. If I could — and I must — find even the tiniest reference to my existence on The Wall I'd have something of which to boast for the remainder of my untalented life and the need of a well-supported boast was the starkest hunger I had ever felt.

Half a line would make everything right. Just the date and my name and 'born.'

'You ought to have a step ladder to keep in here,' my father called to Mr. Syl. I was near the door and I heard Mr. Syl sigh and say softly, 'If that ain't a chip off the old block I never hope to see one. He'd tell a spider how to spin.'

I was trembling with excitement and my hand left a damp mark on the wall as it hunted among the even rows of dates, along the door facing, up the side of the window. Finally, tiptoeing, I found the day that was my own, and read: 'Pouring rain. Set dishes out to get washed.' I looked again at the date, hoping I had misread it, counting on my fingers to make sure of the year.

'Just you wait until I tell you about me!' How many times had I held that promise up as a shield between me and the reminders of my short-comings! And now it was another withered boast and there was nothing to take the place of what I had lost. On The Wall before me bad weather and a bachelor's dishes had been made immortal in space which in a just world would have been rightfully mine.

When I thought I could speak without sniffling I went around the huddle of furniture in the middle of the room and asked my father if it had rained the day I was born.

'There you go talking again,' he complained, his broad forefinger tracking the elusive cholera along the north wall. 'Your mother ought to do something about you.'

I wished he had denied the rain. An error in the record would have shocked but comforted me. I went back to the window and sat down and read the entries near the floor, half hoping that some belated mention of me might appear there. In the light of my grievance none of the items seemed important and I no longer took pleasure in them.

'Judd come by with his new teeth. They sure look good but he has to take 'em out to swallow.'

'Pneumonia got Grover Robbins. Wouldn't want to praise pneumonia but even when he was sober Grove was a troublemaker.'

'Les Jones was picked to teach the Bailey Bridge School. Good thing. Upstart they had there last year couldn't spell hoe-cake without his mammy's help.'

'Tent meeting commenced back of the mill. They got what they call religion but from this side of the creek it sure resembles cramp colic.'

'Helped dig grave for Widow Brunner. If she don't have her pick of crown

stars it ain't fair. She raised five boys without no help and had a roll of due-
bills left over.'
'Brice Ridd's little red-head and Touchy Adams got married this morning.
Good match. Been too bad to spoil a *couple* of households with them spitfires.'
'Aunt Bea sent me word to put down she'd started a Lend and Borrow quilt.
She won't put a worldly quilt name in the Bible and anywhere else she loses it.
Her housekeeping ain't much better than mine.'
'Brady bought a red automobile he says can go twenty miles a hour easy.
Can't hold up long at that rate. Sorry I wrote that. I sure hate to hear a old
man run down progress.'
'Young Bill Holt made a speech at the political rally. Wind held out ex-
cellent. If his ideas ever come to him he'll sure be first rate.'
My father was standing on a chair when Mr. Syl came in. Beyond the
black walnut secretary that stood facing the fireplace I could see my father's
jeans elbow moving in and out among the dates.
'You ought to always put down the temperature, summer *and* winter,'
he told Mr. Syl.
'You're 'way too high for the cholera, Bud.'
Mr. Syl came over to my window. 'You cholera-hunting, too, Sister?'
I shook my head, remembering to put my hair back in place afterward. 'I
was trying to see did it say when I was born, and it doesn't.' I didn't look at
him.
'How old are you?'
'I'm nine.' I hoped my father wouldn't think that was talking too much.
'And how many months and days?'
'I'd have to count.'
He went over and opened the door to the clock. There was a ship painted
on the door and the waves of the ocean were of heavy blue-white paint that
stood out enough to catch the dust, and fine ashes from the fireplace. At
another time the thought of a dusty ocean would have pleased my fancy, but
now it didn't matter. I wanted to be up behind my father on Old Bay, with
no further need to keep the tears out of my eyes.
Mr. Syl had taken a short pencil out of the clock and put a point on it. He
snapped his big knife shut and put it in his pocket and brought me the pencil.
'There's a new shingle by the door you can figure on. Be sure you get it
strictly accurate. There ain't no possible point to all this if it ain't strictly
accurate — like Pa himself would had it.'
I looked at him questioningly.
'Tonight I'm going to set down that you're nine years old and so many
months and days this date, and a mighty promising-looking little sister.'
He glanced to where my father was still standing on the chair looking for the
cholera, and winked at me. 'If being on The Wall evens things up for you any
you're sure welcome.'
'No cholera here,' my father announced, getting down. 'You ought to be
more particular about stock diseases than you are.'
Mr. Syl went over to the west wall and put his finger on a plank near the

mantel and a little higher than my head. 'Come get your cholera, Bud, and then set down and calm yourself. Sister's got some figuring to do and she don't want to be interrupted.'

'We got to be going,' my father said as he bent over the date he had hunted. That young one's so slow when she figures that the moon would be full before she'd added one and two.'

'Sit down,' Mr. Syl said firmly, 'or go look at the pigs. Sister's going to do her figuring and eat a honey biscuit before she leaves here.'

My father said, 'Thunderation, Mr. Syl!' but went on outside and we heard the weights on the gate rattle.

Mr. Syl smiled. 'He's gone to tell the pigs how to root. He makes you feel like two cents, don't he, Sister? Well, don't you care. You get your shingle.'

That night I hurried through my supper and slipped back into the family room before the others had finished eating. I had a table knife hidden under my apron and I did my best to put a fine point on my pencil before I wrote on the wall beside the window 'I am nine years and two months and seventeen days old this date and Mr. Syl Faulkner is sure a good man.'

The room had been freshly papered in the spring and I was sure of being punished but it seemed like the least I could do for Mr. Syl.

I stood off and looked at what I had written and then carefully erased a flourish that had been part of the 'I.'

Note: Now read the published version; carefully observe the change of emphasis and the development in characterization.

Limbs is a Flourish Word

BY LUCRETIA PENNY

(Reprinted by permission of the author and the *Saturday Evening Post*)

I figured my age out afterwards on a shingle, trying not to cry. That's how I know I was nine years and two months and seventeen days old the Saturday morning I rode with my father to have a look at The Wall. The only hope I had that day was that Mr. Sylvester Aquila Willoughby might have thought my being born was important.

If Mr. Syl had thought my being born was important he'd have set it down on The Wall. And if my name was on The Wall the King David thing was as good as blotted out.

What everybody called The Wall was really all four walls of the square front room at Mr. Syl's. The room had never been painted or papered — it was just naked pine — and Mr. Syl wrote on the four sides of it anything he thought was important. It made a sort of diary or history or whatever you'd call it, and people came from as far off as the Kentucky line to prove things by it. I didn't see any reason why Mr. Syl should have thought my being born was important, but then Mr. Syl was a great man — strong and smart and not afraid of anybody — and great men don't always think what other folks think.

The night before, when I was crying into the knitted lace on my pillowslip — before Aunt Sethella came to bed — I wouldn't have thought of telling that I wanted to go to Mr. Syl's. I knew what they'd say if I did. My father would look out from under his eyebrows that were a lot too bushy for such a little man and say, 'What in thunderation for?' and 'Think me and Old Bay's got nothing better to do than travel six miles off and six miles back with you?' and 'Leave it to a girl young-one to think up the eternalest things to want!' Aunt Sethella would sniff the way I'd heard her do lots of times. 'Syl Willoughby and his wrote-all-over walls! Every stitch of his furniture in a huddle in the room's middle!' And then she'd sigh and pretty soon she'd be singing about Love and Hope and Beauty's bloom are blossoms gathered for the tomb and nothing's bright but heaven.

That's a good song, all right, for when you're gloomy. I'd been saying it over that night, before Aunt Sethella came to bed. It helped to keep the King David thing from coming to the top of my mind where I could see how awful it was. I had to keep it weighed down with anything I could because it didn't want to stay down any more than a cat wants to be drowned. I was so gloomy

I didn't think even heaven could be solid bright. Not for me, anyway. Likely I'd no sooner get there than they'd take me for a smart aleck the way Miss Helen had right after she came to be our teacher.

Miss Helen's taking me for a smart aleck was something else I couldn't stand to think about, so I put my mind back on the song. Aunt Sethella had a copy of it in her trunk and the writing was so nice you wouldn't believe anybody could have done it. I begged her to let me take it to school, but she wouldn't. It would have been something to brag about at school. I asked her who wrote it out and she said somebody she used to go to singing school with. I said, 'Don't you even remember his name, Aunt Sethella?' and she said it would be a pity if she had to go around gabbling about all she could remember. I said if anybody ever copied off a song for me that good, I'd gabble.

Thinking about all this the Friday night I was so gloomy reminded me of The Wall, the way good handwriting would. That was because everybody said there wasn't a line Mr. Syl ever wrote but what would take first prize at a writing school. As soon as I thought of The Wall I knew what it was that could save me. Suppose my birthday had been set down there! That would be something to brag about! A brag like that couldn't be bettered. It could blot out the King David thing like it hadn't ever been.

Just for a minute I lay there and imagined Monday was going to be all right, for of course I knew better. Mr. Syl might as well be a million miles away. Nobody would take me to his house. Saturday would come and go, and Sunday. The school bell would ring and nothing I could do would make Monday easier to stand.

All this, though, was before I knew about my father's wanting the date of the hog cholera. I found that out at breakfast next morning.

I had to try to eat my breakfast because I didn't want my father and Aunt Sethella to know how gloomy I was. My father would have heard about the King David thing at the store, of course. Checker players always got news of what happened at school because Shucks Sloan, whose father kept the store, was a great hand to tell all he knew. He'd told about the banjo thing the fall before and it shamed my father so he lost a checker game he by rights would have won. All I could do was pretend I didn't care. I didn't know then that pretending is an unworthy flourish and I reckon Aunt Sethella didn't either.

There were dried apples, and side meat cut thin, and biscuits and sorghum for breakfast. My father pressed the top of a biscuit down with his fork and watched the butter run out on his plate. He said, 'Either it's seven or it's eight years since the hogs had cholera. No way you take it could it be ten.'

Aunt Sethella said, 'Don't look to me for the answer. I didn't come back to keep your house till five years ago come Easter. The five years back of that I was on the Kentucky side taking care of Miss Triphy, and hog cholera wasn't one of my worries.'

Aunt Sethella always smiled like she hated to when she said, 'Miss Triphy.' All I knew was that Miss Triphy had promised to will Aunt Sethella a farm and she hadn't done it. I didn't see any reason to smile any kind of a smile over her. If she'd done what she said, I could have gone over on the Kentucky side

to live with Aunt Sethella, and my father wouldn't have had such a load t(
carry.

My father touched the red squares on the tablecloth with the handle of his
knife. 'Here was Jeff's. Here was mine. These three of his, kings. These two
of mine. You'd said I didn't stand a chance.'

Aunt Sethella didn't look to see where the crowned and common men had
been. She just said, 'Checkers!' and made the way it sounded tell how well
she could get along without that game.

I didn't need any talk of kings to make the King David thing commence
burrowing to the top of my mind. I tried to swallow a bite of side meat and the
lump in my throat was bigger than the thistle blossom on the sugar bowl.

My father said, 'Well, I beat Jeff twice right together. Last time I got two
together off of him was year of the hog cholera. Jeff says that was ten years
back, but either it was seven or eight.'

Aunt Sethella said, 'Hush, Bud. Hush. I can't see how it matters.' She
stood up and dished the dried apples out of the bowl onto our plates. 'Eat
'em. I got more soaking for tomorrow's pies.'

She had finished her breakfast way ahead of my father and me, like she always did. She was taller than my father, but she was skinny and what satisfied
a sparrow would do for her. She went over to the stove and started washing
the cook things, the way she did every morning, and watching us like she
wished there was some way to make us hurry, and sort of looking past us
too.

My father took another biscuit and got quiet. Once in a while he'd touch
the tablecloth with his knife handle and you could tell he was memorizing
those two games and feeling good.

I reckon Aunt Sethella noticed it, for she sighed. Her sigh was like something dead tired going down a long stairsteps, going slow and stopping and
going on. I'd heard she took it after her mother's mother and I wondered if
when I was grown I'd sigh that way, thinking of King David and all I'd been
through at school.

Aunt Sethella said, 'I don't crave to hear checkers and hog cholera the
whole blessed enduring Day of Rest. If you've got to know how long it's
been, saddle Old Bay and ride over to Syl's.' She had a way of favoring him
like that, giving him an easy out and making like she did it to spare herself;
the way your mother'll talk, if you have one. She was a lot the oldest and
she'd raised him after their other folks died.

My father said, 'I aim to,' and he creamed butter into the sorghum on his
plate and plastered another biscuit with it. He said, 'You ought to let the
cook things wait till you've washed the dishes.'

I crammed a forkful of apples into my mouth so I wouldn't be gabbling
out of turn and I tried to watch his face and not let him see enough of mine to
start him prying into what I had hope of.

Aunt Sethella commenced to hum When the Roll is Called Up Yonder to
show she wasn't paying any attention to advice. I waited for him to finish
eating and cross his knife and fork. Then I dropped a spoon, and while I was

under the table after it I said what was on my mind. That way nobody'd notice how much it meant to me.

'I reckon it wouldn't hurt anything if I rode behind you to Mr. Syl's to help hunt the cholera date.'

'Leave it to you to want to help do what you don't know how to!'

He stood up and put his foot on a chair and commenced to lace his shoes, like he always did after breakfast. I watched the rawhide strings go over the hooks on his shoe tops and I tried to think what words I could use to sound like I wasn't asking the same thing over.

He said, 'Dud's after me to trade him this place for half interest in the store and the stock scales.'

'And we could set up housekeeping on the platform of the scales, I reckon!' Aunt Sethella sniffed. 'Anybody come and wanted a bunch of hogs weighed, they could drive 'em right in the kitchen.'

'I never said I traded. Man with the load I carry's never free to look out for his own good.'

Aunt Sethella just looked at him and I moved over by her. 'If I was to go I reckon it wouldn't hurt anything if I wore my guimpe dress.'

'If you was to go you'd wear what's on you. Nobody's to see you but Syl Willoughby. A man that'll eat his own cooking won't notice brier stitching on a guimpe.'

My father said, 'Never since the Lord made Eve has a man had to eat his own cooking.'

Aunt Sethella turned around to put a pot lid in the rack on the wall, and standing with her back to us, she said, 'There could be things not known to you, Bud. I'm not saying there are, but could be.' The way she said it was just like Love and Hope and Beauty's bloom being blossoms gathered for the tomb. It all just meant luck for me, for my father changed the subject in a hurry and he said, 'Get your hair out of your eyes, King David, and try not to talk my arm off all the way there and back. Funny to me that every time you see a girl young-one with tow hair it's flying every which of a way.'

Aunt Sethella said, 'Can she help it if she's towheaded?' Then she said to me, 'Don't go off without your stocking cap. Weather could change. Spring's set in before it's due.'

I said, 'Yes, ma'am, spring has,' and tried to make my voice match hers and not sound hopeful and start them wondering.

The first milestone would be just beyond the buckeye tree and the next one opposite Cousin Les Greer's springhouse. After that, if I wanted to count off the miles, I'd have to watch over my shoulder. But until we came to the Greer place all I had to do was sit sideways on Old Bay and hold to the saddle and think about how, if I found my name on The Wall, everything would be as changed for me as ever things were for Cinderella.

Why, just to be able to say you'd been to Mr. Syl's would gather a crowd around you at school in no time. And if you'd eaten one of his honey biscuits you had a brag that couldn't be bettered. There wasn't a child who wouldn't beg to be the one to go take a look at The Wall when folks got to arguing about what year Cousin Captain ran for sheriff or when the high water carried off the swinging bridge.

There wasn't any end to the stories you'd hear about Mr. Syl and The Wall. Whatever Mr. Syl set down was truer than history books and, not being afraid of anybody living, he didn't leave off anything he thought was important. He sharpened his pencil and he made his letters all the right size and shape, and he told the bare, bald truth and let the chips fall on anybody they pleased.

Mr. Syl didn't have any more use for pretending than a toad has for spit curls. There was a story about the time Mr. Joe Kester did something mean to his own aunt about a mortgage. Mr. Syl just sharpened his pencil and put down that Mr. Joe was a low-grade skunk to do a thing like that. Mr. Joe found it out and sent Mr. Syl word it had to be rubbed out. Mr. Syl said he didn't keep erasers, he just made sure he wasn't setting down anything that wasn't so. Then Mr. Joe wrote him a letter and said that plank better be sawed out by Saturday or he'd shoot it out and all hell and high water couldn't stop him. So Mr. Syl got on his horse and rode over and told Mr. Joe, like manners was all that mattered, that high water was in the hands of Providence, but hell could sure be had for the asking. Then Mr. Joe took down with a bad stomach-ache and stayed in bed a week and never opened his mouth again about Mr. Syl's Wall.

And there was that time when Mr. Stin Smith — Stin's for Stingy — went over to Mr. Syl's and asked for a pencil and said he was going to write on The Wall that he'd put $100 in on the new church. Mr. Syl knew all about how Mr. Stin wouldn't buy his wife a cookstove, not even when the door came off her old one and nobody could fix it. So Mr. Syl said, 'Not on my Wall, Stin. You'd make flourishes on all your letters and I sure hate a flourish. Way I look at it, Stin, a man's writing ought to be plain, and easy to make sense out of, same as his life ought.'

I'd heard many a story like that and I knew a lot of the lines on The Wall. Some were just weather, like 'Sure a bleak bad day' or 'Good growing weather.' Some were what used to be news about folks I knew, like 'Brice Ridd's little redhead and Touchy Jones got married this morning and I hope they make out all right.' Some were about things far off, like 'Benjamin Harrison elected president. There's still no law against hoping for the best.' And somewhere in among these things that Mr. Syl put down there'd be, I hoped, a line for me.

I wondered what my father'd say if he knew what I was hoping, and me just a towheaded girl. I wondered if when he was little he'd ever gone to Mr. Syl's and seen the furniture in a huddle in the room's middle and eaten a honey biscuit.

I didn't ask. It wasn't any time for me to start talking anybody's arm off. We'd come in sight of the Greer place and as easy as not my father could make me get off there and stay until he came back.

Cousin Lura Greer always washed on Saturdays to get her boys' school things in. My father looked at her line of overalls and shirts and said, 'Les and Lura sure have it lucky. Another year or two and the boys'll be doing all the feeding and milking and helping make the crop.'

Cousin Lura came out to the fence with the bucket she had clothes in and commenced to hang socks and stockings on the wire. She'd shake them a little, but not enough to make them hang straight.

My father said, 'You ought to make Les put up another line or else swap me some of your boys. Don't know what year it was the hogs had the cholera last, do you?'

She didn't answer right away and I set my mind on making her shake her head. I'd heard it could be done if you tried hard enough.

'Ten years back,' she said after she'd hung up some more socks.

My father said, 'No. Seven or eight, it was.'

She gave her shoulder a shrug. 'Then why'd you ask me? It was the year Juddy was a baby and Juddy was ten last month, or what's set down in our Bible record won't do to trust.'

'You're thinking about distemper or limber-neck or something.'

'I'm thinking about hog cholera.' She smiled at me. 'They're guying you at school again, aren't they? You have bad luck, don't you?'

I shook my head, not meaning for anybody to know it worried me any what happened at school.

My father said, 'She goes woolgathering; that's all she does. Hog cholera was seven, or it was eight, years back. Reckon I've got to ride all the way to The Wall to find out which.'

'Ten's what you'll find, Bud,' Cousin Lura said.

He clucked to Old Bay and we moved on past the second milestone.

Cousin Lura hadn't shaken her head like I'd hoped, but she hadn't stopped my trip either, and I took that for a good sign. I began to make a dream about Monday. I'd stand by the stile block in front of school and Shucks and Sophronia and Luella and Trudie Louise and the Greer boys and everybody would be there. I'd say, 'Know what?' Not braggy, but more like it was some little thing that had just that minute come to my mind. And then I'd tell them and as soon as I'd said, 'Mr. Syl,' they'd stop making jokes about me. They'd forget the King David and banjo things. I could stand up to read or go to the blackboard to write my tables or lose a million games of mumble-peg and nobody'd crack a smile. Miss Helen could see, by the way I was looked up to, that I couldn't be a smart aleck. Nobody'd call me King David and I could eat my dinner without having a lump in my throat bigger than a thistle blossom. I wouldn't have a worry in the world at school. I'd never be so gloomy nights I'd have to say Aunt Sethella's song about Love and Hope and Beauty's bloom being blossoms gathered for the tomb. That was the dream The Wall could make come true for me.

Mr. Syl was sitting on his front steps in the sunshine, smoothing a new axe handle with a piece of broken glass. I eased down off of Old Bay and pushed back my hair and followed my father up to the steps. Mr. Syl and I looked at each other and nodded, and I felt almost certain I'd find my name on The Wall.

Mr. Syl was straight like the silver poplar at the corner of his house. He was tall — a whole lot taller than Aunt Sethella — and his hair was white and thick. His face didn't look near old enough to go with his hair, but I'd heard that all his folks were early to gray. His eyes were brown; not like Aunt Sethella's, but lightish brown. They weren't young or old or anything like that. They were just kind. You could tell it wasn't just that minute they were kind; it was lasting. You needn't be forever thinking what to say and do to keep them from changing.

Just standing there watching Mr. Syl scrape the axe handle and listening to the talk between him and my father made me feel like I soon wouldn't have a worry in the world.

My father said, 'You ought to have a bigger piece of glass to polish with.'

Mr. Syl ran his finger over the handle and smiled. 'Bud, is there anything on God's green earth you won't give advice on?'

My father started talking about the checker games and then, like it didn't have anything to do with checkers, said he wanted the hog-cholera date. I edged around toward the door.

Mr. Syl said, 'Cholera's left of the mantel, Bud.'

'Don't worry. If it's down I'll find it.'

'About head-high to your daughter here, maybe two-three inches higher. Throw on a stick if the fire's too low. I'll be in soon's I've slickened this hickory some more.'

I didn't ask which side to look on. That might be gabbling too much. I just waited for my father to get inside and then I went in and began looking for my birth date.

Just the date and my name and 'born' was all I asked. That would give me a brag to take to school, a brag every woolgathering thing I've ever done could hide behind.

The front door was open and my father said to Mr. Syl, 'You ought to keep a ladder in here.' Mr. Syl sort of laughed and said, 'You'd tell a goat how to graze.'

I was shaking all over with hope and everything and my hand was making a damp mark on The Wall along the rows of dates. The mark went up the door facing and down one side of the window and then stopped on the other side at a place I had to tiptoe to read. It stopped at the day that belonged to me. I remember how pretty the G was that started off the line there.

I looked at the date again and it was mine. I counted on my fingers and made sure the year was right. Then I just stood and looked at the line that said, 'Gentle rain fell after long drought,' and the hope that had held my heart up settled down flat, and where it had been, the place hurt like a stone bruise. The brag I'd been going to blot out the King David thing with had been gathered for the tomb. I wasn't even sure that now I could keep from showing how gloomy I felt.

When I thought I could talk a little without sniffling I went around the huddle of furniture in the room's middle — the bed and table and things that had been moved to make way for a record I wasn't in — and over to my father. I asked him if it had rained the day I was born.

He was hunting cholera as high as he could reach on the wrong side of the room and he didn't look down. He said, 'There you go gabbling again.'

I wanted him to say it hadn't rained. A mistake on The Wall would have made it easier to stand being left off. I went back and knelt by the window and read what was near the floor. I hadn't any hope my name would be there, and it wasn't.

'Pneumonia got Grover Robbin. Wouldn't want to praise a disease, but even when he was sober Grove was a troublemaker.... Helped dig grave for Widow Brunner. If she don't get her pick of crown stars it won't be fair, after raising five good boys and not using credit.... Bill Creel spoke at the political rally. His wind held out good. If his ideas ever come to him Bill will sure make a speaker.'

None of it seemed important. My interest in it was dead. All I wished was that my father would look for the date where Mr. Syl had said, so we could go home. Past the tall chest of drawers in front of the hearth I could see my father's jeans elbow moving down another wrong row of dates. I stared at a stain where a dirt-dauber's nest had been knocked off the chest, and staring helped keep back the tears.

My father got on a chair and read the top lines. He said, 'Temperature for every day ought to be set down here.'

Mr. Syl came inside and I made like I was reading The Wall, so he wouldn't see my face.

'You're way too high for cholera, Bud,' he said.... 'You cholera hunting too, sister?'

I shook my head and remembered to push my hair back again.

'I was looking to see did The Wall say when I was born,' I said, and tried to make it sound like I was just killing time.

'I should have set that down, sister. I've left off a right smart that's more important than a lot I've put on. How many years and months and days old are you?'

I said I was nine, but I'd have to count the months and days. I hoped my father wouldn't think that was talking anybody's arm off.

Mr. Syl went to the mantel and moved the can of lamp lighters and opened the clock door. There was a ship painted on the door and the ocean waves were made out of paint that was heavy and stood out and caught the dust and ashes. Any other time a dusty ocean would have been something to think about, but not then. All I wanted was to be up on Old Bay, behind my father's back, where nobody'd guess how I felt.

Mr. Syl took a yellow pencil out of the clock and put a finer point on it. He snapped his knife shut and handed me the pencil. 'Get that new shingle by the steps to figure on. Be sure you have it strictly accurate how many years and months and days old you are.'

I didn't see why anybody'd care how long I'd been alive, much less somebody that hadn't thought my being born was important, but it would be a help to get off by myself. I went out and sat on the steps, that were all trashy with hickory scrapings where Mr. Syl had worked. I could hear Mr. Syl's words and my father's, and I left my ears listening to them, but I didn't think about them. It wasn't that I was woolgathering either. It was because I couldn't think of anything but adding, if I was going to get a strictly accurate number of days.

My father said, 'Time that slow-figuring young-one gets two and two added the moon'll be up.'

Mr. Syl said, 'Bud, what do you get out of making her feel like thirty cents?'

'Here's the date they started laying the railroad. We boarded some of the hands and the boss and his wife.'

'Sethella did, you mean. She'd told me she reckoned she'd best stay single so long as she had you to raise. It took me a right smart time to catch on that she had you to spoil and was afraid I'd hinder her.'

'Thunderation, Mr. Syl! If ever there was a self-made man I'm him!'

'I'm owning to my share of the blame, Bud. A smarter man than me might have made Sethella see it different, but I figured the thing to do was wait. I didn't know that by the time you was grown Miss Triphy'd be along with that good farm she said she'd will Sethella for nursing her the rest of her life. All I could think of then was that my farm wasn't near that good.'

'First-rate farm, it was; but Miss Triphy's nephew's got it. If we'd got it I was going to sell off part and buy a store.'

'By the time old Miss Triphy went to her reward — which I hope was suitable — you'd lost your wife and you and the little one needed Sethella. She's given me no sign that she's changed her mind from what she decided way back yonder. Things happening the way they have, I've brought up no arguments. That leaves me without right to meddle. Only I'm sorry, Bud, about the little one being made to feel like thirty cents. What would she want her name on my Wall for?'

'Thunderation, Mr. Syl, how'd I know! What would any girl young-one want with anything it wants? Cholera's not here. I've looked all over.'

'Here, Bud, by the mantel. Come get your cholera. Ten years ago, it was.'

'I knew it was about that.'

'And speaking of hogs, I got a red sow that's prettier'n a speckled pup in a street parade. I want you to go look at her.'

'We got to be going, Mr. Syl.'

'Not till sister's done her figuring. And she's to eat a honey biscuit, too, before she leaves.'

My father said, 'Oh, thunderation, Mr. Syl!' But he came out and went around the house toward the pump and then the weights on the side gate rattled.

Mr. Syl came to the door and smiled. He said, 'Mack's patching fence close to my hog pen. Your pappy'll get to telling him how. That'll start talk that'll last no telling how long.'

'I'm two months and seventeen days more than nine years old,' I said and dropped the shingle down by the butter-and-egg flower.

'Come in,' he said. 'I'm going to set down that you're that old this date and mighty promising.'

I said 'I'm much obliged, Mr. Syl,' and I didn't try to make it sound like it was just a little thing he'd done for me. I stood by him and watched him sharpen the pencil finer and write. He made letters that were perfect. My name, when he had written it, looked strong and steady and no foolishness about it and like whoever wore it needn't be afraid. I stood there and looked at it and then at him, and I wasn't sure I'd need to brag about being on The Wall. Maybe just knowing would be enough for me.

Mr. Syl went to put the pencil back in the clock, and before he'd turned around again I knew what I was going to do. In a way, I knew it was wild and unheard of. Still, at the same time, it was just what was coming next and there wasn't any changing it, no more than if it was over. I reckoned nobody'd ever done such a thing, but I was going to talk somebody's arm off without pretending any.

Maybe he knew what I was going to do. He got out his pipe and he sat down in the rocker by the hearth. I sat on the edge of the wood box part of the time and part of the time I stood up. And I brought out, from where they'd been weighed down, the King David and the banjo things, the way my father had of saying 'girl young-one,' and there not being any color in my hair, and the way, no matter how I tried, everybody but Trudie Louise beat me playing mumble-peg, and she was six.

I came right out and said that some nights Aunt Sethella's song didn't seem like it told things half as gloomy as they were. I said all three verses of the song over for him, so he'd see what I meant, and I told him Aunt Sethella wouldn't let me take it out of her trunk to brag about the writing at school.

'I'm a woolgatherer, Mr. Syl, and I can't play mumble-peg worth a bawbee. I'll forever be towheaded because if you're not going to be you start being something else by the time you're nine. My father'd swap me for a boy, Mr. Syl, any boy. Miss Helen, when she was new last fall, liked me all right until the banjo thing. Then she thought I was a smart aleck.'

Mr. Syl just sat there and smoked like many was the time he'd had his arm talked off by somebody that wasn't pretending. For all he cared I could just look the way I felt and sound the way I felt. I tried to show him the schoolroom in the fall on Friday after recess when it was time to say speeches. We'd erased the blackboards and beaten the erasers on the window sills. All you could smell was chalk. In streaks of sunshine on the boys' side of the room the chalk dust was so thick you'd hate to walk through them and breathe it. Miss Helen had on her silk shirtwaist — her green-and-blue-plaid one — and the pin in the collar was blue and matched her eyes. The speech I was going to say was named To Helen and I was the first to say it since she'd been our teacher.

'I knew every big word without stumbling, Mr. Syl. I'd been swapping words around and trying out new ones in it the way I do just for fun, but I knew it, Mr. Syl, like A B C's. Miss Helen was sitting at her desk and she looked kind and sort of pleased. She smiled at me and I went woolgathering, and first thing I knew I'd said, "To the glory that was Greece and the *banjo* that was Rome."

'Luella'd said that same speech the last of school and when I said "banjo" she laughed out loud and Miss Helen knocked on her desk, and when I sat down she said that wasn't nice of me. I knew she thought I was a smart aleck and when everybody laughed at me from then till Christmas I made out like I didn't care.'

Mr. Syl held his pipe off and looked at it and said, 'It was something, I suppose, like the summer the boys worked my name over into "Silly Willie."'

It was a lot to ask me to believe that anything like that ever happened to Mr. Syl, but I couldn't stop to think about it. I wasn't through talking his arm off.

He said, 'I can see how it would be easy to get a banjo in it. Nero's fiddling the way he did makes it come natural to think of string music when you think of Rome.'

I took a long breath and began on the King David thing that I hadn't even been letting come to the top of my own mind. I went back to how, ever since the banjo-Friday, I'd been scared to say a piece and I'd say the shortest one I could find. Then I found Absalom, and it was so sorrowful I thought maybe my saying it would make Miss Helen know I wasn't feeling smart alecky. When I'd practice saying it I didn't even change the words any just for fun, except one place in the first line. I got up to say it and I looked at Miss Helen and hoped she'd catch on about I wasn't a smart aleck and right away my tongue slipped, and I said, 'King David's *limps* were weary.'

Mr. Syl nodded. 'Way that line reads in the book, sister, I never thought much of the piece. Couldn't see why Mr. McGuffey would want it in his reader. King David's limbs is enough to make a plain-spoken king fidget in his grave. "Limbs," sister, is purely and plainly a flourish word, and King David's bound to have hated a flourish. I'd said change it to "King David's legs," but way you had it is better still. Limping he must have been, because the next line says he'd come a far piece.'

'He had come from far Jerusalem,' I said, and the King David thing didn't seem any more awful, right then, than a sore toe.

Mr. Syl said, 'I'm not claiming it wouldn't pay to go by the book and what Miss Helen wants, and all that, but still I'd say the changes you made have got sense to them. You sure did King David a favor.'

'I was woolgathering.'

'I know. I don't uphold woolgathering and I don't uphold pretending not to care. Pretending's an unworthy flourish. It's fit for nothing but to mix things up.'

'Sometimes, though, it's all you can do,' I said. 'Aunt Sethella says you can make better use of your face than to let it give away everything you think.'

The way he looked at me I thought maybe he was about to say his arm was talked off and I'd have to rest my tongue. His eyes were still kind, but he just looked at me and didn't say anything. I wasn't half through, but I waited. If he wanted me to stop, I'd stop.

After while he said, 'I'm much obliged to you for bringing that up. Your aunt's saying that, sort of opens up a new viewpoint.'

'Aunt Sethella's got no more use for coming right out and giving away your feelings than a squash bug has for side combs.'

Mr. Syl said, 'A man can study the human race a right smart and still learn out of a primer.'

I was eating a honey biscuit when we heard the weights on the side gate rattle and then somebody working the pump handle. My father'd be in as soon as he'd pumped himself a drink. I didn't think I had time to tell Mr. Syl that sitting there eating his honey biscuit I'd had my doubts that Love and Hope and Beauty's bloom are always gathered for the tomb. Or that I'd decided if pretending's a flourish that mixes things up I'd come right out and tell Miss Helen I hadn't meant to be a smart aleck. Or that I was same as satisfied Monday would be all right at school. I just said, 'This is a good honey biscuit, Mr. Syl.'

'I'd trade a lot like it for one of your aunt's fried pies.'

'That's what's for tomorrow's Sunday dinner,' I said and wished there was a way I could get one to him.

Like his mind had been already made up, Mr. Syl said, 'Tell your Aunt Sethella I'm coming for dinner tomorrow. I'd waited to be invited, you can tell her, but today a new viewpoint opened up to me.'

The paper on the room where Aunt Sethella and I slept had red roses on it and Aunt Sethella'd had a hard time getting the roses' edges matched when she pasted it on.

I sharpened my pencil and wrote something by the window that Saturday night. I was pretty sure she'd be mad, but it seemed like the least I could do for Mr. Syl.

I wrote 'I am nine years and two months and seventeen days old this date and Mr. Syl Willoughby is sure a good man.' I backed off and looked at it and there was a bad flourish on the 'I.'

I didn't hear Aunt Sethella come in. She wanted to know what I was doing and I said I was rubbing out a flourish and Mr. Syl sure hated flourishes and that he said pretending was one and fit for nothing but to mix things up.

From where she was standing Aunt Sethella could read what I'd put down, but she didn't say a word and she didn't sigh. The way Aunt Sethella'd been acting ever since we got back wasn't any more like herself than anything. I didn't know the song she was humming while she iced the two cakes and dressed the hen, but it wasn't the one about blossoms gathered for the tomb. Those two cakes, on top of fried pies, ought to have put me past being surprised at anything, but I still sort of thought she'd start acting like herself when she saw what I'd done.

There was plenty she could have said and it wouldn't been more than I had coming to me. But what she said was, 'You ate one of his honey biscuits, did you?'

I said, 'Yes, ma'am, and it was good.'

She said, 'Well, if you fancy eating a man's cooking — which I don't — you did well to eat while you could. I don't look for Syl Willoughby to mix many more batches of biscuits. You go on to bed now and get yourself some sleep.'

I said, 'I'm fixing to. I haven't got a worry in the world.'

COMMENT

The writer who will carefully compare these two versions of 'Limbs is a Flourish Word' will discover ways of solving many of his own problems of revising and developing a story. He will see how this particular story was built from a germ-idea to a dramatic, unified, and emotionally satisfying story that sold in a top market. In this connection it might be interesting to note that the story was carefully slanted toward the *Saturday Evening Post*, the magazine to which it was sold. The writer was told that her material was more suited to that market than any other, and she should keep that in mind as she worked on her story. As you will see, the gap between the first and last versions of this story is a wide one, but it was bridged by carefully directed revisions aimed toward achieving a definite and unified effect.

Briefly stated, the main suggestions made to the author in the criticism of the first draft were as follows:

1. Focus reader-attention on 'sister' instead of on Mr. Syl, 'sister' being clearly the main character, since she is the one who has a purpose for the story.

2. Begin with interesting action, and not with long explanatory passages.

3. Tell the story from the point of view of 'sister' as the action takes place, not as a memory of something that happened long in the past.

4. Characterize all actors more sharply and by means of definite character traits, especially 'sister.' Make the reader like or dislike each one heartily. Characterize them much more than you have done by action, speech, personal appearance, setting, and locale, and all the other ways in which it is possible to characterize story-actors. Add specific details and sensory appeal.

5. Give the story a distinct and strong plot by making 'sister's' problem much more important to her. Make this problem specific, highly emotional, and set a time-limit very near in the future when this problem must be solved. Make it very hard for 'sister' to solve her problem, by putting almost insurmountable difficulties in the way. Plan a Black Moment at the climax when it seems that 'sister' has failed. Then have her succeed.

6. Expand the story by interesting scenes, each one necessary to the plot-unfoldment, by two or three thousand words.

In the second draft the writer did all that was suggested and *added* the character of Aunt Sethella, with a slight hint of early romantic feeling between her and Mr. Syl.

From this point on until the story was ready for editorial submission, the criticisms and revisions were concerned with problems of presentation. Crises were sharpened, characterization was built up and made more complete, the thread of interest concerning the romance between Aunt Sethella and Mr. Syl was strengthened, used as a unifying force, and brought to a satisfying conclusion at the close of the story.

'Limbs is a Flourish Word' is a practical example of the way in which a slight character sketch can be developed into a strong, intrinsically interesting, emotionally moving, plotted story that sells.

Index

Action, writer likes to use, 24; characterization, 35, 43; progressive, 73; and reaction, 92; as in dialogue, 207; important to show character, 233

Art, conscious, 7; Corot, 10; photographer, 71; novel highest form of, 214

Artist, should make fullest use of his medium, 211

Attitude, by sympathetic, writer may enter into characters, 14

Awareness, developed through observing, 42

Background, characters, 133
Biographies, popularity of, 11
Biter Bit, plot form, 124
Brevity, necessary, 147

Calmness, contrast valuable, 153
Camera, angle in fiction, 158
Camille, bad women made attractive by beautiful souls, 207
Cause, and effect, 92
Character, more important than plot, 1, 3; analysis, 21; bizarre, 21; description, environment, setting, delineation of, 74; direct, telling the reader, indirect, 22; dynamic, 35; in fiction, 229; radio, 194; stage, 208; static, 29, 31, 32; short story, 214
Characterization, many kinds and degrees, 184; individualized by contrasting, 186; for radio, 209, 210; for screen, 209, 210; static, pathos and curiosity, 3, 44
Character-trait, dominant, ruthlessness motivated by acquisition, 190; ambition, loyalty, pride, 132
Clothing, important means of characterization, 36, 207
Conclusions, reader wants to reach own, 55

Consonants, express rugged strength, 32
Contrast, arrests reader's attention, 80; between motive and action, 142; pictorial, 148; high relief, 153
Conversation, one of most important ways of individualizing, 68
Courage, 27, 45; shown by posture, 35; moral, 131; and fear, 143, 175; dominant trait, 186; and determination, 189; and self-control, 191
Crowd, psychology, 213

Death, 45; readers do not like to lose their fictional friends by, 158
Decision, chief characters forced to decide between two courses of action, 131
Delineation of character, 74
Description, must be used with care, 23
Details, observe with meticulous care, 39
Determination, 27; and ingenuity, 131, 161, 175
Dialogue, properly handled, 73
Dickens, Charles, 13; *Oliver Twist*, 2
Doctor, unusual opportunities of, for observing, 13
Doyle's (Conan) Sherlock Holmes, lives in mind of reader, 2
Dramatist, radio, depends on sound, 14
Dramatization, difference between transcription and, 11

Effect and cause, 92
Emotion, try to feel, 51; express anger, 60; effect on voice, 69; use of hope, 90; interest, 104; fear, 143; to mind of reader, 151, 171; dominant, admiration, pity, 190; build-up, 191, 232
Emphasis, toss of head, 49
Environment, includes surroundings, 23, 141; influenced by, 217
Experience, can enlarge by reading, 13